Freebooters and Smugglers

Freebooters and Smugglers

THE FOREIGN SLAVE TRADE
IN THE UNITED STATES AFTER 1808

by Ernest Obadele-Starks

THE UNIVERSITY OF ARKANSAS PRESS
FAYETTEVILLE • 2007

11   10   09   08   07   5   4   3   2   1

TEXT DESIGN BY ELLEN BEELER

⊗ The paper used in this publication meets the minimum requirements of the
American National Standard for Permanence of Paper for Printed Library Materials
Z39.48-1984.

Library of Congress Cataloging-in-Publication Data

Obadele-Starks, Ernest, 1959-
    Freebooters and smugglers : the foreign slave trade in the United States after
    1808 / by Ernest Obadele-Starks.
        p. cm.
    Includes bibliographical references and index.
    ISBN-13: 978-1-55728-858-5 (hardcover : alk. paper)
    ISBN-10: 1-55728-858-5 (hardcover : alk. paper)
    1. Slave trade—United States—History—19th century. 2. Slave traders—United
    States—History—19th century. 3. Pirates—United States—History—19th
    century. 4. Smugglers—United States—History—19th century. 5. Slave trade—
    Africa—History—19th century. 6. Slavery—Law and legislation—United
    States—History—19th century. 7. Slavery—Southern States—History—
    19th century. I. Title.
    E446.O23 2007
    973.7'1—dc22
                                                                      2007030918

To my parents, Ernest K. and Mary E. Starks

Contents

Photographs and Illustrations

Acknowledgments

This book is the result of several years of collaboration with historians, students, archivists, and friends. The final product owes much to a collection of individuals who offered insight, analysis, recommendations, and sometimes their gut-level opinion about the project. In reflecting on its evolution, this study benefited greatly from two individuals in particular. In the embryonic stages of this work, Cynthia Bouton, being the true colleague that she is, took time from her own hectic academic schedule to offer several critiques, probing questions, and trenchant comments about the manuscript. At a later stage in the writing, Gwendolyn Midlo Hall canvassed the study, detected gaps, and then pointed me toward additional sources without which the final product would not have been as thorough.

Several others had a hand in the development of this book. I offer my thanks to Larry Yarak, Alan Karras, David Eltis, Randolph Campbell, James McMillin, Richard Blackett, Steven Mintz, Barbara Krauthamer, Amilcar Shabazz, Emma Christopher, Robert Resch, Walter Kamphoefner, Gerald Horne, Cary Wintz, Charles Robinson, Bobbi Jo Howard, Terri Beane, Ervin James, and Thomas Paradise. Stephanie Attia and Janis Wilkens edited the entire manuscript in a timely fashion. Paul Springer chased down citations and edited the bibliography. I also thank Abir Raslan for her willingness to help edit the bibliography and notes.

Among the library and archival staffs to whom I am indebted and grateful are those at the United States National Archives in Washington, D.C.; the Regional National Archives in Fort Worth, Texas (Barbara Rust); the Library of Congress in Washington, D.C.; the British National Archives in London, England; the Historic New Orleans Collection in New Orleans, Louisiana; the Department of Archives at Louisiana State University in Baton Rouge; the Center for American History at the University of Texas at Austin; the Texas State Library in Austin, Texas; the Sam Houston Regional Library in Liberty, Texas; the Galveston & Texas History Center at the Rosenberg Library in Galveston, Texas; Special Collections at the University of Texas at El Paso; Special Collections at Kansas State University; the Kansas State Historical Society; the Massachusetts Historical Society in Boston, Massachusetts; the Austin Public Library, Austin, Texas; Xavier (New Orleans) University Archives and Special Collections; Special Collections at the University of Virginia at Charlottesville; the Library Company of Philadelphia; the Institute of Texan

Culture in San Antonio, Texas; the Corpus Christi Public Library, Corpus Christi, Texas; the Georgia Historical Society, Savannah, Georgia; the New York Historical Society, New York, New York; the Woodson Research Center, Rice University, Houston, Texas; the Hartley Library, Southampton University, Southampton, England; and the New Bedford Whaling Museum, New Bedford, Massachusetts. I especially want to thank Joel Kitchen at the Sterling C. Evans Library at Texas A&M University-College Station for his professionalism in helping me locate sources and Angelita Garcia-Alonzo for translating key documents.

The students from my Readings on the African Slave Trade class at Texas A&M University-College Station offered incisive comments and conducted extensive research that expedited the completion of this study. For this, I owe thanks to Jason Burris, Aaron Cottrell, Jason Fair, Cristen Gerdes, Matthew Lagesse, Jace Martin, Tamiko Matthews, Nathan Nelson, Katherine Sacra, Krista Scott, Mark Spence, Kathleen (Katie) Swan, Nicholas Tate, Ricardo Torres, and Angela Williams.

With all the latest crazes and innovations in internet technology the completion of this study would have been slowed considerably had it not been for several friends and coworkers who graciously rendered their computer skills. Among those who helped me with my technology deficiencies are Jude Swank, Judy Mattson, Naguib Ktiri-Idrissi, Kelly O'Callahan, and Homer E. Carter.

This project also required moral support. There are several people who in their own way played a key role in the completion of this book. I thank Konjit Selassie, who motivated me in her own unique way; Bethlehem Arefaine, who spent quality time with my daughter when I needed a release from my parental duties to conduct research or to write; Steve Palmer, Sara Palmer-Williams, Chelsey Palmer-Williams, and Miles Palmer-Williams, who invited my daughter and me into their cozy English home during my research trip to the British National Archives; Richard and Susanna Finnell for their enduring friendship; Iyad Abdel-Jawad for inquiring about the manuscript and expressing his eagerness to see it in print; and Zoe Davis, whose unconditional love means more to me than she will ever know.

Financial support was also essential. Generous funding from the Scholarly and Creative Enhancement Grant Program at Texas A&M University-College Station helped cover my travel, research, and editing costs. Funding from Texas A&M University at Qatar and the Qatar Foundation also helped defer many of my expenses and was vital in the completion of this project.

Freebooters and Smugglers

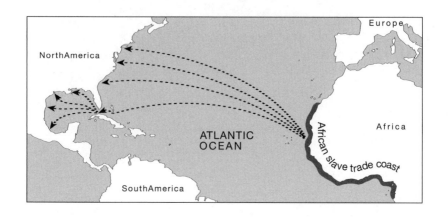

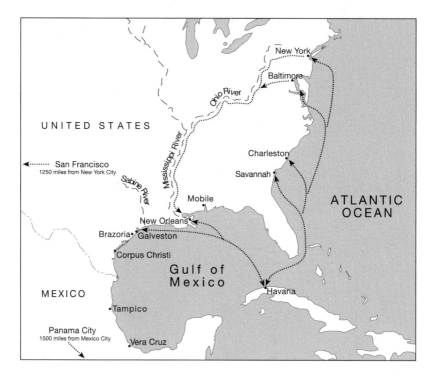

Introduction

In the winter of 1819 the infamous Jim Bowie and his two brothers, Rezin and John, transported a coffle (a group of slaves chained together) of bewildered Africans from Texas into Louisiana and stashed them in the wilderness not too far from a federal marshal's office. Once again the Bowies had avoided arrest for their part in smuggling slaves into the country in violation of an 1808 law that prohibited the introduction of foreign slaves into the United States. As Louisiana land speculators, the Bowie brothers increased their wealth by engineering ruses that afforded them the leeway to bid on and purchase the registration of title for illegally imported slaves. Their role as unofficial government informants, over time, led to the formation of an illicit business alliance with several federal agents. The brothers had routinely informed United States marshals about groups of slaves hidden away in the secluded forest regions of southern Louisiana. Federal law required that unclaimed and undocumented slaves be sold at government-sponsored auctions to the highest bidder, and that informants, federal agencies, and their employees share the proceeds derived from any sale.

The Bowie brothers had devised perhaps the most successful smuggling scheme on the American frontier. "James, Rezin, and myself," John Bowie wrote, "fitted out some small boats at the mouth of the Calcasieu River and went in to trade our shares. Our plan of operation was as follows: We first purchased 40 Negroes from Lafitte at a rate of $1 a pound, or an average of $140 for each. We brought them into the limits of the United States and delivered them to a customs house." When no other prospective buyers showed up for the government sale, the Bowies walked away with a new batch of slaves, many of which they sold on the domestic market. For the Bowies, the ownership of new and valuable slaves enhanced their social status and gave them access to the upper crust of frontier society.[1]

The mission of the United States Marshals Service was altered dramatically by slave smugglers and traffickers from the time when George Washington made the agency's first appointments to the years when the Bowies and others used the agency to assist them in circumventing the Abolition Act of 1808. The office of United States Marshals and Deputy Marshals Service was initially created in conjunction with the federal judicial system by the first Congress, under the Judiciary Act of 1789, as a support organization for federal courts within their judicial districts. The primary function of federal marshals was to serve subpoenas, issue summonses, enforce writs and warrants, make arrests, and to carry out all lawful orders issued by judges, Congress, or the president. By the time the Bowies began their smuggling careers the agency was consumed with the task of policing the illegal slave trade.[2]

The Bowies' role in maintaining the post-1808 foreign slave trade was neither random nor occasional, but rather part of a rationally conceived informal economy. Smugglers like the Bowies relied on the bustling New Orleans slave-smuggling operation of Jean and Pierre Lafitte, two siblings who—after being run out of Louisiana for engaging in illicit business practices—played a major role in the foreign slave trade after 1808.

During the first half of the nineteenth century, the Lafittes had abandoned their New Orleans-based wine import business in exchange for a place in the foreign slave trade market. They built an immensely lucrative contraband-slave industry that extended from Spanish Florida across the Gulf of Mexico coastline southward to the Mexican border. Unless they coordinated their smuggling operations through Louisiana's Calcasieu Lake with the Lafittes, the Bowies had but one other option: to first ship their slaves through Galveston Bay in Texas and then overland into Louisiana.[3]

Although the Lafittes had established a substantial financial empire, which they coordinated from their New Orleans blacksmith shop, the two brothers could not resist the monetary temptations of the foreign slave trade. From their Galveston headquarters they spearheaded a slave-smuggling operation that for a good part of the nineteenth century served as a chief supply source for slaves in the region. Relying on a fleet of pirate vessels that their father, Marcus Lafitte, had accumulated over the years, and with a complement of loyal crews, the Lafittes bullied slave ships and confiscated the human cargoes of their competitors to form an unrestrained slave-smuggling racket.

Who were the gatekeepers of the post-1808 foreign slave trade in the United States? What were their motives and incentives? How were they able to maintain and sustain their participation in the practice well into the 1860s? *Freebooters and Smugglers* explores the entanglement and relevance of porous borders, boundary claims, lax enforcement (including corruption within the American judicial system), misrepresentation of ship documents and registries, and the heavy propaganda and enforced conformity in defense and sustaining of the foreign slave trade in the United States after 1808.

This study is an inquiry into the fundamental challenges facing the implementation of the Abolition Act of 1808. Its goal is to draw attention to the actions of individuals and groups of adherents—especially those on the front lines of the trade who struggled to maintain the practice. It analyzes the interplay and tension between economic motivations (self-interests), ideology (politics), and institutions (government and government agencies).

The Abolition Act of 1808 had marked the end of one period in the crusade to dismantle the foreign slave trade in the United States, and the beginning of another. The law was conceived during the United States Constitutional debates of the late 1780s. Under pressure and duress to ratify a national constitution, state delegates were compelled to accept a compromise on the foreign importation of slave labor. While some had called for its eradication as well as the institution of slavery, some southern delegates resisted efforts to cut off the external supply of slaves. The agreed-upon compromise required that Congress would pass no laws for twenty years from 1787 that would interfere with the introduction of foreign slaves into the United States.

Congressional debates regarding the foreign slave trade resumed in 1806, and by 1807 a new bill prohibiting the practice was signed into law. State laws banning the introduction of foreign slaves—as well as other federal laws such as the Act of 1794, which prohibited the outfitting of ships to be used in the foreign slave trade, and the Act of 1800, which banned American citizens from selling foreign Africans into slavery—predated the Abolition Act of 1808. The latter law was broader in scope and more restrictive in its objective than its predecessors. It mandated that Americans cease in their participation in the foreign slave trade. Passage of the 1808 Abolition Act in the United States occurred in concert with a similar British law that also banned its citizens from introducing foreign slaves onto its soil and into its colonies.[4]

Slavery in the United States after 1808 was augmented by, but not limited to, the existing slave population. Because planters and merchants relied on both domestic and foreign slaves after 1808, foreign slave movements into the United States played a key role in the overall strategy to supply the country with slaves. Smugglers and traffickers, in their attempt to enjoy financial gain, were essential figures in this redistribution.

Not all slave movements in the United States after 1808 were innocent voyages with legal intent. Slave smugglers and traffickers had for years formed networks from which they employed their creative energies and defied the legal and political proscriptions designed to end the foreign importation of slaves.[5] Their vocation, which had survived colonial regulations, territorial expansion, and legal restrictions, was advanced by a preexisting culture of ambivalence among merchants, planters, citizens, and public officials. Patterns of illegal slave trading during the nineteenth century were part of an extended legacy of smuggling activities that had permeated frontier societies in the Western Hemisphere. English colonists in Jamaica, the *London Times* reported just six days after the Abolition Act of 1808 became law in the United States, took "their own view" of the measure and regarded it as blatant "interference with their internal regulations," particularly upon the "transitory accession of revenue" derived from the African slave trade between the island and the states.[6]

Participants in the post–1808 foreign slave trade necessarily adopted strategies to maintain their vocation as time and circumstances dictated. These singular and collective acts of resistance create possibilities for understanding the meaning and significance of these activities that might otherwise be construed as a series of unrelated or unimportant events. In many respects, the story of the post–1808 foreign slave trade is also the story of the United States, and it is difficult to understand the latter without fully appreciating the former. While the slave trade had always been a part of American society, the post–1808 foreign trade represented a unique and constant presence in America until the Civil War.

The demand for slave labor required unique increases in the slave population at a time when many states had banned the foreign importation of slaves. By the mid-1780s all of the New England and the middle states, plus Maryland, Virginia, and Delaware, had banned the importation of African slaves. South Carolina and Georgia enacted laws as well. In addition to violating these state and local restrictions, slave traffickers and smugglers trampled on the rarely enforced federal antislave-trade laws of 1794 and 1800. According to United States census records, the black population of southern slaveholding states nearly doubled in two decades, increasing from 676,637 in 1790 to 909,910 in 1800 and to 1,251,188 in 1810—a net increase of 574,551 in twenty years. The growth in population of slaves in individual states is also informative. Between 1790 and 1800 the slave population of Georgia more than doubled, increasing from 29,264 to 59,699 workers. Farther south in the Mississippi territory the number of slaves soared from 3,489 to 17,088 in the first decade of the 1800s. By 1810 even more slaves could be tallied in Tennessee, Missouri, Arkansas, Alabama, Florida, Louisiana, and Texas. H. C. Carey attributed these population surges to natural growth and estimated that between 1790 and 1810 internal reproduction among slaves contributed seven times (505,000) as many people than did the foreign slave trade. After 1820 white immigration slowed in slave states, but the number of slaves entering the region increased. From the mid-Atlantic states alone, Robert Fogel and Stanley Engerman have argued, 835,000 slaves were imported into the Deep South and Southwest between 1790 and 1860. Combined, Alabama, Mississippi, Louisiana, and Texas accounted for approximately 75 percent of these redistributed bondservants. It is unclear precisely how many of them traveled overland in coffles with their migrating masters, through the legal coastwise slave trade or as captives in the foreign slave trade.[7]

Economic expansion after 1808 encouraged this trading. As the frontier opened up to cotton production, a voracious demand for slaves developed in the new cotton states of the Southwest. The gold rush in California in the late 1840s also required slaves for mine work. Because slaves were in constant demand in these emergent regions, both domestic and foreign slaves were needed to fill the labor voids. Slave supply did not always keep pace with demand. For remedy, slave buyers often turned to slave smugglers and traffickers or to just about anyone willing to offer them a decent deal on a slave.[8]

Frontier communities attracted their fair share of these characters. The frontier, Edward E. Baptist explained in his study on middle Florida plantation society, shaped the United States, and the essence of the United States was the frontier. Simply broaching a discussion on the "frontier," Baptist pointed out, conjures loaded images of a place that tested and refined white men and distilled the nation's deepest tendencies. The essence of the frontier was to defy authority and the mandates they attempted to impose. Unstable and unpoliced, frontier regions provided a base from which slave traffickers and smugglers tested the limits of the Abolition Act of 1808.[9]

The urbanizing of the frontier economy created stiff competition for jobs, and the lack of institutional urban support systems, combined with the precarious financial status of most individuals and families, were chief inducements that lured new participants into the illegal foreign slave trade. This type of criminal culture in the United States prior to the Civil War had become woven into the country's political, economic, and social tapestry. Most people had little money. It is estimated that, around 1850, thousands of families in the cotton states received average annual earnings of less than $100. In 1860 the daily wages paid to a day laborer in the aggregate of all states and territories averaged $1.18, whereas the illegal sale of a single slave during the nineteenth century could bring $400 to $1,500.[10]

Participants in the post-1808 foreign slave trade forged a culture that unified them around the idea that the trade was an economic imperative for themselves and their customers and that the financial returns justified their actions. Thus, the schemes they engineered and the networks they established were, in their minds, practical and valid.

The African American scholar W. E. B. Du Bois spent several months between 1889 and 1891 thoroughly examining contemporary sources and secondary accounts of the foreign slave trade and analyzing United States efforts to end it. Du Bois delved into the records of the very institution (the United States central government) responsible for suppressing the trade. Through a meticulous critique of presidential messages, government reports, records of collectors of revenue, letters of district attorneys, congressional committee reports, navy records, documents of antislavery societies, and eyewitness accounts, Du Bois found more than an adequate number of credible sources to reconstruct the role of Americans in maintaining the foreign slave trade after 1808. From the House Reports of the Seventeenth Congress, and with evidence from the African Society of London, he concluded that as early as 1816 a significant portion of the slaves shipped illegally from Africa into the United States were transported by Americans. From personal testimonies, Du Bois was also able to trace patterns of conduct among smugglers. "I soon learned how readily, and at what profits . . . Negroes were sold into the . . . American States," one smuggler had confessed, later admitting that "many American citizens grew rich by trafficking in Guinea Negroes, and smuggling them continually, in small parties."[11]

In December 1891 Du Bois offered his findings to Harvard scholar Albert Bushnell Hart, who in turn arranged for the young black intellectual to present his early conclusions to the 1891 annual meeting of the American Historical Association in Washington, D.C. "The Enforcement of the Slave-Trade Laws" was a scholarly assessment of the realities of the post-1808 foreign slave trade in the United States and an indictment of its advocates and participants. "If slave labor was an economic gold," Du Bois announced, "then the slave trade was its strong right arm. Northern greed joined to Southern credulity was a combination calculated to circumvent any law, human or divine." For clarity, Du Bois, in his expanded work on the subject, elaborated on the double jeopardy of slavery as an institution and the vexing "international" crisis of the foreign slave trade.[12]

Du Bois left his contemporaries and future scholars with one final observation. Some Americans, he asserted, chose to enrich themselves through the earnings of the foreign slave trade, a devious bargain of dollars and cents, rather than adhere to the principles of "liberty" that compelled them to eradicate both slavery and the foreign slave trade.[13]

The beneficiaries of such conspiracies, Du Bois argued, were many of the planters, merchants, smugglers, and traffickers who had responded to the lure of profit and migrated south from the slave-inundated Chesapeake region into Georgia, then westward through Alabama and Mississippi, and ultimately into Louisiana and Texas, where soil was better suited for cotton and sugar production and the need for slaves was greater.[14]

Giving attention to the post-1808 foreign slave trade will necessarily reveal what we know and how we know what we know about the practice. Several theories regarding its suppression have emerged over the past several years. Nineteenth-century writings examining the attempts of Great Britain to regulate the foreign slave trade suggest that England was urged to reconcile its own moral failings. These scholars argued that British action was a response to its own hypocrisy. British suppression, some writers concluded, was driven by its zeal to dominate the world economy and to impose its will upon other countries. British and American failure to fully pursue the prescribed policy of suppression and enforcement led an additional set of historians to examine the effects of the Abolition Act on the structure of the post-1808 foreign slave trade. Historians have also demonstrated a strong inclination to confine themselves to quantitative analysis through the use of documents and databases when studying the post-1808 foreign slave trade, rather than studying the methods and strategies that prolonged the practice.

A cursory review of the literature on the post foreign slave trade in the United States reveals the absence of a well-developed historical framework. There is, however, an important starting point in the work of Philip D. Curtin. Using sophisticated analysis, Curtin estimated the extent of the entire trans-Atlantic slave trade from its inception to its end at 9,566,000 slaves. He estimated that about ninety-two thousand enslaved Africans were imported into the United States between 1783 and 1810. Joseph Inikori argued that about 15,400,000 slaves were transshipped over the life span of the Atlantic slave trade but made no particular effort to study the distribution of slaves into the United States after 1808. James A. McMillin has injected new energy into the discourse. Although McMillin's study begins in 1783, the author offers supportive evidence of a significant foreign slave trade network in the United States after the American Revolution in which slave traffickers, smugglers, and many others cashed in on as late as 1810.[15]

By reassessing slave manifest records, court cases, and the inner workings and culture of slave-smuggling networks, it becomes clear that foreign slaves were imported into the United States after 1808. Using Curtin's calculations the number of slaves imported into the country following passage of the Abolition Act could be estimated around, at the low end, 3,500 annually. Stretched over fifty-five years (1808–1863), it is safe to conclude that approximately 192,500 slaves were introduced into the United States. Using slave manifests records an even higher estimate can be made. According to these documents, around ten slave ships per week entered the Port of New Orleans between 1808 and 1863. Each vessel carried on average 15 slaves. In at least half of these cases discrepancies arose regarding either the legality of the ship, the integrity of the crews as many were prosecuted for participating in the post-1808 foreign slave trade, or the legal status of the Africans on board. Thus, around 75 slaves a week entered New Orleans under these questionable legal circumstances. Over a fifty-two-week period the number increases to approximately 3,900. When slave imports from other major slave-trading ports (Mobile, Pensacola, Savannah, Charleston, Norfolk, Baltimore, New York, and Boston) where slave manifests recorded about one-third of the number of slaves entering New Orleans during the same time period (1808–1863) are included, it is reasonable to argue that of the approximate 4.5 million blacks (slave and free) in the United States by 1860 as many as 786,500 were introduced into the country from foreign ports following passage of the Abolition Act in 1808 until slavery ended in 1863.

Freebooters and Smugglers does not quantify, in a formal way, foreign slave shipments. It does, however, appreciate the relevance of such quantities. While relying on some quantitative analysis, this study demonstrates that the foreign slave trade did contribute to the growth of the slave population in the United States after 1808. It unearths pockets of conspiracy and collusion regarding the trade and invests more perspective than have previous studies on how the trade crisscrossed frontiers and permeated cultures.[16]

The initiators of much of this activity were slave smugglers and traffickers. The line of distinction between these two groups and slave traders was often convoluted. Slave traders generally operated within the boundaries of the law. Their legal domestic slave-trading firms were professionalized. They kept depots, hired salaried and commissioned employees to monitor their businesses, announced slave sales, bombarded newspapers with graphic solicitations, and redistributed and resold the slaves by legally moving them between owners. Slave traffickers and smugglers violated laws that prohibited the distribution of foreign slaves. They resisted the admixture of political dispensations against the foreign slave trade, preferred more clandestine transactions, created pseudo-corporations, and found reputation and word of mouth to be more suitable forms of advertisement.

Slave traffickers and smugglers came from various occupations, endeavors, backgrounds, and locations. Upon passage of the Abolition Act of 1808, the Bowies, the Lafittes, Renato Beluche, Juan Antonio Pereira, Samuel Glover, Louis de Aury, James Morgan, Monroe Edwards, James Merrill,

Samuel May Williams, Richard Royall, Sterling and Pleasant McNeil, James W. Fannin Jr., David Byrdie Mitchell, John A. Quitman, Beverly Chew, James Long, and Nathaniel Gordon all found considerable interest in maintaining the foreign slave trade from the Gulf Coast to New York.

In January 1817, for example, Lieutenant Commander B. V. Hoffman of the United States Navy wrote to Captain Charles Morris and B. W. Crowninshield, secretary of the navy, and informed both that he had seized "the private armed Mexican schooner *Eugene* about four miles from the bar" near the Louisiana and Texas coastlines "for having no papers and a number of blacks on board, said to be slaves" from Africa.[17]

Participants in the post-1808 foreign slave trade devised schemes to avoid their pursuers; welcomed the help of American military leaders; skillfully manipulated United States marshals and customs agents; exchanged financial and material perks for favors; and tactfully maneuvered their way through the judicial system. They also relied on free and enslaved African sailors and seamen for much-needed seafaring expertise and labor as they renovated commercial ships, modified whaling brigs, and built alliances with filibusters. They colluded with slaveholders to disrupt the movement of slaves seeking refuge outside of United States jurisdiction. Their activities posed some of the greatest obstacles to the freedom of all Africans. Those captives who had succumbed to these pursuers, Reverend Peter Williams Jr., son of the founder of the African Methodist Episcopal Zion Church in New York, warned, were in dire need of immediate and "convenient asylum."[18]

The foreign slave trade in the United States was a visible enterprise during the nineteenth century. Using the 1839 eyewitness account of Reverend Horace Moulton, a Methodist Episcopal minister from Boston who had traveled extensively through the American South, Theodore Weld was able to draw attention to the foreign introduction of slaves into the country. Reverend Moulton recounted that the foreign slave trade was carried on so openly that a short visit from outsiders would suffice to convey that the horrors of the traffic had not yet ceased. Moulton was "surprised to find so many [Africans] that could not speak English." He found the port areas void of any significant enforcement and concluded that foreign slaves could "be landed safely at any port of this [American] continent." The 1820 law that had made the illegal importation of slaves a capital offense, Moulton suggested, was "a dead letter."[19]

No single source gives a clear view of the extent of the post-1808 foreign slave trade. Slave voyages to the United States after 1808 were rarely documented in European or American archives and are unlikely to be included in most recent slave trade databases. The slave manifest records of the United States Customs Office did, however, offer a foundation from which to launch this study. At first glance, these records appeared to provide very generic and repetitious data regarding slave movements. Closer scrutiny of these informative sources allowed me to tap into a historical rhythm regarding slave transshipments. They provided useful demographic information about the slaves themselves, names of slave ships, dates of departure, ports of destination, and the investigating customs agents. By placing these manifests in a broader historical context it is possible to draw certain conclusions and to make plausible inferences about the post-1808 foreign slave trade. These manifests do not offer a complete picture of the trade or its participants, but when referenced against other sources they do help establish a more accurate representation.

The testimonies, pleas, and alibis found in slave-smuggling court case profiles, many of which are highlighted in the work of Helen Tunncliff Catterall, validated some of my judgments. A significant number of these cases involved the seizure of suspected slave vessels and the forfeiture of the property found on board in incidents from New England to Louisiana. These cases allowed me to investigate more fully the patterns of behavior among slave traffickers and smugglers.

The reports of the United States Marshals Service, which compiled information about illicit slave trafficking along the frontier, informed my understanding of how government agencies responded to the enforcement of federal laws regarding the foreign slave trade. Analyzing their stories altered many of my own biased images and judgments of federal marshals as ten-gallon-hat-wearing, pistol-toting, saloon-carousing keepers of the peace. These sources revealed that marshals held interests in the post-1808 foreign slave trade, which they secured and protected through their own political, economic, and social connections. Their job title afforded them virtual immunity from prosecution and granted them broad discretion to confiscate smuggled slaves and to auction them for cash. While United States Customs Office agents addressed the trade in maritime circles, federal marshals focused much of their attention on the overland illegal trafficking schemes between borders and boundaries.

Analysis of official diplomatic correspondence contributed significantly to my study. Diplomatic leverage and international credibility were the primary concerns of most governments. Multilateral dialogue on the post-1808 foreign slave trade addressed several issues. For proponents of an international ban, prestige and enforcement prevailed as major points of contention. Other nations, typically those in the embryonic stages of their own political development, found the Abolition Act of 1808 and the slave-trafficking crisis to be useful tools in diplomatic negotiations. The balance between diplomacy and labor necessities often swayed from one year to the next.

Navy records were another crucial source for this study, and from them I have discerned a story within a story. Most nineteenth-century naval squadrons had tandem obligations. On the one hand, they protected borders and waterways. On the other hand, they were responsible for the suppression of the foreign slave trade. For navy crews, suppression was a matter of perspective as vigorous and effective enforcement of the Abolition Act of 1808 was so often linked to the availability of resources. Insufficient revenues and shortages of enlistments hindered efforts to disrupt the trade as destitute naval officers and crews turned from the politics of enforcement to the politics of opportunity.

Although limited in their scope and volume, slave narratives, personal testimonies, and newspapers helped me trace the development of the post-1808 foreign slave trade. Nineteenth-century newspapers provided, in some cases, inconclusive and inconsistent data. Many encountered financial difficulties and struggled to survive. Although their accounts of ship clearances for the foreign slave trade, their profiles of court cases, and their synopses regarding the runaway crisis were not always pinpoint accurate, the articles and editorials they produced form a database of useful information regarding awareness among local populations.

The foreign movement of slaves into the United States after 1808 was linked in a large way to the political and economic transformation of Louisiana following the American purchase of the territory. As the Port of New Orleans rose to commercial prominence, slave smuggling and trafficking emerged as a vital and viable profession. The methods slave smugglers and traffickers used to elude criminal prosecution and serious punishment is a complicated but central part of this story. Arrests were frequent but convictions were rare. The social, economic, and political clout of smugglers often influenced the decisions of judges and juries. Because most classes of people understood the intrinsic value of slave labor, they too exploited the judicial system to help extend the life of the foreign slave trade. As boundaries and borders shifted, the post-1808 foreign slave trade brought to surface latent issues regarding Mexican independence from Spain, the Texas War for Independence from Mexico, and political disputes between nations over suppression strategies. Although eradicating slavery and ending the legal domestic slave trade were focal points for most abolitionists, the abolitionist campaign itself failed to place the post-1808 foreign slave trade at the center of its critique. Confronting the practice at home carried obvious advantages over grappling with it abroad. Regulating the activities of slave smugglers, monitoring the behavior of government officials, and keeping pace with the movement of slaves across porous borders complicated their task. Because of its relationship to abolitionism, expansion, foreign consuls, the gold rush, filibuster societies, the ship industry, the southern business community, secession, and the Civil War, the foreign slave trade drew considerable attention among its supporters and detractors.

Freebooters and Smugglers is a departure from the numerous studies on the legal domestic slave trade in the United States as well as from the pre-1808 foreign slave trade. It is a follow-up to Du Bois's critique of the practice. It assesses the nature and character of the trade after 1808 and chronicles its significance in the campaign to sustain slavery in America. This study places the often-overlooked and understudied but important universe of the post-1808 slave trade in proper historical context. An assessment of circumstances and conditions from which it thrived is informative and instructive and offers a starting point for truly understanding its role in American history.

1

"A View of Opening a Trade"

POST REVOLUTION, LOUISIANA, ABOLITION, AND THE FOREIGN SLAVE TRADE

As William C. C. Claiborne, the American governor assigned to the Louisiana Territory, stood along the banks of the Mississippi River in New Orleans in 1809 observing what he believed to be slave ships entering the port, he was convinced that Louisianans were determined to maintain a steady supply of slaves to help bolster their economy. Claiborne faced a litany of legal questions regarding the jurisdiction of the United States in the region and the extent to which the Abolition Act of 1808 applied to the inhabitants of Louisiana. The law, as far as he was concerned, was ambiguous at best. One thing was certain; changes in the borders and boundaries along the emerging American frontier had unpredictable consequences. Claiborne could not have foreseen the effects that the combination of the foreign slave trade and the Louisiana Purchase would have on the territory. He had not anticipated that slave smugglers and traffickers would be drawn into the center of the region's political and social transformation. Because slavery was such a critical part of Louisiana's economic transition, there was little Claiborne could do to enforce the Abolition Act of 1808 or to mitigate the movement of foreign slaves into the region.[1]

Implementation of the Abolition Act of 1808 in Louisiana was beset by several obstacles including under-resourced customs houses, the emergence of free and enslaved African sailors and seamen as co-participants in the foreign slave trade, the competing commercial and political interests of foreign nations, and the advent of prominent slave traffickers and smugglers in the region. The combination of these issues laid the foundation on which the foreign slave trade was able to survive well into the nineteenth century.

These circumstances and the post-1808 foreign slave trade itself is more easily understood when considered within the context of the years following the American Revolution. Territorial expansion into the frontier during this period gave rise to new commercial centers. The American purchase of Louisiana helped develop and shape the city of New Orleans into one of these major hubs. The Abolition Act of 1808 forced slave traders to generate new strategies to accommodate Louisiana's demand for slaves. Slave smugglers and traffickers acted upon this occasion to enhance their financial status and to improve their relationship with central authorities—though the foreign slave trade was not a panacea for planters and merchants in the region. It was, however, an issue in which most people, directly or indirectly, were forced to negotiate. The post-1808 foreign slave trade exposed the motives of those who confronted and tested the limits of abolitionism.

Post-Revolution Foreign Slave Trade

The foreign slave trade in the United States was as much a topic of concern for Americans in the years proceeding passage of the Abolition Act of 1808 as it was in the years after the law went into effect. The provenance of slave shipments into the United States before passage can be traced to the post-Revolutionary-era. Before the American Revolution, slave traders were wealthy and respected merchants who generally perceived the distribution of foreign slaves as normal commerce. Despite the emergence of a small northern-based domestic slave trade in the mid-eighteenth century and after the Revolution, most slaves sold in the United States were imported from Africa.

It was also during the mid- to late eighteenth century that antislavery supporters boasted important gains of their own. Massachusetts, New Hampshire, and Vermont had all abolished slavery; Connecticut, Rhode Island, and Pennsylvania had passed gradual abolition laws; New York and New Jersey debated abolition. The crusade against the slave trade itself claimed more success. By the time the American Revolution ended, all of the New England and middle states, including Maryland, Virginia, and Delaware, prohibited slave imports, and within a few years all had permanently banned the foreign slave trade. At the 1781 Constitutional Convention in Philadelphia, the state of South Carolina and its allied states sought to preserve their right to import slaves from outside the country. They sacrificed other interests to win a twenty-year barrier against congressional regulation of the foreign slave trade. Soon after the compromise, however, the South Carolina state legislature voluntarily closed its foreign and domestic slave trade. Over the next ten years overwhelming antislave-trade majorities in its statehouse government extended the ban, and by 1802 its antislave-trade laws were firmly in place.[2]

In the face of these restrictions planters and merchants sought to repair and renovate their damaged plantation economies and to replace slaves lost during the war. It was a small group of Charleston, South Carolina, individuals and merchants such as George Austin, Samuel Brailsford, Henry Laurens, Thomas Middleton, Miles Brewton, John Hopton, Roger and Thomas Loughton Smith, and Hugh Young, who were responsible for maintaining the post-Revolution slave trade in their state. Economic factors rather than federal or local laws ruled their actions. Capital, credit, and the slow pace of slave imports were their biggest obstacles. It was not long before calls for a direct trade in slaves from Africa were made. After examining the federal census records for his state in 1801, Governor John Drayton estimated that slaves introduced into South Carolina accounted for about 50 percent of the increase in its slave population from 1790 to 1800, a time when slave smuggling was condoned. Two of Samuel Brown's ships, the brig *Don Galvez* and the vessel *Pacific,* were engaged in this trade. Joseph Hawkins authored a book that described his involvement as a slave smuggler around South Carolina aboard the ship *Charleston,* but Hawkins never did reveal the intended landing site of his ship's cargo, perhaps to protect himself and his shipmates from incrimination. In 1797 Hawkins and his crew attempted to deliver a shipment of slaves but diverted their vessel to Antigua after experiencing structural problems. The ship was seized and its cargo of slaves sold. In 1798 South Carolina officials confiscated the schooner *Phoebe* and its forty-five slaves. During the last six months of 1799 officials filed six actions against South Carolina slavers for violating the federal antislave-trade law of 1794.[3]

By the 1790s, slave shipments began arriving into Georgia directly from Africa at more regular intervals. Between 1780 and 1790 its volume of slave arrivals increased from 2,200 to 10,400. Between 1783 and 1810 Africa was listed as the origin of 34 percent of slaves disembarked in Georgia. After the Georgia legislature banned further imports in 1798, large numbers of slaves were still smuggled into the state. The introduction of more than 3,600 slaves between 1798 and 1810 has been documented. The colonial Georgia slave merchant Joseph Clay contended that along the Windward and Gold Coasts of Africa slaves were always in demand. This was confirmed in newspaper advertisements that indicated that Georgia slave traders, planters, and merchants solicited slave labor from Africa and other foreign lands. The *Georgia Gazette* announced the sale of slaves "Just Arrived from Cape Mount, on the Windward Coast of Africa." Several Savannah newspapers advertised the sale of 330 "New Negroes from Angola." A few years later the Savannah City Council assembled a coastal patrol force to prevent the illegal landing of 700 to 800 slaves from the Island of Guadalupe. When the schooner *Hannah* was captured near Savannah in August 1803, one local official complained that the "business of smuggling the Negroes of St. Domingo into this state" was "truly alarming." Georgia's legacy in the foreign slave trade was evident several years after its legislative ban on the importation of foreign slaves. In 1815 northern-based slave ships maintained routes that carried slaves between New England, Africa, the West Indies, and eventually to Georgia.[4]

After Georgia banned the foreign slave trade in October 1798, its neighbor to the south, Florida, became a much more important slave-trading region. Census records and local observations indicate that foreign slave trading was very active in the Florida Territory, where Spaniards and Anglo-Americans were immigrating and importing slaves simultaneously. Many settled along the northeast coast of Florida near St. Augustine, on St. Mary's Island not far from the Georgia border, and close to Mobile on the Gulf Coast. Census records suggest that eighteen hundred foreign slaves were transported into Florida during the 1780s. Some Florida planters and farmers brought slaves into Florida for their own use, but as many as two-thirds may have been imported to sell on the United States slave market. This was especially true between 1798 and 1804 and after 1808, when foreign slave imports were prohibited in the United States. Florida shared a long and unguarded border with the United States, making it a simple exercise for smugglers to transport slaves between states and across regions.[5]

Slaves from Greater Senegambia in Africa tended to be more clustered in regions that would later become part of the United States. When considered in context with their transshipment into the country during the pre-Revolution period, perhaps general conclusions regarding the origins of those shipped during the post-Revolution era and beyond can be drawn. The

1739 Stono Rebellion (often referred to as the Kongo revolt) in South Carolina caused residents in the state to fear West Central Africa as a source for African slaves. Thereafter, Greater Senegambia became the focal point of Atlantic slave-trade voyages for the remainder of the eighteenth century. West Central Africa did not become a significant source of slaves for South Carolina again until 1801.[6]

From the study of transatlantic slave voyages, evidence suggests that during the eighteenth century the United States was an important destination for Greater Senegambians after the northern European powers legally entered the Atlantic slave trade. The unknown and perhaps unknowable is the ethnic composition of new Africans transshipped to the United States. It is highly probable that Greater Senegambians were significant in this traffic as well, because of selectivity in the transshipment trade between Africa, the Caribbean, and the United States.

From the standpoint of African ethnicities arriving in the United States, the artificial separation between Senegambia and Sierra Leone is a bit ambiguous. There is evidence that Senegambians were clustered regionally in the Chesapeake and probably elsewhere as well, particularly Georgia and Florida. Five out of six Atlantic slave-trade voyages to British West Florida ports along the north coast of the Gulf of Mexico came from Senegambia narrowly defined.[7]

Greater Senegambians also played a significant role in populating Louisiana with slaves. In the French slave trade to Louisiana, 64.3 percent of Africans arriving on clearly documented French Atlantic slave-trade voyages came from Senegambia narrowly defined. Based on evidence presented in the *Trans-Atlantic Slave Trade Database* for British voyages to the entire northern coast of the Gulf of Mexico, as well as additional Atlantic slave-trade voyages found in Louisiana documents that were included in the *Louisiana Slave Database* but not in the *Trans-Atlantic Slave Trade Database,* Gwendolyn Midlo Hall suggests that slave-trade voyages coming from Senegambia comprised nearly 60 percent of all documented voyages coming directly from Africa to Louisiana and the northern coast of the Gulf of Mexico between 1770 and 1803. The African origins of Louisiana slaves during the Spanish period was not as consistent. A large majority of new Africans arriving in Spanish Louisiana between 1763 and 1803 were transshipped from the Caribbean, mainly Jamaica, where Gold Coast Africans were in demand and were retained rather than shipped elsewhere.[8]

Excluding Atlantic slave-trade voyages and only considering descriptions of slaves in internal documents, Africans from "Senegambia" were 30.3 percent and those from "Sierra Leone" were 20.8 percent, or a total of 51.1 percent from Greater Senegambia arriving in Spanish Louisiana. Eliminating slaves described as being from "Guinea" or the "Coast of Guinea" from the Sierra Leone category, Africans from Sierra Leone drop to 6.7 percent. The result is a minimum of 37 percent of Africans of identified ethnicities from Greater Senegambia.

Because states offered only modest resistance to the foreign importation of slaves during the post-Revolutionary era, and the United States put forth less-than-aggressive efforts to suppress the foreign slave trade in the initial years following the ban of 1808, the slave-trading patterns of traffickers and smugglers revealed little noticeable difference from one period to the next.[9]

The Foreign Slave Trade and the Louisiana Purchase

The American purchase of Louisiana in 1803 marked a key transition in the history of the foreign slave trade in the United States. It ushered in a new set of issues regarding the limits of American jurisdiction over slave transshipments into the region and altered the dynamics of American interest in the trade. In South Carolina, the legislature promptly reopened the state's foreign slave trade in virtual concert with the purchase of Louisiana. John Drayton, who had endorsed the antislave-trade ban in his three years as governor of South Carolina, shifted his position and voted against prolonging the ban as a state legislator in 1803. In Louisiana, John Watkins, an official sent to the territory by its first governor, William C. C. Claiborne, observed what Drayton and others had suspected: "No subject," Watkins announced, "seems to be so interesting to the minds of the inhabitants of all that part of the country [Louisiana], which I have visited, as that of the importation of brute Negroes from Africa." The impact of South Carolina's renunciation of its slave-trade ban and the consummation of the Louisiana Purchase were felt almost immediately. Both had a distinct effect on South Carolina's major port city of Charleston, which had become the workstation for numerous slave merchants and consignees. In February 1804 the American brig *Maria* transported five slaves from Charleston to Hernandez, Cuba. Three months later the ship had returned to carry twelve more. By the end of the same year several vessels, including the American ships *Eliza, Baltic, Warren, Leon, Jane, Betsy Polly, Fair,* and *Mentor,* made at least one trip from Charleston to Cuba. Each carried numerous slaves. In 1806 and 1807, only Liverpool, England, merchants sponsored more slaving voyages than did Charleston slavers. In Liverpool, the firm of Baker & Dawson operated under an exclusive contract that transported slaves to Cuba. After 1805, American slave shipments going into Louisiana were legally bound to pass through Charleston. The March

1807 Charleston to New Orleans voyage of James Gordon and a "negro man with a collar around his neck," aboard a brig belonging to Hugh Young, indicated that a link between the two cities had been established.[10]

The ambivalence of some government officials provided encouragement for slave traffickers and smugglers to transgress borders. Thomas Jefferson, a prominent slaveholder and chief architect of the Louisiana Purchase, displayed sober indifference toward the introduction of foreign slaves into the fringes of the frontier during his tenure as secretary of state. Jefferson offered a cold response to a Spanish complaint that Georgians had crossed over into Spanish Florida to kidnap several slaves belonging to a Florida resident. His ambivalent reaction to another charge by French West Indian officials that an American sea captain had made off with slaves from Martinique, which he intended to sell in Georgia, was indicative of Jefferson's attitude toward the issue. In this case, Jefferson coolly instructed Georgia's governor to see that justice was done in the interest of international amity. As president, Jefferson deployed forty naval gunboats to the mouth of the Mississippi to defend the region's harbors, assist its customs agents, and to protect its merchants from the plunder and pillage of pirates; he allocated fewer resources, however, to suppress the foreign slave trade along the frontier.[11]

Louisiana was among those frontier regions where questions regarding the foreign slave trade had a distinct history. Creation of the national territorial system in 1787 had cleared the way for the eventual establishment of the Louisiana Territory. The Northwest Ordinance called for the entire region north of the Ohio River to be divided into as many as sixteen rectilinear states, each to be self-governing, and each to achieve equal status in the Confederation once its population reached that of the least populous of the original thirteen states. Originally, the 1787 ordinance had contained no mention of slavery, but two days before its passage, Nathan Dane of Massachusetts proposed "articles of compact" that called for the prohibition of slavery in the territory. Dane's amendment, however, predated the Louisiana Purchase, and therefore applied specifically to those territories north of the Ohio River. Unlike the Northwest Territory, where the exclusion of slavery was perceived neither as threatening to the expansion of slavery nor as a great concession from the nation's slave interest, the American purchase of Louisiana from France in 1803 marked a critical transition in the history of the foreign slave trade. During Louisiana's years as a territory, the federal government pandered to the needs and desires of its dominant planter class. The 1804 congressional bill that divided the Louisiana Territory into two distinct regions prohibited slavery north of the 33rd parallel, but allowed for the importation of slaves within the boundaries of what would later became the state of Louisiana, while the remainder of the Purchase was incorporated without mention of any restriction on slavery.[12]

The southern and northwest American frontiers were true tests of Jeffersonian republicanism, and the extension of slavery west of the Mississippi represented expansion of the ideals of decentralized government in which local populations dictated their own affairs. Although it had become accepted that slavery was legal in any American territory from which it had not been barred by federal law, both houses of Congress approved amendments banning the introduction of foreign slaves into Louisiana in 1804 to the dismay of disgruntled parties who alleged that it was "truly, impossible for lower Louisiana to get along without slaves." Some questioned whether American lawmakers had fully comprehended the logic behind prohibiting a trade so vital to Louisiana's economic interests.[13]

The Abolition Act

Before passage of the Abolition Act of 1808 slaveholding regions in the United States confronted a growing movement to dismantle the very commerce that had helped build the foundation of their economies. The international campaign to eradicate the foreign distribution of slaves had spread from Europe to America. Denmark outlawed the trade in 1802. The British followed when English abolitionists mounted a major crusade and pressured their government to impose its own version of a foreign-slave-trade ban. The English law was enacted in 1807. England's "Act for the Abolition of the Slave Trade" prohibited slave traders, citizens, and subjects from outfitting vessels in British ports for slave voyages. It also banned them from trafficking slaves except in the British West Indies, where intracolonial slave trading was permitted. This regional movement of slaves persisted for several years beyond 1808, and thousands of slaves were transported from Barbados and Dominica to the less-developed colonies of Trinidad and Demerara. Slave trading in this region, as the historian Eric Williams has pointed out, reached "proportions which could not be reconciled with the high-sounding pretensions of humanitarianism which had characterized the Abolition Act" of 1807.[14]

Although several European nations had passed similar laws against the foreign slave trade, enforcing them was a greater challenge. When compared to other countries, England conducted a continuous and more serious campaign to eradicate the trade. During the nineteenth century its navy interdicted several hundred illegal slave voyages. It confiscated the cargo and property of slavers in the northern regions of the Atlantic and turned this evidence over to its Vice-Admiralty Court in Nova Scotia, Canada. Although slave traffickers and smugglers in this region rarely admitted that their voyages involved the purchase of slaves from Africa, the court repeatedly identified inconsistencies in their behavior and stories. The *La Merced,* for instance, had engaged solely in commercial trade in New England before it abruptly altered its typical trading pattern in 1810 and began sailing to the coast of Africa with cargo that did not "consist so much of mercantile articles, as of stores" as it did an "outfit for the slave trade." The court arrived at the same conclusion about the Spanish vessel *Severn* in 1811, which at initial glance, with its tobacco, rum, wine, gunpowder, butter, rice, beef, pork, flour, soap, and candles, appeared to be engaged in legitimate commerce between Canada and the West African coast. Had it not been for published reports about the ship's cargo—which included the storage of "things peculiar to the slave trade"—the vessel might have escaped seizure. British suppression of the foreign slave trade in Latin America not only secured its immediate purpose of preventing slave smugglers and traffickers from adopting the flags of Latin American nations, but also enhanced its prestige as a defender of morality and diplomacy. Because its primary goal was the universal abolition of slavery, England focused much of its attention on the more prominent slave-trading nations as well as those that legally supported the practice but did not participate in it.[15]

Additional evidence of British efforts to disrupt the post-1808 foreign slave trade occurred when the frigate *Solebay,* commanded by E. H. Columbine, and the sloop *Derwent,* operated by Lieutenant E. Parker, were dispatched to the slave coast of Africa. Although England demonstrated more resolve to mitigate the trade than did its contemporaries, the vessels assigned to Columbine and Parker represented two of Britain's more outdated and ill-equipped navy ships. Both vessels were small and old. Their combined fifty guns were hardly adequate for the challenge of effectively suppressing the slave trade. Together, they formed but a minute portion of the 601 ships that Britain had certified for general sea operations. Most of England's naval resources were used to protect its own coastline from foreign aggressors, a practice that continued for several years.[16]

The 1808 congressional act prohibiting United States participation in the foreign slave trade differed in many ways from the British version. One contrast was the disposition of African captives. The British law stipulated that they "should in no case be liable to be sold, disposed of, treated or dealt with as slaves" by the crown or any of its subjects. In short, Britain assumed custody of all slaves illegally imported into its empire. It also implemented a plan to assimilate "liberated Africans" into British colonial society. United States law required that illegally imported slaves be sold for the benefit of the state and the informant—a provision that Congress grappled with before enacting the legislation. Most northern legislators resented the notion of state-sponsored slave selling. Some proposed compromises that would free or transport illegally imported slaves to regions where slavery had been abolished. Other Americans, however, vowed to relegate any African introduced into the country, legally or otherwise, to slavery.[17]

Evidence of a foreign slave trade between Africa, the United States, and the Caribbean was visible almost immediately in the years following passage of the Abolition Act of 1808. Adolph LaCoste was indicted for sailing the ship *Science* from New York to Africa to procure Africans to be disposed of as slaves. The slave trafficker Battiste sailed from New York to Africa in the brig *America* to round up slaves as young as fourteen. Battiste made several stops along the African coast and loaded slaves at each point before his return trip to New York where he was eventually prosecuted and sentenced for his offense. John Smith boldly appeared in a Connecticut federal court in 1809 to demand double value for his interest in a group of slaves which had been confiscated by American authorities. As owner and master of the brig *Heroine,* Smith had transported more than one hundred slaves from Africa to Cuba. Because the sale had allegedly occurred prior to the enactment of the Abolition Act, Smith escaped punishment for his activities. He graciously accepted the courts favorable ruling. Joseph Peabody of Salem, Massachusetts, had his slave ship, the *Mexican,* seized by Spanish pirates off the coast of Africa. After confiscating its cargo the bandits set the ship on fire.[18]

Difficulties emanating from the identification and misidentification of slave vessels hindered cooperation between nations and made enforcement of the Abolition Act of 1808 problematic. Some slave traffickers and smugglers avoided detection because of a procedure instituted in 1792 by the United States Department of State. In order to stimulate the shipbuilding industry, the agency required its foreign consulates to grant sea-letters (the right to own and operate ships in foreign countries) without restrictions. Americans who purchased vessels abroad often did so as fronts for slave traffickers in exchange for handsome payoffs. Others conducted their activities through the illegitimate use of foreign flags. The American operators of the slave ship *Amedie* took refuge under a Spanish flag and identified themselves as Spanish slavers just as British officers were seizing and condemning their vessel. They maintained this claim until legal matters concerning their situation could be sorted out. That the *Alerta,* carrying 170 slaves from Africa to New Orleans, was "bearing French colors" was, perhaps, the most important factor in the decision by the United States District Court in New Orleans to return the seized ship and slaves to Blas Moran, the owner of the vessel. Moran successfully persuaded the court that he knew little about the activities of the ship's commander, who he alleged had engineered a scheme to buy, sell, and trade slaves at sea from a group of "residents domiciled in New Orleans." American ship captains, the American Consul to Sweden wrote, often fronted for Swedish slave dealers. Much of this activity occurred between Africa and the Swedish Caribbean island of Ile Fourchue, usually called Five Islands, which was part of the Swedish colony of St. Barthélemy. American trade between these islands had been active for several years. Its coves were adequate for small swift vessels, and it offered an ideal place to conceal smuggling activities from the main island. In 1815 a Boston-based slave ship that had been outfitted in 1799 as a slaver had taken on 150 slaves from Africa after making an intermittent stop in Georgia. The slaves were eventually sold at St. Barthélemy before its capture. In the summer of 1821 a former United States navy brig was outfitted in Cuba for the Guinea slave trade. It returned from Africa with 380 slaves but was captured by a pirate boat crew that transported the slaves and ship to Five Islands, where they were sold to a group of islanders.[19]

The Five Islands dilemma was part of a larger problem in the Caribbean. England's ban on the foreign slave trade was designed to end trans-Atlantic slave transshipments altogether and to confine slave selling and trading to its own West Indian colonies. But when it came to its Caribbean islands, enforcement emerged as a significant concern. One American was indicted for working on board a vessel employed in transporting a slave boy from St. Thomas to Cuba where he sold him for three hundred dollars. In Jamaica, Britain's largest island in the Caribbean, where there was a sufficient number of slaves for internal purposes, the tendency was to export them under the guise of indentured servitude. Because the demand and price for slaves were typically higher in Spanish-controlled Cuba, many slave dealers in Jamaica directed their contraband there. In one case, the governor of Jamaica was compelled to admonish a police officer for behaving in gross violation of his duties. The officer had failed to adequately investigate the complaint of a Jamaican slave, who alleged that he had been purchased by a visitor whose intention was to carry him off to the Cuban slave market, contrary to Britain's intercolonial slave-trade laws. British officials in Jamaica and Barbados opposed the exportation of slaves for fear that such practice enhanced the economies of competing nations. The upstart planting communities in the

United States also helped increase the demand for Caribbean slave labor, which led to a pseudo-indentured-servant trade in African captives into the United States.[20]

The expansion of the sugar economy and the spectacular growth of cotton plantations in the American South and Southwest had a direct effect on the outward movement of the Caribbean slave population. Because Cuba's famous tobacco industry grew to depend upon free white and black labor, and the growth of traditional rural industries and new urban jobs guaranteed additional occupational opportunity for free labor, slave dealers who had previously operated within Cuba were compelled to explore new markets. The steady increase in the number of white immigrants into Cuba, the manumission of slaves, and the positive natural growth of freed persons all ensured the continued increase of free labor populations on the island throughout the nineteenth century. It also lessened the need for slave labor and elevated the island's slave-smuggling and trafficking industry which thrived along Cuban ports well into the 1860s.[21]

The movement of slaves into the United States from the Caribbean following the ban of 1808 was also linked in large part to white slave masters (mainly French) who had fled the region for the United States with their bondsmen to escape brutal slave uprisings. In 1809, fifty-six French immigrants who had been expelled from Cuba because of Napoleon's occupation of Spain had the slaves they were transporting confiscated and sold in Louisiana in accordance with its territorial law. Similarly, a second wave of French refugees from St. Dominique also jeopardized their slave property upon entering Louisiana. One historian estimated that more than 11,000 St. Dominique refugees, whites, free persons of color, and slaves landed in New Orleans between 1790 and 1811. At least 3,226 of the 9,059 refugees that arrived in 1809 were slaves. According to a New Orleans mayor's report, the number of slaves entering the city via Cuba outnumbered those of whites and free persons of color. The report was consistent with previous counts that a total of 9,059 immigrants had arrived by the start of January 1810, of which 2,731 were whites, 3,102 were free persons of color, and 3,226 were Africans imported to perform slave labor. *El Aviso de la Habana* indicated that several ships had also left Havana in the winter and spring of 1808 bound for New Orleans. Included in these voyages were the American frigate *John Jones,* mastered by Captain Fittermay, carrying 217 slaves, and the American schooner *James* under the command of Captain James Shearman, which left Cuba with 43 "negro bozales [Cuban term for slaves imported from Africa]." On April 14, 1808, Andrew J. Ehrenshion steered the American frigate *Franklin,* which hauled rice, house furniture, and 45 slaves to New Orleans. Because of his uncertainty about the legal status of these transshipments, William C. C. Claiborne decided to stop "all vessels with slaves on bord [*sic*] . . . at Plaquemine [*sic*]," and to refuse them entry into the Port of New Orleans until the Africans in tow were verified as legal imports and until clarification regarding their disposition could be established.[22]

Although the entry of white refugees and their slaves into Louisiana was approved by the United States Congress and was not construed as smuggling, serious questions were raised about the limits of Louisiana's territorial ban and the Abolition Act. Legal ambiguities regarding jurisdiction left many Louisiana planters and merchants with the impression that slaves could be imported into the territory from foreign ports. Governor Claiborne explained his position for allowing white refugees to enter Louisiana with their slaves even though they had done so with the help of slave traffickers: "Under the law of 1808," Claiborne contended, "the slaves were reported to me by the Collector of Customs, and I was requested to name a person to whom they should be delivered. As to their disposition I had to consult my own discretion, for neither the laws of the United States, or of the Territory had made express provisions on this point." Claiborne refused to send the Africans back to the Caribbean or to confine them to jail. To do so, he argued, would have constituted "an inhumane act" and would have "thrown the slave owners" "as paupers upon the community."[23]

In the midst of these legal uncertainties the Abolition Act of 1808 bolstered competition between the legal interstate domestic slave trade and the foreign slave trade. It also fueled political rivalries between the supporters of each.[24] One reason for these clashes was the passage of a congressional amendment that sanctioned a coastwise slave trade, one that provided an important link between the slave-trading regions within the United States. During the 1806 and 1807 congressional debates over the abolition of the foreign slave trade, the issue of discontinuing the coastwise legal domestic slave trade in the United States was also discussed at length. Despite efforts to end both, southern lawmakers put up formidable opposition to such proposals. Representative Peter Early of Georgia was one such dissenter. Early was a voice for many southern slaveholders. He introduced an amendment which stipulated that "nothing shall prohibit the taking on board or transporting of any Negro, mulatto, or person of color, in any vessel or species of craft whatever, from one place to another, within the jurisdiction of the United States." Besides, said Early, "What honor will you derive from a law which will be broken every day of your lives?" Representative John Randolph of Virginia embraced Early's proposal and concluded that failure to legalize the coastwise trade would effectively undermine slavery in the country. The amendment ultimately passed and required captains, masters, and commanders of slave ships to submit duplicate copies of manifests and affidavits that identified their slave cargo and ports of destination. An 1816 federal law further stipulated that all slaves shipped in the coastal waters be described by name, sex, and height.[25]

The coastwise slave trade expedited the movement of slaves, but at the same time threatened Louisiana's territorial ban. It also highlighted many of the challenges facing implementation of the Abolition Act. The coastwise legal domestic trade allowed slave dealers to transship hundreds of bondservants between regions without the dealers themselves having to leave their headquarters. The captain of a slave ship was responsible for the bondservants until the vessel arrived at port, where speculators had often arranged for someone to meet the ships at the dock. Maryland's Austin Woolfolk had many of his traders who were stationed around New Orleans, prepared to receive slave ships as they entered the port. Woolfolk and his relatives succeeded in expanding their coastwise operations, establishing a preeminent slave-trading firm by participating heavily in this commerce. Instead of asking for fifteen to twenty slaves to go to the Georgia market, Woolfolk alerted the public in 1821 that he planned to pay the highest prices in gold and silver for one hundred slaves that could be shipped to New Orleans.[26]

The economic significance of the legal domestic slave trade has been carefully charted. Its importance in the United States rests on two basic premises. First, the trade augmented the westward flow and resettlement patterns of American immigrants from where they were less valued to regions where their social, political, and economic value improved. Second, the trade earned profits for planters in the more established slaveholding states and thereby prolonged the life span of slavery.[27]

The laws governing the domestic slave trade were sometimes unenforceable. This often made it difficult to distinguish between it and the foreign slave trade. Participants were usually required to obtain certificates of good character for their slaves. This document was to accompany any slave transported from one state to the next. Good character certificates were used to regulate or restrict the introduction of incorrigible slaves and to inhibit the illegal importation of slaves. In most states, the laws requiring the certification of slaves, however, were short-lived. Although the large number of certificates reflected a high level of compliance, slave smugglers and traffickers found ways to circumvent or violate the law. Some used counterfeit documents to bypass customs and to deceive authorities. The *Baton Rouge Gazette* noted that no slaves, "save those of good character, shall be admitted; but persons engaged in this business, whence the trade is carried on, publicly announce their willingness to purchase, without certificates required by law, and yet when needed, certificates of the necessary kind are forthcoming!" Because the level of enforcement on slave certificates was suspect, it is difficult to determine the number of slaves illegally introduced from one state to the next.[28]

Distinguishing slaves introduced legally from those that arrived illegally was also made more difficult by the numerous routes that slave traders, traffickers, and smugglers used when transporting them. Mount Vernon, Virginia's Bushrod Washington—slaveholder, prominent leader in the American Colonization Society (ACS), and nephew of the country's first president—ran into financial difficulties resulting from ill-advised spending. His subsequent drastic actions undermined his involvement in the ACS and contributed to the unchecked and unregulated movement of his slaves. Washington attempted to rescue his declining fortune by selling fifty-four slaves to two Louisiana gentlemen who lived along the Red River. He netted $10,000 on the transaction. Washington understood the potential consequences of his actions and worked as best he could to keep the deal secret. Sending freed slaves and free blacks to Africa was a critical part of the ACS' agenda, but selling enslaved Africans into the frontier violated a fundamental tenet of the organization. Concealing the transaction was easier than hiding his slaves. It was not long before someone had spotted Washington's slaves trudging through Leesburg, Virginia, bound in chains. Although Washington's actions were legal, the subversive sale was so similar to an illegal transaction that unfavorable comparisons were often made.[29]

Washington faced stiff criticism because he had chosen to move his slaves across many of the overland slave-trade routes that smugglers and traffickers had often used. Some of these roads and paths passed through or near port cities. One artery went from Alexandria, Fredericksburg, and Richmond, Virginia, to Columbia and Hamburg, South Carolina. This upper route along with others became less traveled by smugglers as new markets proved more valuable to slave traders. In the mid-1820s, Natchez, Mississippi, and New Orleans, Louisiana, for instance, emerged as the two major termini for overland slave-trading routes. Transporting slaves downriver was another option for getting them into these new markets. Andrew Durnford used this method when his original plans to travel by sea failed. After much deliberation, Durnford heeded the advice of a fellow traveler, rented a wagon, purchased some horses, and transported his slaves across Virginia to a port along the Ohio River. From there, they dodged abolitionists and floated down the Mississippi River to New Orleans.[30]

Indeed, New Orleans played a key role in this traffic. Smugglers' Anchorage, located on the island of Grande Terre—a "place visited by sugar planters . . . who bought up . . . stolen slaves . . . from 150 to 200 dollars per head"—, in particular, offered a convenient place to unload slave contraband before moving them on to New Orleans. As one New Orleans eyewitness noted: "The whole adjacent coast was disquieted and kept in terror by pirates" and smugglers. Countless transactions demonstrated that a premium had been placed upon both smuggled and domestic slaves. At one New Orleans slave auction in 1810, the price of smuggled slaves averaged $400 for healthy men, while desirable slave women sold for $325. The comparable retail market value hovered around $500–$1,500.[31]

New Orleans and the Foreign Slave Trade

Slave trafficking, slave smuggling, the coastwise, and overland slave trade all contributed to the movement of bondservants across state, territorial, and international lines between 1790 and 1860. The convergence of Louisiana's urban and rural economies, and the realignment of the ports-of-entry and customhouses between Mobile and New Orleans in 1804 (which eased the traffic strain and ship congestion) helped to quicken this process. As new merchants entered Louisiana they often purchased cotton, sugar, and produce from planters, sold manufactured wares, or started plantations of their own. Specialization in business was rare in early Louisiana, and the volume of business in New Orleans was not enough to sustain the rural economy through legitimate means. Instead, nonspecialists dominated the business circles of the urban areas, and many of the most successful business folk eventually invested a share of their profits in agriculture and slaves so that by the nineteenth century, the struggle for control of the foreign exchange of slave labor was evident throughout the city.[32]

The emerging Louisiana economy placed the port at New Orleans within a class of rising commercial harbors. As the territory fragmented into a random collection of organized and unorganized interests, New Orleans inhabitants learned early that American rule could not unilaterally define their economic future. At the heart of its culture lay the conflict between those who enjoyed the lucrative returns of illicit commercial transactions and those who procured their goods and profits through legal channels. To some, an unrestrained smuggling culture unnecessarily handicapped honest merchants. To others, all forms of commerce, illicit or otherwise, helped gird the economy and increased fortunes. The growth of Louisiana businesses affected slave traffic and shaped the legacy of New Orleans, which served directly as a catalyst for the proliferation of the post-1808 foreign slave trade into the expanding frontier.[33]

Nineteenth-century New Orleans was, by the numerous accounts of its admirers and visitors, on the brink of becoming one of antebellum America's leading cities. It had grown from an imperial outpost, parceled between European powers, to become an international commercial mecca. No other city in early nineteenth-century America possessed its commercial potential. The Mississippi River and its tributaries provided exclusive access to population centers to the north and along the Gulf of Mexico for New Orleans, while the major ports along the East Coast, such as New York, Philadelphia, Boston, and Baltimore, competed for their share of the national economy. Unlike these towns, New Orleans's river system extended to nearly every crop region and commercial center in the United States, turning the city into an entrepôt for virtually every type of cargo, domestic and foreign, legal and illegal. Steamers along the Mississippi River flowed in daily, while foreign vessels cruised in from the Gulf of Mexico. The city buzzed as merchants bought and sold an array of merchandise including cotton, sugar, paper, clothes, shoes, buttons, guns, tobacco, china, books, wine, indigo, cattle, hogs, corn, textiles, books, livestock, flour, and beverages. A short distance from the New Orleans levee, one could also find North America's largest slave market—a market given life by the rise of cotton and the movement of slaves into the region.[34]

As stevedores and draymen unloaded their cargoes at New Orleans's bustling port, criminal networks transformed the city into one of America's most recognized centers for the post-1808 foreign slave trade. Slaveholders benefited from the large numbers of slave traders and buyers who flooded the streets and blanketed the walls of the city with their bills and graphic advertisements. Some came as independent business people or salaried employees of small and large trading firms from as far east as Virginia, while others journeyed from the states of the Deep South. Those who came by sea from the Caribbean no longer relied on small wind-propelled schooners, which limited their capabilities of transporting slaves into the region, but instead trusted in the more technologically advanced steam-powered rigs. As steamboats increased in numbers and improved in design—in some cases sporting triple-decked structures—shippers were able to navigate their vessels more easily through the strong currents, shallow waters, shifting sands, and mud bars of coastal Louisiana.[35]

Although the British impounded nearly sixteen hundred slave vessels between 1808 and the American Civil War, the business of introducing foreign slaves into New Orleans benefited from a failure of American authorities to effectively enforce its own slave-trade ban. Efforts of the United States Navy to suppress the foreign slave trade during the nineteenth century were lethargic and spasmodic. Problems with navy gunboats and crews, and an understaffed and poorly funded New Orleans naval station, hindered the navy's ability to uncover slaving conspiracies. During his first term as president, Thomas Jefferson pared down the meager United States naval fleet, which in its pre-altered state could hardly ensure prudent oversight of most slave transshipments. Because United States Navy ships lacked modern technologies, its flotilla of gunboats, which primarily defended the nation's ports and harbors from foreign attacks, was less than capable of adequately chasing down vessels suspected of slave smuggling.[36]

Once the Abolition Act of 1808 became law, the United States Navy did send Master-Commander David Porter to New Orleans to intercept foreign slave transshipments. Enforcement was a difficult task for Porter and his naval crews. Using vessels made from unseasoned and decaying timber, Porter, who had arrived in New Orleans in 1808 to replace Captain John Shaw as the station's commander, was asked to patrol a long stretch of the Gulf of Mexico coastline. Navy officers had often acknowledged that the discipline among Porter's sailors had become "much relaxed" and that their vessels lacked the required number of seamen needed to round up slave smugglers. Captain Shaw was creative in his response to this issue. He turned to the local Creole population to complete his gunboat crews, and with these makeshift gangs, he successfully apprehended three slave vessels by the end of 1808. In January 1810 Porter reported seizing the British slaver *Alexandrina,* which had illegally left Jamaica carrying 127 slaves; and in May he impounded a Portuguese vessel transporting 104 slaves. He also pursued the Portuguese brig *Moreveto,* the French privateer *Le Guillamne,* the Spanish ship *Alerto,* and the brigs *Adherbal* and *Neptune.* Some of Porter's ad-hoc navy crews were often recruited from the very ships engaged in the post-1808 foreign slave trade. The financial benefits of confiscating foreign slaves led some traffickers and smugglers to turn informant. Often, these sailors presented, perhaps, the best chance for naval officers to apprehend and prosecute law breakers. The slave-trafficking crew aboard the slave vessel *Clara,* for instance, agreed in 1809 to testify against the ship's owner in exchange for a share of the proceeds derived from the sale of the ship's slaves.[37]

Porter's operation was hurled into a state of confusion in February 1810 when the seizure of the *Amiable Lucy* (which had allegedly transported slaves from the West Indies to Louisiana illegally) was ruled unconstitutional. The *Amiable Lucy* decision reflected a growing trend in American jurisprudence. As chief justice of the United States Supreme Court, John Marshall presided over the *Amiable Lucy* case and several others involving the rights of citizens to be secure in their property claims. Because Congress had passed laws regulating the foreign importation of slaves into Louisiana in 1804 but the territorial legislature of Orleans "had never passed any laws prohibiting the practice," the court concluded that the United States Abolition Act of 1808 did not apply to Louisiana.[38]

In the years following the *Amiable Lucy* case, slave traffickers and smugglers went from being mere informants to becoming enlistments in the United States military service. Their willingness to join up with American armed forces earned them favorable treatment from government officials. When the United States Navy seized the ship *General Bolivar* in December 1814, William C. C. Claiborne, by now the former governor of the Louisiana Territory (which had become a state in 1812), challenged the confiscation on legal grounds. Claiborne was known to make allowances for those who had contributed to American military causes during the War of 1812. He used every coercive tool he could to suspend writs of habeas corpus against slave traffickers and smugglers, especially those against persons who were skilled "canoneers and bombardiers." Claiborne also called upon the state legislature of Louisiana to draft bills halting the detainment of smugglers who agreed to enlist in the country's armed forces. Some officials supported complete exoneration for slave traffickers and smugglers. Andrew Jackson believed that military service should absolve their crimes. United States district judge Dominick Augustin Hall, who presided over several slave-smuggling cases in New Orleans, dismissed numerous charges against some of the more prominent smugglers in the region.[39]

An 1815 promulgation by President James Madison granted smugglers "a free and full pardon of all offenses committed in violation of any act or acts of the Congress . . . touching the revenue, trade, and navigation . . . and commerce of the United States." Madison's declaration afforded smugglers favorable conditions under which to continue their nefarious vocation. He carefully constructed his proclamation and paid specific attention to the "inhabitants of New Orleans and . . . Barataria" who, by presenting "a certificate in writing from the governor stating that such person has aided in the defense of New Orleans," would be entitled to a full pardon from "all suits, indictments, prosecution, fines, penalties, and forfeitures."[40]

Among the many slave smugglers having strong ties to American military service and the foreign slave trade was the Venezuelan war hero and shipmaster

Renato Beluche. In New Orleans Beluche's name appeared on numerous slave transactions. According to Gwendolyn Midlo Hall's *Louisiana Slave Database,* Beluche consummated deals for slaves of numerous racial designations between 1788 and 1815. As a master wigmaker and native of the city of Tours, St. Etienne Parish, Beluche had assisted numerous French slave masters in immigrating to Louisiana from Cuba and Haiti. He initiated his own slaving activities by first capitalizing on Louisiana's growing demand for flour, grain, and other badly needed staples. The lion's share of Beluche's prosperity in the early 1800s, however, stemmed largely from slave smuggling. He frequently crossed the Gulf of Mexico aboard the *Two Sisters.* On March 5 and November 15, 1805, he set sail from New Orleans for Vera Cruz. On July 2 and August 30 of the same year he cleared for Havana. In each instance, Beluche remained away for six to ten weeks. His numerous trips and the length of his stays raised suspicion about his activities. Eugene Marchand, a New Orleans resident, suspected that Beluche was hiding smuggled and stolen Africans in his New Orleans home. In an attempt to recover his own slave Suzanne from Beluche, Marchand petitioned the New Orleans mayor to have Beluche's house searched. Beluche, however, consistently outwitted Marchand and other pursuers. By the time federal agents had targeted Beluche's businesses and possessions for seizure, the shipper had assumed a new identity. Under the alias Pierre Brugman he avoided arrest by David Porter, of the United States Navy, who had anticipated a generous payoff for himself from the confiscation and selling of Beluche's slaves and property.[41]

Slave smugglers such as Beluche often frustrated efforts to enforce the Abolition Act. When United States customs agents at New Orleans apprehended Juan Antonio Pereira in April 1815 on suspicion of slave smuggling after he refused to pay a modest duty, they confiscated only twenty bags of coffee from Pereira's *San Christopher.* This left government agents speculating about his motives and activities. They suspected that Pereira had already used one of the many passageways leading into the interior of Louisiana to unload slaves. Officials were particularly suspicious of small schooners, such as the one Pereira used, which they generally associated with slave smuggling.[42]

The military and criminal activity of the brothers Lafitte was another significant source of frustration. Despite writs for their arrest, the brothers paraded freely through the streets of New Orleans and Barataria. Having learned from their father, Marcus Lafitte, and his business associate Renato Beluche, Jean and Pierre Lafitte became the most ruthless of all Gulf Coast slave smugglers. There were three Lafitte brothers in all—Pierre, the oldest, Jean, and Antoine, the youngest. Pierre was so well recognized that the patch he sported over one eye, one local newspaper wrote following a jail escape, meant that no further description was necessary to identify him. Pierre became the chief lieutenant for his brother Jean, who masterminded their piratical and smuggling business. Flamboyant, charming, and well-dressed, the English-, Spanish-, and French-speaking Jean Lafitte, with an army of nearly one thousand pirates, several brigs, and a fleet of schooners, pillaged and plundered slave vessels at sea. From Barataria and New Orleans the Lafittes built a profitable blacksmith and wine import business, both of which they used as fronts to traffic and sell smuggled slaves.[43]

Like Beluche, the Lafittes are also on record for having purchased and sold slaves through legal channels. Gwendolyn Midlo Hall's *Louisiana Slave Database* provides numerous examples of these transactions. What is more difficult to ascertain is the precise number of slaves the Lafittes vended illegally. Civic heroes to many, the Lafittes used a loyal base of slave traffickers who ignored legal proscriptions, and whenever possible they imported slaves.[44]

The Lafittes promulgated a culture of fear. Their combative demeanor demonstrated a willingness to challenge those who threatened their vocation and property. One eyewitness reported seeing Lafitte's skilled marksmen patrolling the streets of New Orleans. Pierre Lafitte himself murdered one customs inspector and severely wounded two others. Customs agent Gilbert also experienced the wrath of the Lafitte brothers after he confiscated a quantity of their merchandise from one of their smuggling gangs. Before the goods could be turned over as evidence, Pierre Lafitte had accosted Gilbert, wounded him, and recovered his cargo. The economic and social standing of the Lafittes made prosecuting the brothers a difficult task. James R. Grymes, a noted New Orleans attorney, declared his appreciation for the handsome legal fees they were willing to pay and expressed his admiration and affection for the elegance that Pierre Lafitte displayed during court proceedings.[45]

The Lafittes' smuggling operation became their most fruitful enterprise and a very important source for purchasing slaves. Slave traders often relied on the wholesale prices of the Lafittes, who refused to accept anything other than specie as payment. The Lafitte's slave auctions attracted buyers from remote regions and they demonstrated that the selling of smuggled bondservants was a valued activity. One German merchant stated that slaves obtained from smugglers for less than two hundred dollars often sold at New Orleans slave auctions for six hundred dollars or more. "Fresh imported Guinea negroes," another one reported, "were sold in NOrleans [*sic*] at $1500."[46]

The poorly policed and porous Louisiana coastline called into question the ability of the United States to regulate commerce at New Orleans. Decades before the phrase "Manifest Destiny" had become a popular concept, James Madison recognized the ferment on the Western and Southwestern frontier and acknowledged the risks facing United States political and economic interests. "I understand that there are persons of respectable character and fortune in Upper Louisiana," Madison said, "who had gone into" the frontier "with a view of opening a [slave] trade" in a place that is "almost defenseless."[47]

War, Smuggling, African Sailors, and Customs

Louisiana's porous borders, boundaries, and coastlines combined with British plans to incite slave uprisings and filibuster schemes in the region led to calls for its annexation into the United States. Its defenselessness was highlighted during the War of 1812, when slave traffickers and smugglers were invited to join up with the American military to resist British aggression along the Gulf borderlands. Although statehood would subject Louisiana to American antislave-trade laws, the prospect of being governed by the more rigid suppression guidelines of England was far less appealing. It was not necessary for American officials to seek out sympathetic slave traffickers and smugglers as most rejected British overtures for enlistment into its Royal Navy. Jean Lafitte and his smuggling crews refused land, service rank, and a $30,000 allowance from British major Edward Nicolls, commander of the English forces at Apalachicola, Florida. Lafitte's rebuff is not difficult to understand. British decrees calling for slave insurrections, combined with its demand that slave smugglers put an end to their vocation, helped reinforce their bond with the American military.[48]

Informal alliances between slave smugglers and American military forces were strengthened during the War of 1812. A beneficiary of this relationship was Andrew Jackson, a man whom most Louisianans revered and trusted to protect them from British invasion. Jackson's reputation for being a disciplined and firm commander stirred enthusiasm among Louisiana dwellers. His greatest military successes at New Orleans can be largely attributed to the help he received from slave smugglers and traffickers that he used as enlistees. At Jackson's behest, they eagerly placed their resources under his command. In addition to obtaining seventy-five hundred flintlock pistols, gunpowder, and ammunition from Jean Lafitte during the War of 1812, Jackson also secured one thousand of Lafitte's most reliable sailors and cannoneers. Before meeting Lafitte, Jackson had regarded the smuggler and his associates as hellish bandits. He later recanted and lauded the outlaw for his bravery and patriotism. He considered him a committed and trusted lieutenant.[49]

Several months before Jackson was called upon to participate in the New Orleans campaign against Great Britain, he had his own encounter with slave trafficking that left him open to scathing rebukes. Jackson had entered into a partnership with Horace Green and Joseph Coleman. The trio intended to earn some quick cash by transporting commodities from Nashville to Natchez. In 1810 they profited from the sale of cotton and tobacco and purchased slaves from Richard Epperson the next year. They paid $10,500 for the slaves, $2,500 of which they gave in advance with the balance payable in two 6-month installments. Somehow Jackson became responsible for the balance. To resolve the matter he traveled back to Nashville and sold the slaves to satisfy the debt. Whether or not Jackson profited from the sale is unclear, but the transaction allowed his adversaries to place him in the company of rogue slave dealers and smugglers. His detractors believed he had escorted a coffle of slaves into Louisiana to sell and that his slave dealing was unbefitting of a public figure.[50]

If the military support that slave traffickers offered to Jackson was essential for his successes during the War of 1812, then the free and enslaved African sailors that the Lafittes had placed under his command were as valuable as any weapon of war. The participation of free and enslaved Africans in American military service has been recorded from the years of the Early Republic to the Civil War. When the British warship *Leopard* forcibly stopped the United States frigate *Chesapeake* off the Virginia coast in 1807 and removed some if its crew, three of the detainees were Africans. During the height of the British and American conflict of 1812 most American navy ships had "no difficulty in procuring a 'fiddler' especially among the coloured men, in every American frigate," who could "play most of the common dancing tunes" to help motivate all sailors to take part in healthy exercise routines. Free and enslaved Africans served with Oliver Hazard Perry at the battle of Lake Erie. Commodore Thomas MacDonough was surprised by the moral deficiencies of a white chaplain on his ship during the war and refused to use him for any religious functions. Instead, he designated a pious steward of color to offer prayers before the battle of Lake Champlain.[51]

British impressments had shielded many free African seamen from the foreign slave trade and offered them better accommodations than the parsimonious opportunities availed to them by merchants, smugglers, and traffickers. The British crown considered forcible conscription a prerogative and felt obligated to bolster its own inefficient military enlistment system by recruiting Africans and guarding them from the foreign slave trade. British naval service held out the promise of prize money, pensions, and hospitalization for aged or injured African seamen. Free African sailors, however, viewed British inducements with indifference. Many refused to sign British muster rolls despite the opportunity it provided to protect them from unforeseen adversity. Some did choose to work for the acceptance of white Americans by offering their military service. More nonwhite than white American sailors opted for British prison rather than service against the United States. In most cases, detainees preferred British incarceration rather than enlistment into the Royal Navy. Free Africans living in America valued family and place, feared the thought of being branded traitors, and dreaded punishment and reprisal for aligning themselves with England. American slaves, however, were offered freedom for fighting alongside British forces—an offer some accepted.[52]

Free African sailors found themselves trapped in one exploitive system after another. If in search of greater gain and a modicum of independence by assisting the foreign slave trade, they barely decreased their own chances of enslavement. While they felt a need to defer to the formal demands of whites for the sake of self-preservation, they also empathized with slaves held in bondage. African sailors appeared as beacons of liberty to these captives and often represented their only contact with the outside world. Wage demands, coupled with high desertion rates among white merchant seamen and sailors, made free and enslaved African sailors essential elements in enabling the objectives of navies, merchants, and smugglers.[53]

Most ship captains realized that they had precious commodities in free and enslaved African sailors. Because of his seafaring skills, Pedro Thomasin and Pedro Esnandez knew they had a valuable worker in José Velasco, a Venezuelan-born African whom they considered a shipmate. Velasco offered the two men their best hope to enjoy financial gain, which might explain their eagerness to obtain his release from a New Orleans jail after he was arrested as a runaway. Africans such as Velasco carried intangible value for their shipmasters and crews and were far too useful to allow them to waste away in prison. Thomas Shields, the purser of an American ship, initiated his own efforts to retain the Africans that operated and serviced his vessel. In May 1813, Shields sent a letter to the mayor of New Orleans requesting the immediate release of his sailors from the city jail.[54]

Ship captains contemplated the ramifications of leaving their African crew members in jailhouses or discharging them to other ship captains after docking at slave-trading ports. Housing them in local jails did not always ensure their return. Releasing them to other ships often meant their disappearance. William Frances, a "colored seaman," deserted a vessel that his captain had assigned him to as an alternative to paying a five hundred dollar bond to have him boarded at a New Orleans jail. Frances's captain had debated his own actions and complained about the exorbitant fee required of shippers who brought African sailors into the city. Frances had worked as a cook and steward aboard the *Osceola* for sixteen dollars per month but when discharged by his captain took work on another ship for eighteen dollars per month.[55]

Some African seamen put to use their seafaring expertise so effectively that they were not only viewed as equals in the industry but also treated as such. Their attraction to the sea, the amenity of working for wages, and the modest protection it provided, afforded them an alternative to plantation life, naval service, or prison. African sailors and crews found considerable maneuvering room within the seafaring workplace, where their color was less of a determinant in their daily lives and duties than it was on the plantation. The innumerable ships on which they toiled and earned higher rank and salary than many of their white shipmates indicated that the African seaman's billet carried precedence over race. In 1807 Stephen Revel, a man of color and cook on board the *Harmony,* a slave vessel owned by a group of Pennsylvania citizens, and his shipmate, James Bowen, a black steward, were each rewarded $3,853 for their role in confronting sea pirates who had attempted to steal the ship and its contents as it sailed from Great Britain to Philadelphia. Six other African seamen had a similar experience when they received their share of goods taken from the wreck of the brig *Catherine.* William, Joe, Europe, Lewis, Jerry, and Peter, all slaves, were granted shares equal to their white shipmates after the ship was libeled for salvage by a Pennsylvania court. The black cook Ferrer was declared innocent by a Massachusetts federal court despite being present on the Spanish pirate ship *Panda* at the time in which its crew captured and incinerated the brig *Mexican* belonging to Joseph Peabody.[56]

Enslaved Africans often took refuge aboard steamboats and other ships where they became co-participants in the foreign slave trade, established their own life rules, and deemed themselves free. Slave owners were alerted about slaves suspected of lingering around wharves and ports with the intent of gaining access to these vessels. Some obtained warrants to have ships searched for escaped slaves. The depositions of schooner master George Clark and his mate Thomas Dailey supported each other's stories about John Nicholas, a mulatto, who had left their ship and did not return until it was time to collect his wages. In 1811 James Mather, mayor of New Orleans, ordered a search of the brig *Argonaut* to locate and capture the slave Shepard, who allegedly had stowed away on the vessel. The ship captain Armand filed an affidavit with the municipal court of New Orleans seeking the return of his slave Ned, who he believed had boarded the *Suffolk*. The slave Jack and five other blacks took refuge on an approaching barge in New Orleans where they assimilated into the seafaring universe after fleeing from the English-born merchant Thomas Durnford in 1816.[57]

The boat skills of free and enslaved Africans aided slave traffickers and smugglers in their subterfuge. Some had constant access to slave vessels and were in frequent demand to work aboard shorthanded slave ships. In many cases, crews "consisted wholly of colored men." In 1816 the slave smuggler Louis Aury thought that he could depend on two hundred Haitian seamen to assist him and his cohorts in their plots. The disgruntled sailors, who had been promised prize money to spend in New Orleans, had often commented on Aury's cohabitation with a mulatto woman. They eventually turned on their leader after voicing discontent about working conditions on deserted sandbars. Aury was shot three times. One bullet lodged in his right hand depriving him use of his forefinger; another struck his left chest, while a third passed through his left hand. After leaving Aury for dead, the seamen commandeered three of his ships, set fire to another, and sailed for Haiti. The fact that most of Aury's troops had come from the first black republic (Haiti) in the Western Hemisphere raised concerns among many whites. The *Savannah Republican* described Aury's black seamen as "brigades who had participated in the horrors of St. Domingo." John Houston McIntosh warned that Aury's crew of "desperate bloody dogs" made them "extremely dangerous to a population like ours" and he feared that if they were not expelled, they would, perhaps, call to their aid "every negro within reach."[58]

Communication and contact between African sailors and slave captives presented less of a concern for slave traffickers and smugglers than did the prospects of prosecution or seizure of their property. Using African sailors on slave ships was, nevertheless, a risky proposition, considering the bellicose behavior that some displayed toward the crews with which they shared responsibilities. Although life at sea offered an alternative to the plantation, some thought more of making life miserable for their criminal captains than they did of offering obedient service. Their collective defiance reflected a consciousness of resistance toward some of the repressive qualities that life at sea carried. Excessive drinking among African sailors played a significant role in some of this unmanageable behavior. Thomas Coates declared that John Francis, an African sailor who was assigned the duty of steward, was so regularly intoxicated that he was unable to perform his functions as a crewman. James Robertson made a similar claim about fellow African Joseph Howin, who, he alleged, behaved belligerently while under the influence of alcohol.[59]

White slaving crew captains responded to episodes of incorrigible behavior either through physical threats, abusive language, or by filing formal criminal charges against African sailors who disrupted the continuity of their commerce. John R. Myrick of the ship *Jackson* had his cook, Alexander Francis, detained for actions that Myrick found unacceptable. Captain Lewis Barnes, who commanded the *Recovery,* arranged to have his kitchen hand, William Sorrel, picked up for similar reasons. Ship master Michael Brown had Jay Robinson expelled from his ship the *Dolphin* and jailed for inappropriate conduct. Captain William Dey explained in a deposition his rationale for having the African sailor Samuel Feney placed in the custody of New Orleans law officers after Feney had behaved dishonorably.[60]

Insubordination, however, rarely resulted in crews leaving behind the Africans that they relied upon to oversee the necessary functions of the slave trade. Virtually no crime was severe enough to imprison an African crew member beyond the anticipated date of departure of the vessels on which they worked. After confirming through an affidavit the refractory attitude of William Payne, Captain William Story made it clear that he preferred Payne's detention to not conflict with his sailing schedule. Although Isaac Johnston had threatened the life of his white captain, C. A. Darbrett, his release from jail for the offense was expedited after Darbrett requested that he be set free before his schooner *Constancia* set sail for the Gulf of Mexico. Even though John Lewis and James Niles deserted the ships they were on, neither of their captains insisted on sentences that required prolonged incarceration. Instead, both crew chiefs requested that jail time not exceed their departure date from New Orleans.[61]

Free and enslaved African sailors were important instruments in the shadowy world of the foreign slave trade after 1808. They labored as carpenters, joiners, caulkers, pilots, mariners, and operators on vessels used to transship slaves. Because the testimonies of African sailors were usually inadmissible in most criminal cases, slave traffickers regularly discharged their white crews before embarking on slaving voyages and replaced them with black ones. Whether to reduce operational costs or to shield themselves from prosecution, the use of free and enslaved African sailors afforded smugglers and traffickers certain advantages.[62]

The high demand for the seafaring skills of free and enslaved African sailors led to legal restrictions against their movement. A Louisiana territorial act of 1806 required that African seamen arrested within the city of New

Orleans were to be disposed of as directed by the mayor and the city council. Only by securing the necessary documents from municipal authorities could they be transported out of Louisiana into the waters of the Gulf of Mexico. During the War of 1812, the New Orleans city council ordered that the transporting of Africans across Lake Pontchartrain be interdicted, because it provided the most expedient access to the Gulf of Mexico where British ships and slave smugglers eagerly waited to employ them in their service or to sell them into slavery. Those who sought to bypass port officials and move Africans beyond New Orleans to remote harbors often did so by coddling relationships with local politicians. These political connections often trumped attempts to restrict the movement of Africans across the lake. Tom Harman and James Bradley were clever enough to secure a passport from the mayor of New Orleans, which shielded them from potential hassles with customs agents. The passport allowed the two men to transport nineteen slaves into the Gulf of Mexico.[63]

Slavers were usually careful to secure proper documentation that would protect their slaving activities around New Orleans. Dominique York guarded his Lake Pontchartrain sailing privileges when he obtained written permission from city officials to travel to Galveston Island in Mexico with the male slave Jean Baptiste Amicar and to return to New Orleans free from interrogation. Felicite Brun, a free woman, submitted a deposition naming and describing sixteen slaves that she planned to transport with her to Jamaica and also declared her intentions of returning to Louisiana. Honoré Fortier used his passport to make frequent trips between New Orleans and Puerto Rico. Sailing for Alexander Harang, Fortier and Joseph Garus were cleared to make several trips, all of which involved the transshipment of slaves. Cuba, however, garnered the greatest amount of attention from slavers, who relied on written assurances from local officials that their vessels would be allowed back into New Orleans after docking at Havana harbor. Jean Simon Stuart minimized suspicion about his activities which involved six slaves who traveled with him to Cuba by registering his trip with the New Orleans city government as a business function.[64]

Beverly Chew

Links to influential government officials helped slave traffickers and smugglers secure the necessary documents for safe passage in and out of New Orleans. Customs agents played an important role in promoting this endeavor. During the first ten years of its operation (1789–1799), the United States Customs Service established the basic mechanics for overseeing the enforcement of most commercial laws. The collectors of customs and their officers imposed fines and penalties, seized goods and vessels, examined cargos, and rewarded informers who helped them confiscate contraband with handsome payouts. The mandate of the Customs Service overlapped those of the Department of Treasury and the United States Navy. Its mission was to combat fraud, detect unauthorized entries into the country, and to confront hostile threats.

Beverly Chew's tenure as the chief collector of customs at the Port of New Orleans was the second longest among those who were named by presidential appointment. Chew was responsible for suppressing slave smuggling in the region. As an aspiring businessman, he understood the economic calamities brought on by poorly regulated commerce and trade. In the face of widespread shipping violations and slave-smuggling schemes, he effectively controlled the confluence of ships that transported slaves into the labyrinth of rivers, bayous, and tributaries along the Western Gulf South. He was known to make smuggling "a little more difficult" for those who failed to acquiesce to his demands.[65] His team of customs agents, for instance, arrested the swashbuckling privateer William Mitchell, a reputed slave smuggler, several times before wounding him at least once. Mitchell had repeatedly challenged Chew's authority and disapproved of his raids on slave and merchant vessels near the southern Louisiana town of Balize, where ships transporting contraband awaited the most opportune moment to distribute their cargo inland.[66]

The legacy of the United States Customs Service at New Orleans was a less-than-admirable one. By the time Chew had obtained his appointment in 1817 the agency was plagued with corruption, misdeeds, subversive activities, and illegal dealings among agents, pirates, privateers, slave smugglers, rum runners, filibusters, narcotics peddlers, renegade politicians, civic leaders, and rogue merchants. Financial gain was one motivation for the participation of customs agents in this nexus of crime. Their connections to informants often led to the collection of large financial rewards.[67]

In Chew's case, the flow of commerce at the Port of New Orleans affected his personal remuneration, which came from the collection of fees. But Chew's appetite for money reached beyond his port responsibilities and employment compensation. As he pursued legal action against slave traffickers, he also cut favorable side deals with them when the prospects for monetary gain seemed certain. Even free Africans who sought the assistance of influential whites looked to Chew, who occasionally granted them special favors. In December 1821, Chew used his political clout to vouch for a slave who needed a temporary reprieve from New Orleans's stringent curfew laws. On one occasion he submitted a letter to Mayor Roffignac of the city requesting that a slave be allowed to retrieve some money that he had found and later hid. When it came to slave transactions, Chew's reputation was an unscrupulous one. In 1803 the New Orleans city council barred him and his business partner Richard Relf from importing West Indian slaves into Louisiana. When his own slaves were arrested for theft, Chew, under cross-examination in court, admitted accompanying them the night they had carried off whiskey and tobacco from the home of a Mr. Bond. In June 1824, Chew authorized the ship *Ceres* to enter New Orleans with slaves despite the fact that its crew presented no manifest. The following year he informed the city's mayor of his intent to allow a free African family from Port au Prince into Louisiana although they lacked the legal documents necessary to enter the country.[68]

Chew and his longtime associate Richard Relf had established themselves as pillars within the New Orleans business community. As members of the city's elite, each man was instrumental in its economic and political development during the decade following the Louisiana Purchase. They organized new forms of capitalistic enterprises, including the establishment of a mercantile house and a local chamber of commerce, which survived the territory years, the War of 1812, and the natural boom-and-bust cycles of the free market system. As pioneers of the New Orleans Insurance Company, which insured vessels, cargoes, and money, Chew and Relf were among the original shareholders of the company's stock and they occupied positions on its board of directors. The two also announced their appointment as the exclusive agents of the London-based Phoenix Fire Insurance Company. While enjoying stockholder status in the Bank of Louisiana, Chew served on the board of directors for the New Orleans branch of the Bank of the United States. Deeply involved in the economic life and business establishment of New Orleans, Chew and Relf were part of a solidly entrenched business circle that dominated the town politically, set its social tempo, and controlled economic development by legal, extralegal, or illicit means. Several dozen of Chew's and Relf's slave transactions were recorded in the public records of New Orleans. The pair also left additional evidence of their slave dealings. Between 1804 and 1807 they vended around 430 slaves.[69]

Chew, Beluche, the Lafittes, and a host of other slave smugglers and traffickers found ways to circumvent the Abolition Act of 1808. Their cause generally prospered because it was so often linked to the political and economic interests of the country. They offered their services to markets dependent upon slaves, and they became a focal point around which their visible response to antislave-trade laws could be observed. To acquiesce to the demands of most slave-trade bans meant lost earnings. Continuation of the post-1808 foreign slave trade, however, meant certain financial gain. Their success in maintaining the trade depended in part on their ability to improvise strategies to help protect their clout and status. In many cases it was the judicial system and the favorable treatment they received from sympathetic juries and judges that helped advance their ambitions.

2

"A Particular Kind of Force"

JUDICIAL PURSUITS, RESISTANCE, DISPERSION, AND THE FRONTIER

When Beverly Chew reported for duty as collector of customs at New Orleans in 1817, he brought with him some issues from his own past that made many in the community skeptical about his ability to conduct fair, impartial, and honest administration of the Abolition Act. Born in Virginia in 1773, Chew settled in New Orleans during Spanish rule and nurtured business relations throughout the city which made him one of New Orleans's most notable personalities. In 1804, Chew was appointed president of the Bank of United States in New Orleans. In 1811 he was named as one of the executors in the will of Daniel Clark, a wealthy New Orleans shipper and trader. It was then that many of his real troubles began. For the next several months Chew was embroiled in a bitter controversy with Clark's daughter Myra Clark Gaines, who believed that the agent had improperly gained access to her father's personal information and shrewdly connived his way into becoming a key player in the allocation of his assets. The fact that one of Chew's companies had fallen on hard times just prior to Clark's passing raised suspicion about his appointment as executor of the businessman's will—an association with controversy that was to characterize his life and professional career. As the lead federal agent at the Port of New Orleans, his credibility was called into question, and more importantly, his sincerity toward the enforcement of American law. Chew's behavior typified life on the frontier, although few criminals feared its criminal justice system. Slave smugglers and traffickers especially manipulated the process, and in cases where they encountered jurisdictional changes that threatened the security of their vocation they casually moved across borders to areas where institutional structures were less developed and less capable of curbing their interests.[1]

Economic and territorial expansion in the United States during the nineteenth century initiated migration and immigration into the frontier, which spawned a movement to redistribute slaves. The post-1808 foreign slave trade was indispensable in this traffic. It was also critical in the early development of the judicial systems along the emerging frontier, where courts provided a means for slave smugglers and traffickers to circumvent the commands of the Abolition Act. As borders and boundary claims shifted, the dispersal of slave-smugglers and traffickers into the frontier tested the limits of slave trade suppression. It stretched resources and exposed corruption among frontier customs agents, U.S. marshals, governors, and other public figures. Boundaries and borders meant one thing to central authorities but something different for slave smugglers and traffickers. To central authorities, jurisdiction, sovereignty, and compliance were of paramount importance. For slavers, opportunity and financial gain through the foreign slave trade lay at the heart of their motivation. For them, geographical lines of demarcation represented minimally restrictive barriers.

Judicial Pursuits

The emerging frontier during the nineteenth century attracted a range of characters, but none more important than those who sought to capitalize on its unregulated economy. The frontier judicial system helped shape this maverick identity. Under-policed and experimental judicial practices provided a base from which judges, juries, and attorneys operated in concert with and deference toward the economic needs of local populations. For those who understood the importance of slave labor, judicial support could function as a benefit to the foreign slave trade. Because American slavery and the foreign slave trade were such critical parts in the transformation of the frontier, juries, judges, and lawyers had to develop their own peculiar rules and procedures to accommodate both. The judicial systems within the slaveholding regions essentially acted to uphold the exploits of slave smugglers and traffickers.

Examination of court cases involving the foreign slave trade uncovers a de-centered legal system that floundered in legal minutiae and handed out an insignificant number of criminal convictions. Although formal legal structures and procedures had been established, the actual judicial practices and conduct of court officials, prosecutors, defense lawyers, and jurists exposed their identification with and legitimization of the trade. Particular circumstances made the application of justice a partial and biased affair. Judges often prosecuted the more flagrant violators of the 1808 Abolition Act, but their accountability to the needs of local societies often trumped the rules of procedural justice. By rationalizing their logic, communities used their courts to protect their interests and to shield themselves and the importation of slaves from the perpetual conflicts brought on by the integration and absorption of judicial superstructures.

Judicial decisions regarding slave transactions were often made by judges who decided cases in the interests of certain individuals and classes of people. Many outcomes were driven by the dominant influence that the institution of slavery had on the legal system. Tradition and laws tended to protect slave buyers, often at the expense of sellers. Out of this prevailing influence evolved the *caveat venditor*—let the vendor beware—principle. In most slave-trading regions slave smugglers and traffickers were guided by *caveat venditor*. One often-cited court decision that adopted a counter position, that being the rule of *caveat emptor*—let the buyer beware—was the 1804 New York case of *Seixas v. Woods*. In a two-to-one decision the court denied a buyer the right to recover payment for a breach of warranty against a seller of "peachum wood" who had advertised and invoiced the shipment of wood as more expensive "brazilletto wood." The majority rejected a legal precedent that for many years had protected buyers in the marketplace when it argued that only proof of false and deceitful statements by the seller was grounds for financial restitution. The *Seixas* decision struck a responsive nerve among slave smugglers and traffickers who applied the decision to their own business practices. The legally tenuous and high-risk nature of the post-1808 foreign slave trade meant that, *caveat emptor* placed slave smugglers and traffickers at an obvious advantage over the buyer in their marketplace activities.[2]

The plethora of court cases involving slavery during the nineteenth century focused as much on the legitimacy and illegitimacy of slave imports as it did on the disputes between slave buyers and sellers. The Superior Council of Louisiana, which was first established in 1712, had served as the primary judicial body for the territory until 1769. It was then that the French gover-

nor O'Reilly dissolved the assembly. Thereafter, Louisiana law was administered by the captain general of Cuba. Spanish law and administration prevailed
until the United States took control in late 1803. From 1803 until statehood
in 1812, the Louisiana territorial governor exercised judicial powers and
authority within the governor's court of the Territory of Orleans. After statehood, legal matters in Louisiana were subject to the American judicial system, where many cases involving the slave trade reached the Louisiana State
Supreme Court as well as the federal appellate court in New Orleans.[3]

The courts, state and federal, selectively protected the actions of some
slave-trade violators and scrutinized the behavior of others. The cases heard
at the Louisiana State Supreme Court had as little effect on the foreign slave
trade as did those in the federal courts. For example, Fernando Antonio
DeSierra, a Havana merchant, was accused in 1813 of using his frigate the
Rosalia to transport 599 Africans from the coast of Africa into the Gulf of
Mexico. As the vessel approached Louisiana, it was captured by Lafitte pirates
and towed to Barataria. When DeSierra traced two of his "lost" Africans to
Antonio Llort, he filed suit for restitution. Although DeSierra did not include
the Lafittes in the suit, his use of supportive testimony from other pirates and
smugglers gained him a favorable decision from the court.[4]

Slave smugglers who did not benefit from the mercy of the courts often
fabricated stories to deceive judges and juries. Renato Beluche was as skilled
at this scheme as anyone. His association with the *Josefa Segunda* vessel raised
suspicion among American and British officials about the ship's mission. The
Josefa Segunda had cleared Havana in July 1817, bound for the Guinea coast
of Africa. There, the ship's captain purchased 314 Africans and loaded them
at the port of Maura before returning to Cuba. The *Josefa Segunda* proceeded
without hindrance until it was confronted by Beluche and his 144 mainly
black and mulatto sailors aboard the *General Arismendy.* They chained and
shackled the crew of the *Josefa Segunda,* confiscated the slaves, and steered the
ship to Louisiana. It was not until the collector of customs at New Orleans
sent an armed United States revenue boat to seize another ship belonging to
Beluche that officers discovered the ship captain's notes indicating that
Beluche and his crew had absconded with the slaves of the *Josefa Segunda.*
The ship's captain had also meticulously recorded his boss's directive to steer
all slave vessels and their cargoes to the Island of Margarita off the coast of
South America, and to maintain a "declaration of being forced into port" if
apprehended by foreign authorities.[5]

Beluche's captains and ship operators refused to reveal the real intent of
their voyages. They offered the alibi that the Africans aboard their ships were
commodities to be exchanged for much-needed "provisions," and that none

were to be transacted on the slave market.[6] Beluche made coordinated attempts to safeguard his property but on several occasions American officials forced him to surrender his cargo. Such was the case with the *Josefa Segunda*. The reward for the seizure placed a considerable amount of cash into the pockets of customs agents, marshals, naval officers, and crews. Beverly Chew staked out his claim for a share of the ship's cargo, as did naval officer Edwin Lorrain and William Emerson, surveyor of the Port of New Orleans. Because the trio had made arrangements for Louisiana planter and medical doctor William Flood to provide care and shelter for 152 of the slaves taken from the *Josefa Segunda,* they felt obliged to bill the government on Flood's behalf. In exchange, Dr. Flood received several weeks of the slaves' labor and a portion of nearly forty thousand dollars derived from the sale of the Africans and other confiscated property.[7]

Beluche also found legal troubles with Great Britain. His 1818 trial in Kingston, Jamaica, presented an opportunity for England to exact revenge for Beluche's well-publicized alliance with the United States military during the War of 1812. Despite an acquittal, the trial provided an opportunity for Britain to reassert its political authority over its colonies and the high seas by enforcing its antislave-trade laws. Although British citizens had exerted continuous and formidable pressure to eradicate all aspects of the foreign slave trade, the Beluche case indicated that in remote regions English policy and law carried less influence than did the social and economic clout of some prominent slave smugglers.[8] Beluche's arrest, the charges of acts of piracy and smuggling, the seizure of his property, and his detention in an English-controlled Jamaican prison angered many wealthy Caribbean and New Orleans residents as well as an assortment of British military officers, who paraded in and out of the courtroom defending the man responsible for much of their financial success.[9]

Judicial cases against slave traffickers and smugglers became a source of conflict for the American central authority. The failure of local populations to comply with federal law required the government to amplify its enforcement. Collector of Customs Beverly Chew, despite his dubious reputation, conceded what most people already knew: "to put a stop to that [slave] traffic, a naval force suitable to these waters is indispensable." Otherwise, Chew believed, "vast numbers of slaves will be introduced to an alarming extent" in violation of central law.[10]

The Abolition Act of 1808 did spur some federal officials into action. John Dick, United States attorney in New Orleans, who had demonstrated his own biases toward certain slave smugglers, was eager to enforce the law against some. Dick accused William Lee, shipmaster of the brig *Mary Ann,* of smuggling "forty-five Negroes, Mulattoes, or persons of colour, for the purpose of transporting them" for "service or labor" into the Port of New Orleans. When authorities inspected Lee's vessel, they discovered that the items he had designated on his original shipping manifest at the Port of New York included a range of merchandise but no mention of slaves. With little hesitation, United States marshals arrested Lee, seized his loot, and ushered him to New Orleans federal court, where Judge Dominick A. Hall levied a thirty-six-thousand-dollar bond. Lee posted bail but the outcome of his case is unknown.[11]

Seizures of slave vessels and their cargoes usually occurred when slavers failed to produce adequate documentation that verified their legal right to introduce slaves into the country. Samuel Glover and Robinson Rigby lost their sloop *Alteezira* under these circumstances. The ship left Norfolk, Virginia, in March 1819 for New Orleans with forty-seven slaves. Glover maintained that the vessel was participating in the legal coastwise slave trade when it was wrecked near the Bahaman island of Abaco. The men reported losing nineteen of their slaves as well as the manifests that could substantiate their claim. According to Glover's account, he and his partner salvaged a portion of their cargo but not the necessary paperwork. Desperate for help, they contracted John Alden, who helped the men salvage their ship. In exchange for three slaves as payment, Alden transported the crew and the surviving slaves to New Orleans. Glover's alleged mishap, however, drew little sympathy from the United States District Court in Louisiana, where he had filed suit to recover his slaves and Alden's brig, which had been confiscated by federal authorities.[12]

Glover's shipwreck story was not an unreasonable claim as wrecking or "wracking" had indeed become a profitable industry among the island communities of the Caribbean. Customary laws regulating the recovery and repair of wrecked ships in the Caribbean favored local salvagers. As a business pursuit, "wracking" had a well-established legacy. Ship salvaging employed substantial numbers of island workers (usually slaves or former slaves) and played a major role in sustaining segments of the Caribbean economy during the nineteenth century. Skilled African salvagers and ship repairers discovered that their vocation, at times, mitigated the burdens of color. At places such as Elbow Cay, Abaco, unscrupulous profiteers often placed lights to lure ships into island reefs, and then used slaves or free Africans in their recovery operations. They averaged about one wreck per month. Attempts to construct lighthouses that would properly guide ships to safe harbor were not met with jubilation by the natives, who repeatedly committed acts of sabotage against such structures, wreaking maritime havoc for shippers and traffickers.[13]

John Jacob Housman's career as a wrecker exemplified its popularity and profitability. A New Yorker by birth, Housman was reared in a maritime environment. In the early 1800s, he set sail for the West Indies. While waiting for his ship to be repaired following a wreck near the Florida Keys, he became intrigued by the material incentives of the wrecking industry. The customary practice was that owners of vessels were forced to offer a share of their cargo to repair crews. Most shippers and slavers acquiesced to these demands and willingly parted with significant portions of their possessions since local judges and juries, comprised mainly of islanders, sympathized with wreckers, and more times than not, ruled in their favor during civil proceedings regarding compensatory issues. Frustrated by the biased decisions of local courts toward nonnatives, Housman eventually immersed himself in the wrecking business when he established a wrecking operation at Key West, which he relinquished before moving on to the island of Indian Key where he established a state-of-the-art wrecking center complete with paved roads, a town square, four wrecking vessels, wharves, warehouses, workshops, thirty cottages, twelve African workers, and a hotel to house stranded ship captains and their crews.[14] Wrecking became a way of life for many Caribbean islanders, but their bizarre enterprise had little effect on the foreign flow of slaves.[15]

Identifying slavers that routed their ships to the Caribbean before entering the United States was without question a difficult task. For example, when Augustus Púgh's brig *Galigo* left Boston carrying 70 enslaved Africans, or when Virginia resident Abner Robinson's schooner *Bangor* left Richmond in April 1817 with 104 slaves, officials had little way of knowing whether the ships had detoured to foreign ports before arriving in New Orleans. East Coast slave traders often submitted blind advertisements in local newspapers in search of slaves to buy. To protect their own integrity and that of the seller, slave traffickers such as Robinson made "Satisfactory assurances" that the slaves he purchased would "not be bought for re-sale." New Orleans customs inspector William Lake conducted occasional searches to locate Africans purchased in the Caribbean. In the winter of 1818 he took time to verify James Beard's slave cargo. Lake wanted to determine if the slaves that Beard had declared on his manifest before leaving Baltimore matched the number aboard his vessel. Beard had attracted special attention from New Orleans customs agents because his manifests indicated he had contracted his slave-transporting services out to the Lafitte Brothers & Company, which was known to purchase and smuggle slaves from the Caribbean.[16]

Dispersion and Policing

Although New Orleans was generally accepted as a headquarters for slave smuggling, American searches and seizures of suspected illegal slave vessels and the prosecution of slave-trafficking crews prompted westward movements and quests for new sanctuaries beyond the jurisdiction of the United States and out of the reach of its agents and officials.[17]

By establishing new headquarters in Spanish Mexico, slave smugglers and traffickers hoped to avoid prosecution as well as confiscation of their property. By relocating their operations farther into the frontier, they placed the onus of purchasing smuggled slaves upon buyers and planters. Mexico offered a convenient alternative. Seventy miles northeast of Mexico's Galveston Island was the Louisiana border, where traffickers congregated and exchanged the latest gossip about the smuggling world. Galveston presented a unique opportunity for many marauders, privateers, thugs, bandits, and profiteers. When slave traffickers first landed there, they found a small island about thirty miles long and two to four miles wide covered with prairie grass and cane breaks with excellent natural harbors and navigable waters. In 1820 it was the nearest point west of the closest state in the United States where traffickers could smuggle slaves beyond American soil. The use of Galveston Island as a slave-smuggling base hastened its development as a major point of embarkation to smuggle slaves into the United States.[18]

Galveston had attracted an assortment of criminal-minded figures. In December 1817 a group of French exiles boarded the sixty-ton schooner *Huntress* in Philadelphia, Pennsylvania, and set sail for Mexico. These exiles had fled France to continue their lives abroad after Napoleon's defeat at Waterloo in 1815. Charles Lallemand, a former general in Napoleon's army, devised a plan to establish a military encampment in Galveston for these émigrés. Crammed aboard the *Huntress* were ninety French exiles, their personal gear, and supplies. In route to Galveston the *Huntress* was boarded by an officer of a ship bearing a Spanish flag. Upon learning the purpose of the voyage, the officer identified himself as one of Jean Lafitte's captains. He and his officers escorted the cadre to Galveston where they awaited the arrival of other Lallemand recruits.

The Lafittes had recently set up a new headquarters in Galveston to escape the repeated efforts of Louisiana and American officials to dislodge their operation in Barataria and New Orleans. Lallemand's crew was unimpressed with Lafitte's men. They were, one expedition member observed, freebooters gathered from among all the nations of the earth determined to put into practice the traditions of the buccaneers of old. They gave themselves up, he noticed, to the most shameless debauchery and disgusting immorality, and only their chief (Lafitte), by his extraordinary strength and indomitable resolution, had the slightest control over their wild and savage natures. In Galveston, the Lafittes amassed an enviable and "organized system of enterprise" that complemented their operations in Barataria and New Orleans. Their Galveston hub consisted of slave quarters that could hold up to six hundred slaves per unit, an employment base of three hundred traffickers, a large mansion, and a local tavern and billiard room where the "groggeries" could linger when they were not hounding slave ships.[19]

The introduction of slaves into Galveston did not go unnoticed by American officials. President James Monroe recognized that it had become a place "for smuggling of every kind" by privateers of illicit businesses. "From Cape Catouche to La Vera Cruz," the United States consul in Galveston reported in August 1817, "pirate boats are very numerous and commit their depredations without respect to flag or nation to smuggle slaves into Louisiana from Galveston." Most of the goods carried there, Captain Charles Morris of the U.S. frigate *Congress* insisted, are somehow "introduced into the United States" and "several hundred slaves are now at Galveston and persons have gone from New Orleans to purchase them," with the intent to smuggle them back into Louisiana with the help of people who "are but too much disposed to render them every possible assistance." Morris went on to promise that "every exertion will be made to intercept them" although there was "little hope for success." In a report to the State Department, the conniving New Orleans collector of customs Beverly Chew admitted in a report that "the most shameful violations of the slave act by a motley mixture of freebooters and smugglers" were under way at Galveston. No effort alone, he exclaimed, "can be effectual in preventing the introduction of Africans" into the United States from the west.[20]

The presence of slave smugglers in Mexico placed an added burden on the United States. American efforts to suppress the foreign slave trade had, in most cases, been spasmodic. American navy cruisers assigned to the Gulf of Mexico often divided their duties between the Gulf and the African coast. The U.S. frigate *Congress* and the brig *Boxer,* for instance, patrolled the coastal regions of the Gulf of Mexico and played a seemingly crucial but ultimately futile role in intercepting illegal slave ships bound for the United States and Mexico. Both vessels hunted slavers from Cape Catouche to La Vera Cruz, Mexico. The crew of the U.S. *Boxer,* in particular, anticipated the attempts of traffickers "to smuggle slaves into Louisiana from Galveston" and kept special surveillance along the Western Gulf South. In November 1819 Jean Lafitte sent a letter to the commander of the U.S. schooner *Lynx,* which was anchored off the port of Galveston. He demanded to know the crew's intention and warned that if they attempted to enter the port in a "hostile manner" their encroachment would be rebutted with physical resistance. Lafitte eventually softened his demand and offered to hand over several members of his crew as an act of good faith.[21]

Jean Lafitte often sacrificed his own sailors and slaves to protect himself from his adversaries. Lafitte sought to earn favor from his government antagonists. He also demonstrated clever timing when he offered assistance to the American naval slave patrols that pursued him. Just a few days following a contentious exchange of words with J. R. Madison, commander of the U.S. schooner *Lynx,* Lafitte offered to assist Madison's stranded vessel near Galveston. J. McIntosh informed General James Long of Lafitte's benevolence toward the *Lynx* after it had "been blown off by boisterous and disagreeable weather." The treatment Lafitte offered the ship's crew, McIntosh insisted, "has been the most friendly, generous, hospitable . . . making the situation of myself and crew agreeable and comfortable."[22]

Committed to his own military obligations with Mexico, the French pirate and slave smuggler Louis Aury also established a legacy at Galveston through the foreign slave trade. Aury had served as commandant general of the New Granada naval forces during the early and temporary ascendancy period of the Mexican independence movement from Spain and also as the first Mexican provincial governor of Texas. After an initial attempt to establish a slave-smuggling operation in New Orleans failed, Aury used his maritime network to help transform Galveston Island into a depot for slave smugglers, where slaveholders who wished to purchase slaves and to transport them by land or sea into the United States could do so. In 1816, Aury seized Galveston Island in the name of the Mexican Republic and ran a vibrant resale business in condemned slave ships. Using Africans, enslaved and free, as his crew, Aury's successes in slave smuggling grew and rivaled that of the Lafittes. As a privateer, Aury had benefited from the financial backing of the New Orleans Associates. The Associates instructed Aury on how to avoid the legal snares of Mexican customs houses along Mexico's Texas coastline. Intense Mexican opposition to slavery during the volatile years of its revolution, however, compelled the Frenchman to dispose of his Galveston estate, which he did by illegally sending his slaves overland to be sold on the Louisiana slave market. Once Aury had vacated Galveston for Florida, he continued to cooperate with the Lafittes after they had taken control of the island.[23]

Aury began his slave-smuggling career in Spanish Florida where privateers claiming to represent various Spanish American nations had "liberated" Amelia Island from the Spanish empire. It was also a place where several erstwhile "Republicans" began a brisk business in the sale of captured ships and their cargoes, which often included slaves. One of the captured ships had returned from the African coast carrying 290 enslaved Africans, whom privateers seized and promptly sold to zealous buyers. The *Niles Weekly Register* reported that the "trade in human flesh is so profitable, that if that island [Amelia] is not taken possession of by the United States, we shall hear of many slave vessels sent as prizes that have conveniently laid off the port to be captured." Customs agents stationed along the Florida coast estimated that Aury sold more than one thousand slaves in less than two months. Many of these captives were subsequently moved northward to Georgia and other southern states where foreign importation was forbidden.[24]

The Lafitte brothers maintained personal oversight of their operations and kept watch on Aury and other competitors through the letters they wrote to one another. Suffering from scabies, an ailing Pierre Lafitte wrote from Galveston to his brother Jean in New Orleans in July 1817 requesting "a ship with provisions" to supplement his depleted resources. "I am beginning to run out of everything, to which I am not accustomed," he insisted. His request surfaced at a time when the relationship between the Lafitte brothers and Aury had worsened and competition between them for control of the foreign slave trade and the loyalties of black sailors had increased. Pierre was committed to "finish perfectly" their undertaking for the "purchase of Negroes . . . in that there were some doubloons [gold coins] to be earned." Pierre indicated that he had successfully separated fifteen sailors from Aury's service. He later provided passage for "fourteen colored youths" that Aury had depended upon to manage his operation. Pierre insisted that he "might have been able to succeed in separating all of his [Aury's] people" with an adequate holding of resources and provisions. "I am like the Chief and the father of Galveston," he boasted to his brother. His dwindling supplies, however, had placed Lafitte in a tenuous position as he found himself obligated to provide for those he had enticed away from Aury. With a limited number of suitable vessels that included one schooner, a packet-boat seized from Renato Beluche, an American ship on consignment, and the privateer ship *Independence,* the Lafittes struggled to maintain control of their share of the slave-smuggling market.[25]

Aury and his advocates caused the Laffittes considerable distress. "I am very content," Pierre Lafitte wrote to Jean, about "separating a great part of Aury's people and putting into disarray the rest." Pierre relished the news that Aury had fled Galveston. Because "Mr. Aury saw himself obligated to leave for fear of complete desertion and as he was seeing his forces diminishing each day, he was determined to set sail." In September 1817 the Lafitte brothers composed a letter and had it delivered to the captain general of Havana, Cuba. They reaffirmed their loyalties to the Spanish monarch and expressed concern about the revolutionary filibuster Francisco Xavier Mina, who intended to wrest control of Mexico away from Spain with the help of Aury. Such an invasion necessarily threatened the Lafittes' enterprises. By June 1816 Mina had made his way to Norfolk, Virginia. By September of the same year he had left Baltimore bound for Port-au-Prince, Haiti, where he obtained assistance for his expedition. Mina proceeded to New Orleans, conferred with his supporters, and purchased two ships. The Lafittes conveyed their anxieties regarding Mina's expedition when they learned through one of their spies that Aury had escorted a contingent of Mina's crew from Florida into Matagorda, Texas, and had offered military and moral support. The Lafittes agreed to place themselves "at the head of the enterprise" to stifle Mina's campaign.[26]

The Adams-Onis Treaty of 1819, in which Spain ceded all of Florida to the United States (while the United States, seeking a clear title to Florida, gave up its claims to Texas), had enabled traffickers to set up new landing sites in Galveston. Traffickers undoubtedly paid close attention to the details of the treaty, which designated a line of demarcation from the Gulf of Mexico northwestward across the continental United States, established the northern border of the Spanish Empire, and transferred Spanish ownership of the West Coast north of California to the United States. Perhaps the most significant provision of the agreement involved the American surrender of its claims to Texas. While neither the United States nor Spain conveyed assurances about their legal rights to Texas, Jean Lafitte, operating as a Spanish spy at the time, acted upon these uncertainties and effectively persuaded the Spanish monarch to hold firm to its claim of jurisdiction. Spanish ownership meant that Lafitte and others could circumvent the restrictive United States antislave-trade laws and facilitate a substantial portion of their smuggling operations through Texas.[27]

Slave traffickers were reluctant to settle in areas where the introduction of slaves was the focal point of political debates. The protracted brouhaha over land titles in Missouri, for instance, made a lasting impression on slaveholders and slave smugglers. In February 1819 the United States House of Representatives resolved a dispute regarding a long and irregular history involving squatters and slaveholders in Missouri and the remainder of the Louisiana Purchase (which by now no longer included the state of Louisiana). The two groups had become entangled in disagreements over land claims with the territorial and federal governments involving the question of whether the institution of slavery was to be upheld in Missouri. Critics of the slave trade alleged that the spread of slavery into Missouri would increase the smuggling of slaves into the United States. On this account, they attempted to tarnish the legal interstate trade by associating it with the unfavorable image of the foreign slave trade. John W. Taylor argued that an expansion of slave territory would make the entire country west of the Mississippi River a "market for human flesh." The certain result of allowing slaves into Missouri, he contended, would be to promote slave smuggling. For this, slave smugglers found the Mexican province of Texas a suitable choice.[28]

Mexico provided the most feasible alternative to the Missouri issue, although it created a new set of social and political problems. Slave labor had helped bolster the expanding Western Gulf South economy during the early 1800s, and in matters related to prosperity and wealth Spain had encouraged the importation of slaves to meet its labor needs. Slaves from Spanish colonies and other foreign ports had filled a void in Spanish-controlled Mexico's labor supply at a time when the Indian population was at its lowest point. While slave trafficking in Mexico was a common practice, the number of slaves in its slaveholding regions remained relatively low.[29]

The economic landscape of Mexico changed dramatically in the years after its independence from Spain in 1821. Prior to that, its economy had depended upon trade between its northern frontier markets and the more southern ones of Chihuahua, Durango, and Mexico City. Because Spanish trade restrictions had inflated market prices, merchants struggled to protect their own interests. Spain had required that all trade be conducted within designated ports, and it prohibited foreign merchants from competing against Spanish merchants within its colonies. Legally, Mexico was restricted from purchasing certain goods in neighboring Louisiana. The end of Spanish rule meant the eradication of prohibitions against foreign trade. Within a few years following its independence, the economic focus and trade orientation of Mexico shifted from an almost complete dependency on Spain to an interdependent market relationship with the United States, France, and England. Because local populations had already established a viable smuggling system of illicit commerce along the Mexican frontier—of which the illegal movement of slaves had become an important dimension—the Mexican ports of Matagorda Bay and Brazoria, Texas, became important destinations for merchants, shippers, and slave traffickers.[30]

The problem of regulating illegal foreign commerce affected the entire Mexican nation and compelled the new central government to adopt many of the same protective policies that had doomed its economy under Spanish rule. A merchant entering Mexican harbors found its regulations to be capricious and arbitrary. For example, foreigners who were well financed or who possessed special skills were not allowed to compete against Mexican merchants. Another act outlawed foreign vessels from engaging in coastal shipping and required that at least two-thirds of the crew members on Mexican vessels participating in coastal trade be Mexican nationals. Mexico, however, lacked the resources to enforce its own legislation and suffered from an embarrassingly small number of customs houses, as well as from a poorly trained and grossly underpaid customs workforce. Its agents often anticipated and accepted bribes to supplement their meager salaries. Mexican naval and military forces were equally inept in protecting the country's borders and coastline from smugglers and contraband.[31]

The vessels that relayed slaves between Mexico and the United States often relied on the cooperation of American customs agents. Benjamin Godfrey and William Andrews, two Texas slave traffickers, fostered working relationships with New Orleans customs inspectors H. Burroughs, James McCulloch, and Pierre Duplessis. On more than one occasion both Godfrey and Andrews were allowed to deliver slaves into the Port of New Orleans. Inspector Duplessis, especially, was an agent that traffickers could count upon to help clear them through customs despite their unexplained and undocumented activities. In Godfrey's case, Duplessis did not interrogate him about his Mexican slave dealings.[32] Duplessis had also openly allowed slave ships from the Caribbean access to the Port of New Orleans. When the steamship *Robert Fulton* pulled into the New Orleans harbor in August 1820 carrying several Cuban slaves, it did so with Duplessis's blessings.[33]

Duplessis's conduct would have been irrelevant if it were not for the mystery and suspicion surrounding his activities before becoming a collector of customs for the Port of New Orleans. His kinship to the Creole community earned him prominent status among New Orleans citizenry; but it was not until Duplessis maneuvered his way into an American faction in Louisiana, which rapidly increased in numbers and challenged the Creole elite for leadership following the Louisiana Purchase, that he truly exercised influence. When he joined an Anglo-Saxon organization known as the New Orleans Associates, a society so secret that its members identified themselves by numbers only, Duplessis connected with a cross-section of criminals and public figures. The Associates financed a range of profiteering and pirating operations. The organization was bankrolled by several unscrupulous figures, including William Mitchell, who, according to some accounts, channeled more than one hundred thousand dollars into the cabal. While serving as a United States marshal in 1813, Duplessis garnered the admiration of his peers despite the fact that he blatantly ignored three orders instructing him to arrest Jean and Pierre Lafitte. "Not to be found," was the only explanation he offered for failing to apprehend this notorious duo, whom he frequently interacted with at public gatherings.[34]

Slave traffickers curried relations with customs agents, which simplified their efforts to sell and trade slaves. The cooperation of customs agents, combined with the unsettled and virtually unguarded Mexican coastline, provided ample opportunity for them to conduct their business. The Brazos River offered them good anchorage at its mouth and access to the interior of the Mexican frontier during the flood seasons. When the flood rains came, traffickers used Matagorda's two principle rivers, the Colorado and Lavaca, to transport slaves inland.[35]

Evidence that African-born slaves began arriving in Brazoria and Matagorda in the years immediately following the ban of 1808 exists within the United States census records. African names found in this data, however, did not necessarily mean African-born. The significance of African names and naming practices also revealed the extent to which concepts of family, lineage, and kinship were retained beyond the Atlantic crossing. It also exposed certain other aspects of slave life, such as the adjustment or resistance to enslavement, the nature of slaves' kin networks, and the perpetuation and modification of African practices. In some cases African names were linked to nativity. The 5,647 distinctive African names found in Gwendolyn Hall's *Louisiana Slave Database* remain to be fully critiqued. The possibilities and implications are potentially far-reaching. A large number of slaves with African names—5,980—fell into the category of slaves of unidentified ethnicities or birthplaces. Some may have been Africans and others perhaps Creoles. Thus, Hall did not code them as Africans. Had she done so, the number of identifiable Africans would have increased. Unless the names included a clear ethnic designation, "nation" designations, rather than personal names, were relied on to identify African ethnicities.[36]

Fluid naming patterns occurred on both sides of the Atlantic, and Africans often changed their names. Some Africans assumed the names of other Africans out of honor and respect. Enslaved Africans occasionally adopted the name of a friend or a shipmate or a recent acquaintance. An African name, and identifying one's birthplace as Africa, does suggest the possibility of being African-born. According to the 1870 census, Texas ranked third behind Louisiana and Georgia in its number of African persons who recorded Africa as their place of birth. The three states combined held 50 percent of all documented African-born persons in the country. The Mexican port towns of Bazoria and Matagorda accounted for much of this importation, as names of African derivation including Abo, Batta, Bayaa, Dada, Malaka, Omo, Kaloda, Udoo, Fadoom, Shiloah, Addo, Cudgo, and Jorus appeared among those listed for these two towns in government records. Although actual birth dates are difficult to pinpoint, approximating years of birth based on the recorded ages also indicates that many may have been brought to the Americas in violation of the 1808 Abolition Act.[37]

Slavery as an institution in the Brazos Valley of Mexico emerged in conjunction with the transition from tobacco production to cotton production. In 1690 Maryland and Virginia contained slightly over two-thirds of the entire black population. The de-concentration of the Chesapeake slave population and the movement of slave labor did not assume large proportions until the beginning of the nineteenth century. By 1820 the share of slaves in Maryland and Virginia had declined to 35 percent. On the eve of the Civil War these two states contained just 15 percent of the country's bondsmen. After remaining relatively stable for a century and a half, the center of the slave population shifted away from the Chesapeake to the south and southwest as world demand for cotton increased and United States cotton production expanded from 3,000 bales in 1790 to 178,000 bales in 1810, to 732,000 bales in 1830, and 4,500,000 bales in 1860. Eager planters responded to this demand and moved into the areas where soil was more conducive for cotton production. The Port of New Orleans, and improved transportation systems, made it possible for them to export their cotton and other cash crops to remote locations. Despite these factors, Mexico would not have attracted settlers or developed a viable cotton economy without the prospects of a suitable labor system.[38]

The post-1808 foreign slave trade was instrumental in supplementing this much-needed labor force and the infamous Bowie brothers represented just one group of smugglers who successfully engineered schemes to import slaves into Mexico. James Bowie, the hard-drinking slave trader, land speculator, and inventor of the knife that bears his name, and his siblings had grown apace with the variety of fortunes that held them bound to protect their economic interest. James Bowie was born near Terrapin Creek, Kentucky, around 1796. His father (Reason) had operated a gristmill with the help of several slaves during James's childhood. In February 1800 the elder Bowie moved his family to Madrid, in what is now Missouri. On May 2, 1801, at Rapides,

Louisiana, James's father and several uncles swore allegiance to the Spanish government. By October of the same year the Bowie family had settled on farms in what is now Catahoula Parish, Louisiana. Around 1809 the Bowie clan had moved to Atakapa in southeastern Louisiana; there Reason purchased 640 acres of land on the Vermilion River. He then developed a plantation near Opelousas, where he grew cotton and sugarcane, raised livestock, and bought and sold slaves. During the War of 1812 brothers James and Rezin joined up with an American regiment to fight the British. In January 1815 the brothers were on their way to join Andrew Jackson's forces at New Orleans just as the war was ending. Five years later, James started his own family, took an active role in community affairs, established a plantation, and became one of the largest slave owners in his locale. Gwendolyn Hall's *Louisiana Slave Database* records several slave transactions credited to the Bowies. The brothers welcomed most organized and well-planned attempts to free Mexico from Spanish control and they eagerly joined up with filibustering expeditions, including General James Long's campaign to wrest the upper Texas coastline away from the Lafittes. They were part of a growing contingent of land speculators and slave buyers intent upon clearing the way to increase their personal prosperity through the foreign slave trade.[39]

To accommodate the needs of sugar planters and cotton growers, the Bowies often directed the movement of slave coffles between Louisiana and Mexico, stashing them in areas along the Sabine River, where they had constructed barracks. As Louisiana landowners, the Bowies made no distinction between the illegal distribution of recent African captives and seasoned slaves, nor did they distinguish between the illegal overland and foreign introduction of slaves into the United States. They purchased slaves from the Lafittes in Texas, landed them at their plantation in Vermilion Bay, Louisiana, then transported and sold them in St. Landry Parish. Many of their transactions violated the federal laws of the United States and also those of Mexico. Their familiarity with the terrain allowed them to shuttle their slaves to points near the offices of United States marshals. The brothers rarely left a government slave auction empty-handed. They maintained a clear advantage over other buyers who showed up for these public sales as their earnings more than offset the start-up monies they needed to purchase additional slaves.[40]

The Bowies' slave transactions often occurred in collusion with United States marshals, who were given extensive authority within their judicial districts to carry out all lawful orders issued by judges, Congress, or the president. Although free African marshals or deputies were not highly visible, they did exist and were useful sources of information. Using racially integrated law enforcement teams along the frontier, marshals had the dangerous task of enforcing antislave-trade laws. They enjoyed more success when they collaborated with free persons who, in some instances, had been held as slaves themselves or who had some previous dealings with smugglers. A significant number of white marshals benefited from the lucrative financial opportunities afforded them through the confiscation of illegal slaves. In 1819, United States marshal William E. Coale received $600 from a court judgment for "information" he provided to the Department of Navy about twelve illegally imported slaves. Marshal Samuel Hodges Jr. pocketed $870 for transporting eighteen prisoners charged with violating the acts prohibiting the foreign slave trade. United States marshal Morton A. Waring was given $998 "for maintenance and care" of four bondsmen brought into the country in violation of the law. Marshal John H. Morel banked $20,286 for providing food and shelter for several captives placed in his care.[41]

While United States marshals were not the only group of government officals to benefit financially, they did exhibit more diligence than did some who became clumsy and reckless in their dealings with the foreign slave trade. General David Brydie Mitchell, who had served as a special commissioner to President James Madison, was privileged to important information regarding the traffic in foreign slaves—some of which he subversively used to enrich himself. His scheme, however, backfired. Mitchell had assumed control of a substantial land inheritance in Savannah, Georgia. He used his earnings to tactfully maneuver his way into public life and politics. He also secured employment with a local law firm where he worked to revise Georgia's state criminal code. His diligent work and professional conduct earned him the positions of mayor of Savannah, United States attorney general for Georgia, major general of the Georgia State Militia, and twice governor of the state. His appointment as United States agent to the Creek Indian nation was a bittersweet experience. While the assignment was a grand accomplishment and offered Mitchell an opportunity to reconnect with the federal government, it also marked the beginning of Mitchell's legal troubles with slavery, which blemished his otherwise distinguished career and made him the focal point of public scrutiny. Though he had served as governor of Georgia from 1809 to 1813 and again from 1815 to 1817, Mitchell was summarily dismissed from his duties as a federal agent to the Creek Indians in 1821 for his alleged ties to a Georgia-based slave-smuggling ring.

Mitchell was accused of orchestrating the movement of slaves between Georgia and Mexico.[42] Charges and countercharges about Mitchell's alleged involvement in slave smuggling swirled from one source to the next. Foiling his racket was less the object than was vengeance, political chicanery, and personal animosity. At the center of the brouhaha was John Clark, one of Mitchell's ardent opponents and sitting governor of Georgia. Clark found his opportunity to settle an old grudge against Mitchell. The Scottish-born Mitchell came to the states in 1783, at the age of seventeen, and as governor had overlooked Clark for a high-ranking regimental duty with the Georgia militia. When Clark became governor, his informants alerted him of suspicious activities around Mitchell's estate. Clark wasted little time gathering evidence and lining up key witnesses. An undisclosed informant, who was ordered by Colonel David Brearly to investigate Mitchell, observed unusual movements of groups of Africans between Mitchell's plantation and the thickets near his home. Brearly indicated that Mitchell had organized smuggling plots in collaboration with his chief advocate, Captain William Bowen, and the employees from Gross & Company of Augusta, Georgia, a firm with links to the foreign slave trade.[43]

Despite an acquittal, Mitchell's encounter reflected the extreme political and legal sensitivities of the foreign slave trade. The task of satisfying federal mandates to prosecute alleged smugglers such as Mitchell was often thwarted by tainted and sympathetic juries, less-than-credible government witnesses, or government agents, whose pursuit of monetary payoffs compromised their civic obligations. In 1810, Pierre Lafitte had infiltrated the federal government after being deputized a United States marshal in Ascension Parish, Louisiana. His job description required him to enforce antislave-trade laws. The Bowies also enjoyed connections within the American judicial and legal framework. Martha Bowie, sister of the Bowie brothers, had married Alexander Sterrett, whose brother James served as New Orleans attorney general and later a customs officer for the Mississippi district. Beverly Chew, the corrupt collector of customs for New Orleans, openly conveyed his conflict of interest when he protested for his right to a share of the monetary proceeds earned from every successful slave-trafficking prosecution. His claim to a portion of the $68,000 acquired from the sale of the 314 slaves confiscated from the *Josefa Segunda* in February 1818 reflected the clash between his personal interest and workplace duties.[44]

The emergence of slave smugglers in Mexico combined with the visible corruption of American officials hastened American efforts to take control of its coastal lands. In January 1821, the United States brig-of-war *Enterprise,* under the command of a Lieutenant Kerny, arrived in Galveston to forcibly remove the Lafittes and their pirates from the island. Force was not necessary, however. Lafitte agreed to voluntarily leave the island and directed his followers to do the same. Some moved on to the Caribbean. One of the brothers, the *New Hampshire Gazette* reported in March 1821, was spotted in Charleston, South Carolina, fitting out a schooner. Some of their men headed for New Orleans and a few settled along the Sabine River area where they operated as fishermen. A smattering lingered around Galveston and eventually blended in with the area's ranchers and farmers. At least two migrated to Corpus Christi, where one died of yellow fever and the other, "Portuguese Joe," who wore gold earrings and whose rugged bare feet, it was rumored, crushed the jagged oyster shells along the shoreline but suffered no gashes or cuts in the process, settled into the community. The *Orleans Gazette* reported that the Lafittes had actually abandoned their Galveston operation by May 1820. Spanish troops from San Antonio scouted Galveston in October 1820 and found it deserted.[45]

The final days of the Lafittes's smuggling enterprise were eventful ones. As they prepared to vacate the island, Jean Lafitte sent his brother Pierre and William Mitchell to New Orleans for supplies and men. Upon their arrival they immediately began to purchase goods and to recruit sailors for their exodus. Nearly ninety people signed up. Pierre vacated New Orleans for Charleston, South Carolina, and later Cuba, where he hoped to collect part of the promised pay for his and Jean's espionage services they had rendered to Spain. Pierre subsequently reunited with his brother off the coast of Yucatan. The two planned to spend their final years near Havana where they had purchased a ranch. Because the Lafittes willingly vacated Galveston, the American military graciously offered the brothers and their crews unhindered passage from the island. "Permission is hereby granted to John [Jean] Laffite and others," Daniel T. Patterson wrote to the commanders of the United States vessels assigned to the New Orleans naval station and others throughout the Gulf, "to depart with their vessels, goods & furniture, without molestation or hinderance." In exchange, the Lafittes agreed to never use Galveston "as a place of rendezvous for any undertakings." After loading their ships with men and supplies, Jean Lafitte destroyed all that he was to leave behind, torched the village of Galveston, and then slipped out to sea. He sailed along the coast of Mexico where he and his crew seized the Spanish schooner *Constitution* and its twelve hundred barrels of Spanish whiskey, nine hundred bottles of oil, a trunk of belts, two hundred handkerchiefs, and other cargo. After the capture, several of Lafittes's crew pilfered a share of the loot and used the ship to sail to New Orleans. There they were apprehended and charged with piracy. All were Lafitte pirates, which may have contributed to the pardon they received from President James Monroe. Despondent over a series of mutinies by his sailors, Pierre's death at Yucatan, and Spain's decision to withdraw its offer of protection, Jean Lafitte sailed for Cuba.[46]

General James Long, along with the frontier filibusters John Sibley, Stephen Barker, and Joshua Child, organized a militia which set out to replace the Lafittes as chief slave dealers in Mexico. Long's expeditions lasted, on and off, from the summer of 1819 until the fall of 1821. Although Long's death in 1821 marked the end of his quest to seize control of Lafitte's old territory, his campaign revealed his own desire to enjoy many of the benefits that had lured Aury, the Lafittes, and others to the region. Rumors spread that Long had teamed up with the Lafittes to smuggle slaves into Mexico. When the Mexican government captured several runaway slaves, they discovered that many had belonged to Long himself. Bill Mecate, a twelve-year-old African, was apprehended on the Mexican side of the Sabine River in April 1820 and taken to Monterrey by Lieutenant Fernando Rodriguez. Mecate identified General Long as his master and insisted that he and Juan Cortes, as well as two others, had escaped from Long in Nacogdoches, where they were held in chains over four years and transported between Louisiana and Mexico as "his master [Long]" sold slaves. Long's activities followed a distinct pattern displayed by many slave traffickers. His constant movement between borders reflected the seriousness of his aspirations to deal in slaves.[47]

Many free and enslaved Africans had sought refuge from the clutches of slave traffickers and smugglers such as Long. Their efforts often landed them in Mexican prisons where guards tended to their needs. There they revealed the extent of slave smuggling. Most agreed that the movement of slaves across borders had placed them under tremendous duress. Juan Pedro "offered to tell the truth in what he knew" about the practice. Pedro was not a typical run-away. After escaping from his captors, he voluntarily presented himself to a Mexican commander who transported him and several other slaves to San Antonio de Bexar in Mexico. The slave Martin escaped across the Sabine River into Mexico and away from slave smugglers, along with a male and female slave locked together "in the same chains."

Mexican officials in Monterrey interrogated three Africans who had been prisoners of Jean Lafitte at Galveston. Juan, Lorca, and Ennalt all testi-fied to being held against their will and of Lafitte's threat to have them sold on the New Orleans slave market. Juan, who said he was born on the island of Anguilla, had worked as a cook aboard a Spanish schooner before he was abducted by a French pirate near the coast of Campeche. Lorca, who dis-played limited English skills, insisted that he was born on the Guinea coast in Africa where he was seized and carried off to Galveston. Ennalt declared in a deposition that his native land was the island of Antigua where he had been a soldier since the age of seven. Having experienced military hardships, he chose to head for the Mexican border rather than subject himself to the domination of Jean Lafitte and Louis Aury in Galveston.[48]

Sustaining and protecting the foreign slave trade was of primary importance for Mexico's Anglo settlers. When Stephen F. Austin, one of the original American immigrants, arrived in 1821, he did so legally, with the approval of the Mexican government and with a clear vision of becoming a very wealthy man. His social and political odyssey in the country connected him with major Mexican figures as well as an array of personalities linked to the foreign slave trade. Born into a slaveholding Virginia family, Austin's father Moses was a commission merchant in Richmond. He was known to use "hearty and well made" slaves, and Stephen most likely handled the slave sales dimension of his father's general business. The Austins had used slave labor on a large scale in the family's Missouri mining business. Stephen understood how vital slave labor was to economic survival for many white business people and planters and he worked to protect the institution of slavery in Texas, a precept that helped breech his loyalties with Mexico but improved his standing with slave traffickers.[49]

One of Austin's closets allies was Samuel May Williams, who had also journeyed to Mexico during the early 1820s, under the assumed name of E. Eccleston. After gaining valuable work experience in a New Orleans commission house, Williams was among a collection of Americans who made haste in fleeing bad debts amassed during the lean economic years of 1820 and 1821. He vacated the United States in search of a fresh start following the banking panic of 1819 that had destabilized the national economy. By utilizing his numerous international connections and his fluency in Spanish and French, the New England–educated Williams befriended Austin, and the two worked to establish a colony for Anglo settlers. Although Austin's primary objective was to facilitate a fair and equitable distribution of land that would satisfy the desires of newcomers, the mere prospect of acquiring large tracts of inexpensive but good soil inevitably attracted planters who ultimately turned to the slave market for their labor.[50]

Through mere chance or careful planning, Williams's resettlement coincided with the passage of one of America's boldest antislave-trade laws. In 1820 the United States Congress enacted legislation that strengthened the Abolition Act of 1808 which made the illegal importation and exportation of slaves a capital offense, punishable by death. It also allocated $100,000 toward the prosecution of slave smugglers and empowered the president "to cause any armed vessels of the United States to be employed to cruise on any of the coasts of the United States or territories thereof, or off the [slave-trading] coasts of Africa or elsewhere," to seize American slavers acting in violation of the law. The central objective of the 1820 law was to help establish a measure of jurisdictional integrity regarding American borders and to curtail blatant violations of its slave trade prohibitions. The passage of the 1820 law occurred just as northern opposition to the foreign slave trade and the rising repudiation among several nations toward the African slave trade increased. Mexico posed one of the greatest challenges to the foreign distribution of slaves, one that created tension between itself and slave dealers.[51]

Mexico, Texas, and the Foreign Slave Trade

The formation of new republics in the Western Hemisphere figured prominently in attempts to suppress the foreign slave trade. Venezuela abolished slavery in 1821. Colombia and Chile did likewise after each gained their independence in the same year. All these countries, as well as Argentina, pledged the assistance of their navies to help suppress the trade. The Republic of Mexico, however, confronted a unique situation. It faced a resilient and determined group of white settlers in its Texas province who resisted efforts to eradicate the introduction of slave labor, even though several new bills regulating slavery and the slave trade were introduced in the Republic of Mexico.[52]

Because of the influx of slaveholders, land contracts in Mexico had to be reaffirmed by the federal government. The children of bondsmen were to be freed at the age of fourteen and new immigrants were required to speak Spanish. The status of the slave trade in the Republic of Mexico was a touchy subject, although African slave labor had existed in the Mexican interior since colonial times. After independence, Mexican leaders demonstrated their disapproval of the foreign slave trade, but found it difficult to balance their suppression politics with the need to encourage settlement. While it had not been mentioned in earlier land-grant contracts between Mexico and Anglo settlers, the foreign slave trade became a major point of controversy in subsequent colonization laws.[53]

After the Mexican junta government of Agustin de Iturbide seized power in the fall of 1822, it passed the Imperial Colonization Law, which greatly restricted the economic prospects of American immigrants who had aspired to new business opportunities; at the same time, it was vague on the introduction of slave labor. This ambiguous nature of the law offered a measure of hope for slaveholders. The law, however, was annulled in February

1823, following de Iturbide's overthrow. When the new constituent congress met in Mexico City in November 1823 and again on July 1824, it expressly called for the complete prohibition of slavery and the foreign slave trade. "Commerce and traffic," the decree read, "in slaves proceeding from any country and under any flag whatsoever, is forever prohibited within the territory of the United Mexican States."[54] Lucas Alaman, one of Mexico's most important leaders, insisted that the language of the decree could only be interpreted as the total and complete repudiation of slavery and the importation of slaves.[55]

The reaction among Anglo immigrants in Coahuila y Texas, a name given to the Texas province of Mexico after it was merged with Coahuila following Mexican independence from Spain, to the new law was mixed. Although American and Mexican antislave-trade laws forced slave smugglers and traffickers to become more circumspect, the threat of prosecution and condemnation of their vessels and property posed little concern for Mexico's Anglo immigrants or for those who provided them with slave contraband. They recognized Coahuila y Texas as an emerging region for the foreign slave trade and considered it vital to their economic and political survival. Although there is no clear evidence of the number of slaves that ended up in Mexico from the United States, it was apparent that Coahuila y Texas presented real possibilities for sustaining the enterprise.[56]

Mexican antislave-trade laws failed to deter some smugglers from moving into the country. Monroe Edwards, a suave Kentucky native who made a living on crafty business scams that involved betraying and bankrupting his closest associates, settled in Galveston Bay in the early 1820s to deal in the foreign slave trade. Not long thereafter, Edwards emerged as a central figure in the transshipment of slaves between Africa, Brazil, Cuba, and Mexico. Through his mistress's husband, a Mexican official, he obtained a large land grant in Coahuila y Texas, which became Chenango Plantation. The estate served as the base for his slave-trafficking endeavors and later became the focal point of a bitter lawsuit levied by his business partner, Christopher Dart, who claimed that Edwards had swindled him out of his share of the plantation's profits.[57]

While some Anglo immigrants proceeded to import slaves into Mexico with little reservation, others were reluctant to immigrate into the country or to invest their resources without assurances that both slavery and the foreign slave trade would be protected. Despite these uncertainties, William Brown transported fifteen slaves by boat from New Orleans to Brazoria in Coahuila y Texas. John Rowland shipped nine slaves belonging to James Ware of New York into the same port.[58] Stephen F. Austin, however, received numerous letters which indicated that several aspiring planters were apprehensive about crossing over into Mexico in light of the country's antislave-trade laws. James A. B. Phelps, for example, wrote to Austin from Mississippi and offered his concerns: "Nothing appears at present," he claimed, "to prevent a portion of our wealthy planters from emigrating immediately to the province of Texas but the uncertainty now prevailing with regard to the subject of slavery." Charles Douglas of Alabama expressed similar feelings: "Our most valuable inhabitants here own negroes," he wrote, and they were reluctant to move into Coahuila y Texas without guarantees that a steady supply would be "secured to them by the laws" of Mexico.[59]

Uncertainties about the foreign slave trade in Mexico had a direct effect on the political and economic relationship between the Mexican central authority and its Anglo settlers. White immigrants protested that the state government of Coahuila y Texas had failed to effectively address their needs. Slave owners, particularly, risked losing control of their public lands as they had already lost their voice regarding the regulation of the foreign slave trade. Anglo Texans entered a new and more adversarial phase in their relationship with Mexican authorities when they called for the separation of Texas from Coahuila, even though the two provinces combined comprised Mexico's poorest state. Erasmo Seguin, the Coahuila y Texas representative in the Mexican Congress, publicly supported separation. He feared that the burgeoning Anglo population at some point would shift the balance of power in the province away from native Mexicans and that the American immigrants would ultimately do whatever was necessary to protect their interest in the foreign slave trade.[60]

Amid increasing opposition to Mexico's antislave-trade laws, the provincial government of Coahuila y Texas stepped up efforts to counteract any attempt by the central authority to end the introduction of slave labor. Immigrants perceived the colonization law of 1824 as vague, and they looked forward to expanding the foreign slave trade.[61] Thus, some of the most egregious incidents involving violations of Mexican antislave-trade laws in Coahuila y Texas occurred after 1824. Besides enjoying a seven-year exemption from tariffs on selected goods, American colonists in the province had virtually no experience paying duties because the government had failed to assign revenue officers to collect required duties and fees. Foreign slave movements into Mexico awakened the Mexican government to the fact that foreigners had grown accustomed to the idea that the trade was an act of good business rather than criminal behavior.

The Monroe Doctrine, Suppression, and Mexico

While smugglers and traffickers manipulated Mexican antislave-trade laws, President James Monroe was busy fashioning the parameters of a fresh approach to American foreign policy that, by virtue of its repudiation of European colonization in the Americas, shifted much of the primary responsibility for suppressing the foreign slave trade in the Western Hemisphere to the United States. "The suppression of piratical practice," and the policing of depredations committed by slave smugglers and traffickers, Monroe insisted, required "a particular kind of force," one that would be needed to pursue the violators into areas where they found sanctuary.[62]

The Monroe Doctrine was shaped to encourage free seas and open trade. The interruption of commerce of any sort undermined this most-cherished concept. Monroe often rejected, however, recommendations to expand his antislave-trade commentaries. His references to the role of the United States in the policing of the foreign slave trade were generally presented within the context of American naval operations along the African slave coasts and rarely with regard to its activities along the American coasts. His actions complemented his politics and teach an important lesson: despite evidence of a foreign slave trade, Monroe expended few resources to alter the practice along the African coast and scarcely effected any change to it in the Western Hemisphere.

The placement of American antislave-trade navy squadrons along the African coast during Monroe's presidency included Captain Edward Trenchard of the ship *Cyane,* who left the states in January 1820; Captain George C. Reed, who departed in June 1820; Captain Robert Field Stockton, who set sail in April 1821 aboard the *Alligator;* H. S. Wadsworth, who guided the *John Adams* in July 1821; and Captain Matthew Perry, who took the *Shark* over to the African coast in August 1821 to patrol for illegal slave ships. The revenue cutter *Lynx* was the lone American vessel sent to negotiate the foreign slave trade along the Western Gulf South, with special emphasis on the Sabine and Calcasieu Rivers in Louisiana.[63]

Political and judicial influences were partially responsible for the disproportionate attention given to the African slave coasts during the 1820s. Aside from the fact that Monroe was himself a southern slaveholder, lawmakers such as the Whig senator Henry Johnson of Louisiana worked to block legislation that interfered with trade and commerce in the American South and Southwest. Johnson opposed laws that would punish slave smugglers and traffickers. He proposed legislation that would prohibit the extradition of foreign smugglers arrested in the United States.[64]

The response of slave smugglers and traffickers to this unsolicited support was evident in their reactions toward the searches and seizures of their ships and contraband. When the slave ship *Neptune,* which had frequently transported wood and ivory from Africa while illegally transporting slaves, was seized, the ship's captain had little doubt that the courts would render a favorable decision on his behalf and that his property would be returned. His "extraordinary" confidence drew "suspicion" among some New Orleans customs agents and the United States attorney general's office, both of which had testified to confiscating fraudulent manifests from the captain.[65]

The behavior of freebooters was emboldened in 1824 when the Supreme Court, in the case of *The Marino v. the United States,* established a stringent burden of proof for federal prosecutors in slave-smuggling cases. The Court rejected a lower court decision that upheld the legality of the ship's seizure. The Supreme Court argued that evidence of the *Marino* being "employed in carrying on trade, contrary to law" at the time of its seizure was "erroneous." Thus, six years after its confiscation in June 1818, property and slaves were returned to the plaintiffs.[66]

In 1825 Chief Justice John Marshall further shielded smugglers and traffickers from prosecution when he wrote the majority opinion for the *Antelope* case. Marshall argued that United States antislave-trade regulations should be placed in harmony with international law with regard to punishment. No American court, Marshall concluded, could judge or execute the penal laws of another country. Instead, American courts were obligated to restore the disputed property of foreigners once ownership was established.[67]

The *Antelope* ruling reflected the waning commitment of the American central authority toward the suppression of the foreign slave trade. Smugglers and traffickers often took their cue from the mandates and legislation of federal officials. None of the presidents, for instance, who presided over the country during the initial years following passage of the Abolition Act of 1808 organized aggressive campaigns to suppress the movement of foreign slaves into the country. Not much was done to disrupt the practice of a "few citizens" who set their own standards and continued in the "abominable traffic" by "sheltering themselves under the banners of other nations."[68] The execution of the Monroe Doctrine and enforcement of antislave-trade laws meant even less to Andrew Jackson, who, during his first term as president, succeeded in having United States slave vessels and property that were seized by Latin American governments returned to their American owners.[69]

The failure of federal agencies to coalesce their authority to protect the country's waterways and soil from slave smugglers and traffickers helped advance the cause of freebooters. Legitimate slave owners and traders, concerned about the chaotic state of slave smuggling into the Mexican frontier, appealed to ship operators and captains to refrain from confiscating runaway slaves and selling them to the traffickers that loitered around ports in search of any captive African they could disguise as a slave, sell on the market or collect monetary rewards through government-sponsored auctions. The warning that L. S. Bringier posted in the *New Orleans Bee* was typical of the many notices submitted by slaveholders who wanted to keep their property out of the hands of smugglers. Bringier's appeal was directed toward rapacious "masters of steamboats and other seafaring vessels" who exploited the precarious coastline of the Gulf. He cautioned each to avoid association with traffickers who lingered at the wharves with the expressed intent of transporting slaves into Mexico.[70]

Although many enslaved Africans had learned of Mexico's favorable intent toward their unfortunate condition, they found themselves trapped under the heavy oppression of masters, traffickers, and smugglers who, in an effort to retain them, made their yoke even heavier. Fiercely loyal to the institution of slavery and to the foreign slave trade, militant white settlers launched rebellions to protest Mexican antislave-trade laws. Hayden Edwards, a land speculator and patron of eight hundred colonists, seized the town of Nacogdoches along the Mexican-Louisiana border, where he flew the flag of the Republic of Fredonia in a preliminary step toward Texas independence.[71]

Anglo resistance to Mexico's prohibition of the foreign slave trade drew sympathy from several Mexican lawmakers. President Vicente Ramon Guerrero, after decreeing the total abolition, granted an exemption for Texans in September 1829. The original decree first reached them in October 1829 in a letter from Governor J. M. Viesca at Saltillo, who wrote to Ramon Musquiz, the political chief at San Antonio. "Without the aid of the robust and almost indefatigable arms of that race of human species which is called Negroes," Musquiz contended, "the advancement of Texas would greatly suffer."[72]

The Texas exemption helped prolong the life of the foreign slave trade into Mexico. The "particular kind of force," which President James Monroe regarded as a requisite to enforce the Abolition Act of 1808 and all the anti-slave-trade laws that succeeded it, had not yet materialized. The legislative and military strategies of the United States and Mexico proved futile. Culpable government agents were of little help. Even the threat of confiscation, prosecution, or death failed to discourage smugglers and traffickers from plying their vocation. During the 1820s, Mexico assumed an important role in the suppression of the foreign slave trade, a part that continued during the 1830s as Anglo Texans agitated for independence and continuation of the trade.

3

"Turbulent and Bad Men"

SLAVE TRANSSHIPMENTS AND
THE TEXAS DILEMMA

On January 1, 1830, Jim Bowie left Thibodaux, Louisiana, and headed for
Mexico with a close companion. They stopped in Nacogdoches, at the farm
of Jared E. Groce on the Brazos River near San Felipe. There, Bowie presented
a letter of introduction to Stephen F. Austin from Thomas F. McKinney. By
February Bowie and his friend Isaac Donoho had taken an oath of allegiance
to Mexico. The pair joined up with William H. Horton, Caiaphas K. Ham,
and several of their slaves and then traveled on to San Antonio. They carried
letters of introduction to be signed by a couple of wealthy and influential
Mexicans, Juan Martin de Veramendi and Juan N. Seguín. Bowie's party continued on to Saltillo, the state capital of Coahuila y Texas, Mexico, and on
October 5 officially became Mexican citizens. By 1832, however, antago-
nisms between the Mexican government and Anglo settlers over Mexico's
repeal of Texas's slave-trade exemption led José de las Piedras, Mexican commander at Nacogdoches, to demand that all citizens in his jurisdiction surrender their arms. Bowie hurried back to Nacogdoches, and on August 1

helped James W. Bullock and three hundred other armed men seize a garrison near the city.[1]

Territorial expansion fulfilled many of the expectations of aspiring merchants and planters. New lands afforded them fresh economic opportunities and by the 1830s many looked to the foreign slave trade as a bonafide and legitimate means of supplementing their labor supply. While the United States and Mexico implemented their own suppression policies as each saw fit, Anglos expressed anxieties about such plans. They believed that the establishment of an independent Texas republic would increase their political power and ultimately allow them to extend the life of the trade. The irony is that Texas independence aroused the consciousness of abolitionists, who organized schemes to advance the suppression of the foreign slave trade. This chapter examines resistance to Mexican attempts to eradicate the foreign slave trade in Texas. It investigates the effect that Texas independence, the abolitionist movement, the crisis of "Negro stealing," the runaway-slave predicament, and the advent of Indian-African alliances had on the practice.

The Law of April 6 and Mexican Enforcement

When Mexico passed the Law of April 6 in 1830, it intended to end the foreign importation of slaves. The law, however, included few provisions for enforcement, provided limited resources to implement the ban, and offered no countermeasure against dishonest federal agents who placed their personal aggrandizement before their civic obligations. Foreigners often reported witnessing the execution of private deals between merchants and customs agents at Mexican ports and observing slave traffickers exploiting rapacious and corrupt port officials, many of whom were dismissed from their jobs for their part in illicit slave transactions. Mexico's Law of April 6 reflected the country's struggle to gain control of its own sovereignty and was an attempt to prohibit the further introduction of slaves and American settlers, particularly those which the central authority considered "undesireable . . . bad men and vagabonds," who were "destitute of principle," prone to "rebel," predisposed to "produce confusion on the frontier," and committed to promoting the illegal introduction of slave labor. Mexican president Anastacio Bustamante, who had wrested power away from President Vicente Guerrero in late 1829, called for the strict enforcement of the Law of April 6. Other prominent Mexican residents also endorsed the decree. John Horse, a former slave himself, expressed gratitude about Mexico's assertive actions. The poet, lawyer, and senator Francisco Manuel Sanchez de Tagle lauded the sanctions and recommended that all emancipated slaves, including those fleeing into Mexico from foreign soil, be sheltered from bounty hunters.[2]

The Law of April 6 closed all Texas ports except Anahuac, a town that had been established near the head of Galveston Bay through which all Texas-bound commerce was routed.[3] The persistence of slave movement into Coahuila y Texas demonstrated that certain customs agents and traffickers held little regard for these port closings. James Morgan of Anahuac was one of them. Morgan was a pioneer Coahuila y Texas settler, merchant, and land speculator. He was born in Philadelphia and spent a good part of his childhood in North Carolina where he established long-lasting business ties. In 1830 Morgan moved to Brazoria in Coahuila y Texas and opened a mercantile company. Together with his business associate John Reed, whom he had met in New Orleans, Morgan purchased the schooner *Exert* and used it to transport contraband. He also used his connections with Mexican officials to circumvent slave-trade prohibitions. Morgan's popularity had gained him favor from Aquile Murat, Mexico's vice-consul for the territory of Florida, who issued Morgan a signed passport which granted him "free, . . . safe," and unhindered passage into Texas on "any . . . vessel" of his choosing. With passport in hand, Morgan traveled from one Mexican port to the next with slaves "disguised" as indentured servants. The documents he toted were enough to satisfy Mexican officials throughout the region.

Morgan moved slaves freely between Mexico and the United States and openly sold them to loyal clientele. Few of his clients exhibited greater allegiance than J. A. Brown and Redmond Parker of Hartford, North Carolina. In August 1830 Brown and Parker purchased several slaves from Morgan, including a fifteen-year-old named Henry, a sixteen-year-old boy named Turner, a twenty-two year old female called Tamar, a twenty-five-year-old mulatto woman named Hannah, and 2 thirty-five-year-old women who answered to the names of Lydia and Molly.[4]

Port officials were often ostracized and penalized for their role in obstructing Morgan's slave transactions. The Hungarian-born George Fisher jeopardized his career as Mexico's collector of customs at Anahuac when he instigated a feud with Morgan. Fisher had demanded that all foreign commercial traffic clear the Anahuac port before entering Mexico. American immigrants had accused Fisher of acting as a secret agent for former president Guerrero. It was not long before Fisher, who had moved to Texas from Mississippi in 1825, was discharged from his duties at Anahuac and reassigned to Matamoros, where his "demeanor" was "extremely forbidding" and his behavior was widely "unpopular" with coworkers and local merchants. The noted American abolitionist Benjamin Lundy, who had called upon Fisher to gain greater insight into the foreign slave trade in the region, found that Fisher "had no time for conversation" or interest in meeting with foreigners. To meet with Lundy, Fisher required a detailed written account of the matters that the antislavery crusader wished to discuss. "I suppose the aristocrat wanted a letter of introduction," Fisher said of Lundy, "but he will not get one from me." Fisher later moved on to New Orleans where he worked as a commissary general for the Mexican government but never again as a customs official for the country.[5]

Despite restrictions mandated by the Law of April 6 slaveholders continued to immigrate into Mexico with the expectations of enjoying the benefits of the foreign slave trade.[6] Richard Royall established a plantation complex in Coahuila y Texas that relied extensively on imported slave labor. Royall, who arrived in Matagorda in the early 1830s with his wife and children, had spent much of his adult life pursuing wealth and protecting his investment in slaves and landholdings in Alabama and Mississippi. Writing to Samuel May Williams in June 1830, Royall admitted that he "found . . . people" throughout the South "very much in the spirit of immigrating to Texas" and that Mexico should expect a "very considerable and valuable population" of white settlers and slaves from the United States despite its restrictions on slavery and the slave trade.[7]

Royall and other slaveholders had little intention of submitting to Mexican antislave-trade laws. Restricted access to ports, and uncooperative Mexican customs agents, presented the greatest obstacles to their defiance. To counteract these constraints, slave traffickers turned to influential white Texans for help. Stephen F. Austin, who served several years as a political liaison between American settlers and the Mexican government, became their key contact. Austin recognized the risk of investing large capital in the foreign slave trade in the face of Mexican restrictions. He spoke in realistic terms to immigrants who were resolved in their disobedience. He openly discouraged slaveholders from entering Mexico with the expectation of violating antislave-trade laws. His stand was not a popular one. It drew "the sarcasms of slaveholders" from across the region. Even nonslaveholders questioned Austin's motives and logic. In August 1830, Rhoads Fisher asked of Austin, "Do you believe that cane and cotton can be grown to advantage by a sparse white population?" Fisher insisted that slaveholders were left with a choice between abandoning the finest portion of the Coahuila y Texas province to its original uselessness or submitting to the evils of the slave trade.[8]

Slaveholders, smugglers, and traffickers were in no mood to spar with Austin or with the Mexican government over their need to sustain a steady flow of slave labor. Instead, they ignored Mexican law and with the help of port officials, mainly from New Orleans, concocted schemes to import slaves. While some fraudulently packaged Africans as indentured servants, a process legal prior to 1830, others avoided making references to their Africans as slaves when conducting marketplace transactions. "Colloured [sic] flesh" was a phrase often used to describe the slaves they intended to introduce. Listing slaves as family members on immigration documents also enabled traffickers to bypass Mexican restrictions. William Truit, a Tennessee slaveholder who refused to part with his slaves before entering Mexico, secured a family passport that included thirty-six slaves as kin.[9]

The closing of Mexican ports allowed Brazoria and Matagorda Bay to compete for the distinction of being centers for the distribution of contraband slaves in Coahuila y Texas. Each town rested in the Brazos corridor where plantation complexes were linked to an expanding Atlantic economy, much of which was driven by the rise of industrial capitalism. The Brazos corridor was a core region that satisfied the demand for certain raw goods and staples crucial to the European and United States economies. The focal point of this exchange was cotton, a crop that the urban industrial population craved. Some of the richest cotton soil could be found along the Brazos River. It was in this area that planters secured large tracts of land and imported slaves to fill the labor needs of their plantation operations.[10]

As coastal outposts, both Brazoria and Matagorda Bay suffered from neglect. The cost to maintain their customhouses was a financial burden for Mexico. The administration of Mexican antislave-trade laws between these two sleepy ports presented a major challenge. In June 1830 Nathaniel Lewis left New Orleans for Matagorda Bay aboard the sloop *Hetta* with a cargo of slaves. Lewis expected to import the slaves without difficulty. In 1831 Joseph B. Carson of Pensacola, Florida, sailed from New Orleans and headed for Matagorda Bay with forty slaves aboard the *Emblem*. The considerable number of slaves that John Matthews, owner of the sloop *Mario,* transported into Brazoria in 1830 suggests that he, too, operated his trafficking enterprise without much fear of Mexican reprisal. Matthews departed New Orleans in December 1830 carrying thirty-nine slaves to Brazoria. Walter White, A. H. Andrus, and P. G. Bertrand shared the schooner *Nelson,* a New York registered slave vessel, and also found Brazoria to be a suitable drop off point for slave cargoes.[11] Samuel Fuller maintained a busy schedule transporting slaves into Mexico from Louisiana, Kentucky, and Missouri. Fuller used both the

Exert and the *Nelson* to conduct his transactions. From January 1831 to December 1832, he transported no fewer than sixty-nine slaves to Brazoria. And according to documented accounts, Fuller's record for hauling slaves into Brazoria was unrivaled—although John G. Rowland made a significant mark in the coastal town with several voyages of his own. While the vessels that Rowland navigated were registered out of New York and Philadelphia, he catered to southern slave traffickers who competed for a share of Brazoria's foreign slave-trade market.[12]

Mexican customs agents had limited ways of verifying the accuracy of slave manifests or the veracity of legal status of slaves listed on such paperwork. This obvious deficiency emboldened the confidence of slave traffickers and enhanced their deceptive schemes. James Morgan and John Reed exploited this flaw. The two slavers used identical slave names from one year to the next on their slave shipments between Cuba and Brazoria. The names of slaves they sold to J. A. Brown and Redmond Parker of Hartford, North Carolina, in August 1830 reappeared in identical form on another slave manifest in 1831. Such use and reuse of a selected set of slave names indicated that port officials were indifferent to the recorded demographic and descriptive information found on manifests and that slavers themselves were willing to duplicate slave names for expediency. The sober ambivalence of customs agents enabled Morgan and Reed to hasten the importation of their slave shipments. Crews from the schooners *Exert, Sophia, Hope,* and *Nelson* also reused selected slave names between March and September 1831 to account for the fifty-five slaves they imported to Brazoria during this time period.[13]

Traffickers exploited the poorly policed Mexican coastline as the United States Navy reenergized its efforts to clamp down on their activities. Spanish smugglers operating on behalf of American citizens often posed the biggest nemesis to its enforcement efforts. Although the foreign slave trade was forbidden under Spanish law, African captives assumed the status of slave once traffickers succeeded in getting them to the shores of Spanish colonies, where slavery itself was practiced. Spain refused to fully execute most treaties banning the slave trade and strongly objected to the search and seizure of Spanish slave ships by foreign powers. In light of such behavior on Spain's part, slave traffickers often flaunted Spanish flags and pursued their business undaunted. In June 1830 the U.S. Navy schooner *Grampus* seized the Spanish vessel *Fenix,* which housed a group of traffickers who had agreed to transport eighty-two slaves for several American citizens into the United States.[14]

The maritime and overland shipments of slaves into Mexico were sometimes intercepted by American officials. United States marshals played a particularly important role in defusing the interplay between traffickers and the recipients of their business practices. Marshals had a long-standing reputation for coordinating the delivery of captured Africans to slave auctions. When the American navy seized the slaves aboard the *Fenix,* the United States marshal's office was eager to set up a government auction. "The sale of slaves by United States Marshals," the *New Orleans Bee* reported in 1830, "was not uncommon in everyday life of Louisiana." John Slidell, United States district attorney for New Orleans, often acquiesced to marshals and allowed them to conduct sales of African captives that were intercepted in route to Mexico. Slidell offered limited interrogation or investigation in these cases. Once federal marshals interceded in the forfeiture process, it was almost certain that slave captives would be sold on the American slave market.[15]

Mexican legal constraints impacted its own suppression efforts as well as those of the United States. As American slaveholders settled into the country, they exacerbated tensions between themselves and Mexican authorities. William B. Travis and Patrick H. Jack viewed these restrictions as an assault on their political and economic liberties. Together they conspired to attack Mexican forces and to recover any enslaved, escaped, or free black that fell into the hands of Mexican officials or its citizens. One group of Anglos contemplated insurrection against Mexico after Colonel John D. Bradburn, a Kentucky-born officer who commanded Mexico's military post at Anahuac, arrested Travis and Jack and charged both with instigating violence against the central authority.[16]

Signs of Defiance

Mexican prohibition of the foreign slave trade threatened the stability of the immigrant- and capitalist-controlled economies of Coahuila y Texas. Cotton, for instance, and later rice and lumber, had jump-started the economy during the 1820s and 1830s and raised the productivity of previously unoccupied lands, which substantially increased the need for labor. The protection of these nascent industries conflicted with Mexico's legal repudiation of the foreign slave trade. Because the trade failed to internalize itself within the Mexican planting and capitalist classes as it had among white planters, American immigrants seized opportunities to bypass Mexican antislave-trade laws and to import, almost at will, slaves, which they deemed necessary for the perpetuation of their livelihood.[17]

The emergence of a resistance movement among Anglos in Mexico demonstrated that many white immigrants expected to maintain a foreign slave trade. Their pursuit of economic and political autonomy led to two separate political gatherings. Their San Felipe de Austin meetings in October 1832 and April 1833 called for the separation of Texas from Coahuila and for the repeal of the Law of April 6. Although the issue of the foreign slave trade received no special attention at either convention it was an undeniable topic of concern within the province of Coahuila y Texas. Appeals for a separate Texas province increased awareness within Mexico's central government about Anglo anxieities. Although many immigrants did not fully expect Mexican authorities to willingly accept separation, they did assume that the existing provincial status of Coahuila y Texas only undermined their goals. The political configuration of the province hindered the political ambitions and economic potential of its slaveholders. For many settlers, property and slavery were synonymous terms and only separate status, Stephen F. Austin wrote to his cousin Henry, would quiet this country or give security to persons, their property, and business aspirations.[18]

Despite the antagonistic relationship between American settlers and the Mexican central authority, their associates and colleagues in the slave-trafficking underworld felt no particular obligation to honor Mexican law and disregarded the political fallout that surfaced from their continued support of the foreign slave trade. The United States consulate at Brazoria maintained a log of illegal slave ships that systematically obstructed Mexico's antislave-trade laws. Included in this list was the schooner *Crawford,* whose crew regularly introduced slaves into the coountry. An English schooner was also observed unloading several slaves from Grenada at Galveston in January 1836. In the same year, the collector of customs at the port of Velasco, threatened to impound a ship that carried forty slaves from Cuba. The McNeil brothers, Sterling, Pleasant, and Leander of Brazoria, who often advertised the scarification of their captives to help expedite recovery of those that escaped, also used Velasco and the Neches River to import slaves.[19]

Some immigrants displayed their repudiation of Mexican antislave-trade law through firsthand participation in the transshipment of slaves. The wealthy plantation owner James W. Fannin Jr. made slave smuggling one of his primary interests. He personally conducted slave voyages into Mexico. Fannin had arrived in Mexico from Georgia in the fall of 1834 with his wife and two daughters and settled a large stretch of land near Velasco. His initial contact with slave smuggling had come a year earlier when Edward Henrick of Montgomery, Alabama, introduced him to Samuel May Williams. Known to most slavers as a man of little patience, Fannin braved the treacherous waters of the Gulf of Mexico and journeyed to Cuba to purchase 152 slaves of which he transported back to Mexico. Fannin had nothing to lose and everything to gain. In August 1835 he bragged about his unimpeded slave trips: "My last voyage from the Island of Cuba (with 152) succeeded admirably." "Concerning his plans," Henrick wrote of Fannin, he "would not wait . . . but is going on emedately [*sic*] to Cuba," for "he is an enterprising man." Henrick recognized that Fannin was but one of many prosperity-seeking businessmen who were not afraid to venture into foreign land to deal slaves. Like Fannin, Benjamin Fort Smith eventually found his way to influential Americans in Mexico. With Stephen F. Austin's help Smith acquired land in Coahuila y Texas. Between 1833 and 1834, he journeyed to Cuba where he procured and imported slaves to work at his Mexico plantation. Unintimidated by Mexican or American officials, Smith unloaded his slaves at the home of Pleasant W. Rose for safekeeping and later moved them to his own plantation along the Brazos River.[20]

The foreign movement of slaves into Coahuila y Texas was not always fail-safe. To counteract detection, American immigrants often routed their cargoes through the Sabine River, which served as the boundary between Louisiana and Mexico. The mouth of the Sabine River became a useful hideaway. Some preferred it over other waterways. Henry Griffith, a pioneer rancher at Johnson's Bayou located near the Sabine River, supplemented his income by selling beef to slave traffickers and smugglers, who used the meat to feed slaves they intended to transport across the border. In April 1836 W. F. Gray noted in his diary that he had stumbled on "an old shed" near the Sabine River that had once housed Lafitte slaves. In the same year Gray also witnessed the McNeil brothers of Brazoria shuffling nearly forty slaves toward Mexico. In the summer of 1836, a Spanish ship carrying two hundred slaves sailed up the Sabine River to avoid seizure. Captain John Taylor cleverly docked the *Elizabeth* at the Sabine Pass, where it stayed for six weeks. He finally unloaded several slaves who had been stolen from an admiralty court in Barbados.[21]

Monroe Edwards was one of numerous smugglers who utilized the Sabine River for his slave transshipments. His slave-trade network connected Africa, the Caribbean, and Latin America with the United States. Edwards constructed a slave mart on the west end of Galveston Bay. He used this area as a base to expand his slave-smuggling ventures and other illicit activities. In 1832, Edwards rounded up a few of his New Orleans cohorts and sailed for the African coast, where he purchased several Africans and transported them to Brazil. In February 1836 he purchased 185 slaves in Cuba. Only 170 survived the voyage to the Brazos corridor on board the schooner *Shenandoah*. With his share of the loot from these transactions, Edwards invested in a plantation complex on the San Bernard River. There, he built a financial empire and contributed a considerable amount of his earnings to the campaign for a separate Texas province. Monroe was part of a growing list of slave smugglers who devoted monetary resources for this cause. Their contributions figured prominently in the plans of Anglo immigrants to topple Mexican rule.[22]

Slave smugglers and traffickers were some of the closest confidants of the most outspoken critics of Mexican antislave-trade laws. They relied heavily on political and moral support of these doppelgängers. Samuel May Williams and his ties with the Mexican government served many of their needs. Williams had acted as postmaster for the town of San Felipe, the same place where one of the two conventions calling for the separation of Texas from Coahuila was held. He later was appointed revenue collector and dispenser of stamped paper for Coahuila y Texas. As compensation for his services, Williams received eleven leagues (49,000 acres) of land near strategic waterways that slave smugglers often used to execute their illegal slave deals. As revolutionary appeals for separation increased, Williams and others focused their attention on grassroots mobilization of the white immigrant population along the Brazos River, where slaves were most abundant and smugglers tended to congregate. Other districts followed suit and placed some of the most ardent slave smugglers and traffickers in charge of local protest efforts. James Morgan was chosen to represent the municipal district of Liberty, Texas, at the 1832 convention for separation. Likewise, Richard Royall, who in 1831 had moved to Matagorda Bay on the ship *Emblem* with forty slaves, represented the Matagorda precinct at the 1833 convention. Royall had also assembled a militia, collected weapons, and raised revenue for the cause. Equally defiant was James W. Fannin Jr., who represented the Committee of Correspondence at Columbia, Texas. This organization collected complaints against Mexican authorities and kept local citizens informed about the independence movement.[23]

When the campaign for Texas separation festered into calls for revolution, and when General Santa Anna wrested power away from the liberal-minded Gomez Farias and transitioned the Mexican government into an antislavery centralized dictatorship, converting the states into mere departments of the central government, slave owners and slave traffickers exerted fierce opposition against these reforms and proceeded to promulgate their local interests at the expense of national concerns. The *Ayuntamiento* (Council) of Liberty in Nacogdoches issued a manifesto that addressed the difficulties that had emerged between shippers, merchants, and customhouses with respect to the collection of duties and the delivery of merchandise. In 1835 the Committee of Safety for Matagorda insisted that residents adopt all necessary measures to protect their property and to secure the institution of slavery and the foreign slave trade. In the same year, William B. Travis wrote to James Bowie and informed the pioneer that white settlers were divided over the issue of independence and that the Peace Party appeared the stronger. Travis was leader of the War Party and had established strong business and political ties with Bowie.[24]

Bowie and Travis sought military support for their cause from newly arrived immigrants. The movement for a separate Texas province represented an opportunity for Anglo settlers to also impose political reforms and to promote their own cultural values and traditions, among which were their versions of liberty, equality, and democracy. The maintenance of a foreign slave trade also figured in their motives. This subject was much more than "a longstanding irritant" in their relations with Mexico—it was a benchmark of their economic and political outlook.[25]

Mexican criminalization of the foreign slave trade helped focus the consciousness of its critics. It also sharpened the awareness of free and enslaved Africans and those opposed to their illegal introduction. Slave hunters found it difficult to gain access to slaves once they escaped from the entanglement of the foreign slave trade into the shelter and protection of the Mexican government. In 1834 Colonel Juan N. Almonte, acting as an agent for the Mexican authority, promised Benjamin Lundy, the famous northern abolitionist, that Mexico, with the help of escaped and freed slaves, would continue to promote its antislave-trade policies through the colonization of freed and escaped slaves inside its borders. Slaves who escaped from the clutches of traffickers and smugglers often roamed the Mexican wilderness where they interacted with Mexicans and Indians, enlisted for Mexican military service, or plotted slave uprisings. The 1834 murderous attack along the Mexico-Louisiana border on Judge Gabriel N. Martin and his fishing party by several escaped slaves, believed to be "Indian raised" or "Indian trained," reflected the inevitable violence inflicted upon white settlers.[26]

It was precisely this lack of control over the frontier that gnawed at Anglo settlers. This type of lawlessness, which failed to benefit their cause, exacerbated the tensions between white immigrants and the Mexican central authority. It also brought to surface latent issues, which later dominated social, political, and legal discourses. Because slaveholders and slave traffickers rejected any idea or legislation supporting emancipation or abolition of the foreign slave trade, they used this frontier crisis as yet another justification to divorce themselves from Mexican rule. Many offered their services and resources to accomplish this feat. James W. Fannin Jr. sold several of his slaves in order to purchase munitions for the cause. Although scattered about and displaying signs of extreme decrepitude, the ships that white settlers accumulated for military service against Mexico came from the generous donations of slave smugglers. James Morgan donated two ships from his maritime fleet, which had grown considerably since his arrival to Coahuila y Texas. He also

TABLE 1
A Chronology of the Abolition of the Slave Trade by 1836

1794	By unanimous vote the French General Assembly abolishes the slave trade.
1802	Denmark abolishes foreign slave trade.
1803	Slavery and the slave trade abolished in Haiti.
1807	England prohibits engagement in the international slave trade. Allows for an interregional slave trade but only between its Caribbean colonies.
1808	United States outlaws the slave trade onto and from its soil.
1813	Sweden bans the slave trade. Argentina phases out the trade.
1814	Dutch abolish the slave trade by a royal decree. Colombia phases out the slave trade.
1815	France ends participation in the slave trade by royal decree. At the Congress of Vienna, the British persuade Spain, Portugal, France, and the Netherlands to agree to abolish the slave trade (though Spain and Portugal are permitted a few years to continue the practice).
1816	Great Britain and Spain sign a treaty prohibiting the slave trade: Spain agrees to end the slave trade north of the equator immediately and south of the equator in 1830 (but was virtually unenforced until the 1840s). Thus, the trade flourished strongly in Spanish and Portuguese colonies. The foreign slave trade to Cuba and Brazil remained strong long after 1830: Brazil through 1850; Cuba through 1865, coinciding with the Union victory in the American Civil War.
1823	Slave trade abolished in Chile.
1824	Slave trade abolished in Central America. Slave trade abolished in Mexico but exemption is later granted to the province of Texas.
1829	Slave trade is abolished throughout Mexico, including the Coahuila y Texas province.
1830	Slave trade abolished in Bolivia.
1833	Great Britain takes initial steps to end intracolonial trade within its Caribbean colonies.

supplied the civil and military communities of Texas with much-needed merchandise. Richard Royall advanced up to three thousand dollars of his own funds to the campaign.[27]

The Texas war for independence from Mexico exposed the link between the foreign slave trade and the campaign to overthrow Mexican rule. This connection reinforces certain historical interpretations regarding the Texas Revolution and challenges others. Some scholars have advanced arguments ranging from the response of Anglo immigrants toward an intolerant and undemocratic Mexican government, constitutional conflicts between the centralist elements of the country and provincial interests, internal divisiveness over political and economic reform, the problem of Anglo cultural assimilation and conformity, or the expansion of an American version of democracy, combined with the zeal to bring order, discipline, and Christianity to the frontier, as fundamental causes for the conflict. The war was thus a manifestation of an American need to rescue the frontier from people and a government enmeshed in instability and disorganization. Despite these economic, political, and ideological rationales, Anglo immigrants were certain to also clarify their position on the foreign slave trade. Although slavery was identified as a legal institution in the constitution of the new Republic of Texas following the war for independence, and the importation of slaves from the United States was permitted, the laws regulating the introduction of slaves did not carry reciprocity with its northern neighbor. The importation and exportation of slaves between the Republic of Texas and the United States was prohibited under American law.

The Republic, Recognition, and the Slave Trade

The issues of "African negroes," the foreign slave trade, and the diplomatic recognition of the Republic of Texas were atop America's foreign policy agenda within a year of Texas independence. The United States secretary of state, John Forsyth, a Georgia slaveholder with strong proslavery sentiments, alerted agents of the young republic that the movement of slaves between the two nations would be met with stiff political opposition and that it would hinder America's recognition of the new country.[28] Diplomatic and political validation was central to the Republic of Texas's hope of sustaining a foreign slave trade. Because it kept no standing army except at certain posts, lacked the moxie to fend off a Mexican insurgency, and its diplomats courted all the major powers and presented their nation as a place of social, economic, and political stability, it required that they resolve international disputes expeditiously and establish new allies as quickly as possible. When two naval ships from the Republic of Texas, for instance, confiscated the British schooner *Eliza Russell,* Texas officials spent little time squabbling with the ship's owner and agreed to remedy the problem "without hesitation" through a joint resolution of its congress, which granted full restitution and acknowledged the "justness" of the $3,840 claim for damages that the ship allegedly suffered during the seizure. As a precaution, Republic of Texas diplomats were also certain to identify any slaves transported onto its soil as "negroes" in their correspondence with foreign nations. Despite the fact that Galveston had become identified as a hub for foreign slave traffic, Republic officials painstakingly avoided the subject when communicating with foreign officials. Making no mention of foreign slave commerce, a representative of the Republic of Texas wrote to a British official in 1838, claiming that a good part of "our trade" comes from "vessels sailing under the United States flag. No one a year ago could have foreseen the surprising increase of our commerce in so short a period. Of late, about thirty vessels are often lying in the Port of Galveston, several of which are steamboats that ply between the Island" and America.[29]

British support for Texas independence but opposition to Texas statehood within the United States is often viewed within the context of England's need to secure an alternative supply of cotton and its quest to maintain a favorable balance of global power between itself and its chief competitors. Britain's response to Texas independence can also be considered within the framework of British-Mexican relations and assessed by the extent of and limits to British political and economic influences in Mexico. British apprehension regarding Texas independence centered on the belief that neither Mexico nor the United States exercised much control over it in its provincial status. Britain's decision to recognize Texas hinged largely on its fiscal and commercial relations with Mexico. It was less interested in protecting the sovereignty of Mexico and generally intervened when government policies appeared injurious to British interests. British capital and commerce played an important role in certain sectors of the Mexican economy, and the English government occasionally offered informal support on behalf of private commercial investments. British officials hesitantly supported Texas independence not only to contain American hegemony and to cultivate the Texas cotton trade, but also to stabilize Mexico, which was beset by fiscal crisis and internal discord. In short, the effective downfall of Mexican rule in Texas did not pose a direct threat to British commercial or financial interests.[30]

The issue of the foreign slave trade, however, was one of the most paradoxical and problematic of all matters involving British recognition of the Republic of Texas. British dissatisfaction with its treatment of the foreign slave trade had far-reaching implications for the new country. For one, it jeopardized hopes for recognition and imperiled its commercial relations with England. Sam Houston regretted seeing "so much reluctance" on the part of the British government to enter into commerce with the Republic.[31]

Advancement of British diplomacy and its antislave-trade policy depended, in part, on England's handling of the foreign slave trade into the Republic of Texas. The enforcement of its Abolition Act abroad reflected the extent of England's international clout. The English Colonial Government House at Barbados played a key role in this endeavor. The Colonial House coordinated Britain's maritime maneuvers to suppress the foreign slave trade throughout the Caribbean and into the United States through information provided to them by government agents and private citizens. David Turnbull, an English traveler, wrote that the price of a smuggled slave from the time it left Havana to the time it arrived in Houston or Galveston tripled. The English temperance reformer and world traveler James S. Buckingham toured the American South for several months, and observed that large numbers of African slaves were smuggled into the United States from Havana and into the Republic of Texas. Joseph Crawford, the British vice-consul at New Orleans, reported in 1837 that traffickers from Cuba were landing slaves in the Republic of Texas in large numbers. Francis Sheridan, Britain's colonial secretary, visited Galveston in 1840 and found the Republic derelict in its enforcement of antislave-trade laws. Nicholas Doran P. Maillard, an English lawyer visiting the United States, alleged that American ships regularly transported slaves between Cuba and the Republic of Texas.[32]

Much of what these English visitors and officials observed was confirmed by agents of the Republic, although some found it advantageous to convey the impression that their government was busily rectifying slave-trade infractions. Diplomatic recognition from England, however, required evidence of active engagement. In reality, Republic of Texas officials were predisposed not only to protecting the foreign slave trade but also to shielding those who carried out the transshipments from criminal prosecution. The occasional arrest and conviction of a slave smuggler or trafficker, as John Taylor learned, was merely an opportunity for Republic of Texas officials to celebrate its phantom antislave-trade campaign. Taylor was ceremoniously handed over to British officials by agents of the Republic, who, in turn, used his prosecution and fourteen-year prison sentence to boast of its cooperation in the crusade to end the illicit traffic in slaves. The arrest and punishment of smugglers and traffickers in the Republic were rare occurrences. Officials accepted, and devoted little time verifying, the alibis of most traffickers. Following his arrest in 1840, W. John Jay attempted to cover up his smuggling activities. Jay claimed that one slave had drowned; another had left with William Moore of Anahuac and could not be recovered; a third was kidnapped and carried off to the United States; and a fourth was allegedly taken by a W. David Garner and sold into Louisiana. A slave woman whom Garner had purchased along with her three children, he pleaded, had been murdered at Brush Island off the coast of Louisiana.[33]

Despite periodic successes in apprehending smugglers and traffickers, England was limited in its ability to uncover every clandestine scheme in the Republic or elsewhere. "The slave trade is by no means extinguished," an English church bishop wrote. "It is however, more covertly conducted. From most accurate sources I can fairly state that not one out of seven slave ships is caught by British cruisers." British naval captain Frederick Lamport Barnard, by chance, did discover one such secret shipment in 1840 when he boarded a slave ship that had sailed under an American flag from the Mozambique Channel of Africa for the Gulf of Mexico. The *Houston Morning Star* recorded its version of what Captain Barnard found: a brig of unknown origins having on board a Spanish captain and nearly nine hundred slaves, of which three hundred perished from suffocation when the hatches were battened down during a hurricane, and of which an additional three hundred perished when the hatches were closed a second time due to the re-commencing of gale force winds. Another one hundred perished during the passage from Mozambique harbor.[34]

England used coercion, intimidation, sanctions, and a series of diplomatic treaties to safeguard the integrity of the Abolition Act. In its transformation from a great practitioner of slave trading to a nation poised to assert military might in order to enforce suppression, England was determined to successfully prosecute the ban. The 1835 Anglo-Spanish Treaty permitted British officers to board and search ships suspected of slave smuggling under the Spanish national flag. The United States, however, repudiated the searching of American vessels by British authorities. Although John Quincy Adams despised the African slave trade, he believed that the Anglo-Spanish Treaty represented "an investment of power ... so adverse to the elementary principles and indispensable securities of individual rights that ... not even the most unqualified approbation of the ends ... could justify the transgression." Lewis Cass, the United States minister to France, echoed similar sentiments: "Who can doubt," Cass remarked, "that English cruisers, stationed upon that distant coast [Africa], with an unlimited right of search, and discretionary authority to take possession of all vessels frequenting those seas, will seriously interrupt the trade of all other nations" while advancing its own economic and political objectives.[35]

Part of the British search for slave vessels centered primarily on the flow of slave traffic into the Republic of Texas. Shortly before England granted recognition, British Parliament member Barlow Hoy alerted the House of Commons to the pervasiveness of the country's foreign slave trade, and he called upon his government to check the unabated movement of slaves into the region. Hoy was convinced that entering into commercial treaties with the Republic of Texas without first eradicating the country's devotion and legal commitment to the importation of slaves undermined the overall objective of suppression.[36]

England's unyielding zeal to suppress the foreign slave trade into the Republic of Texas stemmed, in part, from its own vulnerable position in the global economy. Its merchant and mechanic classes were roused to the reality of being overwhelmed by foreign competition supported largely by the unrestrained use of slave labor. Thus, antislavery ideology became an integral part of British working-class consciousness that formed the popular base of abolitionism. British abolitionists not only mobilized at the grassroot, they also altered the framework of England's political discourse regarding the slave trade itself. One of their goals was to stifle England's recognition of the Republic of Texas until both slavery and the foreign slave trade were abolished. With fixed determination to protect their economic interests, however, Texans devoted themselves to the preservation of the practice. For many, the foreign slave trade was an economic imperative.[37]

Social, political, and economic stability were realistic concerns for citizens and officials of the Republic of Texas. Maintaining an efficient navy to police its unguarded coastline presented a challenging dilemma—especially when it came to defending itself against Mexico or monitoring the introduction of slaves from countries that prohibited the trade. Texans could hardly boast of being serious about honoring the Abolition Act of 1808 or any subsequent prohibition when its own laws allowed for the practice to exist and its own navy exhausted what limited resources it had in protecting its sovereignty from Mexico rather than allocating them toward suppression.

The Republic of Texas's inventory of navy vessels was on the increase by 1838. Acquiring these ships was no easy matter and did not always result in an effective and capable military force. The benevolence of James Morgan and other financially stable Texans was a less-than-adequate source for building a credible naval force that could meet the Republic's military needs while simultaneously suppressing the foreign slave trade. To increase their inventory of seaworthy brigs, Texans turned to several countries for assistance. Samuel May Williams submitted one of the first proposals for monetary help to

Nicholas Biddle, president of the Bank of the United States. After three months of negotiations, the two failed to arrange an acceptable financial package for Williams to purchase ships on behalf of his country. General James Hamilton had better luck. He persuaded his friend, James Holford of London, England, to advance his government $70,000, part of which was to be used toward a $20,000 discounted purchase of the steamer *Charleston*. The purchases of sea vessels, however, meant very little when the gravest problem confronting the government was the presence of undisciplined and uncommitted enlistments. The size of the crew aboard the Republic of Texas-owned *Potomac*, for instance, declined from fifty-five to eighteen between May and August 1838, mostly a result of desertions prompted by dissatisfaction with inadequate pay, poor rations, and other deficiencies.[38] Some of this discontent culminated in violence—in the spring of 1842 a mutiny erupted on the deck of the *San Antonio*. The crew seized control of the vessel, murdered its lieutenant and several commanding officers, and then steered the ship to shore.[39]

Republic of Texas officials openly commiserated about the sorry state of its navy and the need to spruce it up. Anxious Republic officials and citizens often bluffed their way through this dilemma. They exaggerated their nation's military competence and boasted of a navy poised to strike Mexican armed forces and its vulnerable ports. "Texas wants nothing from Mexico but peace," the *National Register Extra* printed in an April 1839 article. But Mexico, the newspaper reported, "will be at the mercy" of the Republic if ideological differences were not resolved. The functional part of the Republic of Texas navy was concentrated along its southern border near Mexico. Here, its ships presented an impressive maritime façade. Though appearing to be in good condition, most of its naval fleet suffered from rapid timber decay and genuinely poor maintenance. G. W. Hill, Texas's secretary of war and marine, wrote to Sam Houston that the Republic's Galveston fleet was void of any vessel that could "be kept sea-worthy . . . eighteen months . . . as they can barely be considered so at present." To upgrade the Republic's vessels to an acceptable state of sea competence required extensive structural repairs. Because most ship repair contractors were based in New Orleans and demanded cash payments, the badly needed modifications went unattended. Republic officials cringed at the thought of out-sourcing maintenance to Louisiana contractors after learning that valuable equipment belonging to its navy had been parceled and pawned around New Orleans by former Republic navy officers who felt obliged to unload the property as payment for back wages owed to them by the Texas government.[40]

The foreign slave trade benefited from the inept and poorly equipped Republic of Texas navy. Thus, Texas's inability to effectively enforce antislave-trade laws and its unwillingness to help facilitate an end to the international distribution of slaves kept the enterprise functioning. In June 1839 the *New Orleans Picayune* reported that slave traffickers had contrived to elude American and English cruisers to smuggle slaves into the Republic of Texas. The *Houston Morning Star* wrote that "a gentleman [had arrived] from the interior who [lived] in the village of Revnosa, on whose authority [it] is [stated], that smuggling [was] carried on . . . to considerable extent" by "civil authorities" in the Republic of Texas, who "[happened] to be the most deeply engaged in this illicit trade." In New Orleans, Thomas McKinney confided to Samuel May Williams that Republic of Texas landowners were "furnishing all the money to bring Negroes to Texas." The slave schooners *William Bryan* and *Southern* made repeated trips to Brazoria from New Orleans, while the *Pokomoke* consistently appeared at Matagorda Bay. One of the more peculiar series of journeys into the Republic of Texas involved the steamer *Cuba,* which shuttled slaves between the Republic of Texas and New Orleans at unpredictable intervals. The mundane newspaper blurbs regarding the conspicuous sailing patterns of the *Cuba* hardly generated the typical stir that accompanied such activity. The *Pendleton Messenger* subtly announced that the ship and its papers had arrived in New Orleans from Galveston.[41]

Slave smugglers and traffickers enjoyed the expressed support of many Republic of Texas officials who recognized the benefits of their vocation. John Grant Tod was one administrator who joined the ranks of traffickers to help advance the trade's life span. Tod appreciated the need to promote the slave trade. His government assignments in the Caribbean placed him in close proximity to slave-trafficking activities where he learned the nuances of the enterprise. As a commander in the Republic of Texas navy, Tod also served as a purchasing agent in Baltimore. With letters of reference to the Republic of Texas navy secretary Samuel Rhoads Fisher, he secured a position as collector of customs at Velasco in 1837. A year later, he was appointed naval inspector and assigned the task of investigating supply purchases, ship preparedness, and illicit business dealings at Galveston's naval yard—although he rarely received directives from his superiors on how to disrupt these felonious activities. Reuben Potter, who served as collector of customs at Galveston during Tod's absence, wrote to Tod in August 1839 and expressed what he believed to be an accurate assessment of their government's position on the foreign slave trade. In his letter, Potter assured his colleague that the international distribution of slaves offered "a profit which cannot fail to tempt the cupidity of . . . speculators" and that "our total deficiency in the preventive service leaves the road open to anyone who may choose to engage" in the practice. Potter expressed indifference about the numerous "cargoes of Negroes from Cuba . . . lately . . . landed in Texas" and displayed even less concern toward the "many similar importations . . . in progress." It was no great mystery to Potter or Tod that slavers were "taking on board a trifling quantity of trashy cargo at Havana," in order to proceed to neighborhood coves, where they received slaves recently imported from the African continent for the Texas "market." It seemed useless, as far as Potter was concerned, to expend energy and resources pursuing Americans or Anglo-Texans operating in violation of antislave-trade laws.[42]

Abolitionism, Abolitionists, Alliances, and "Negro Stealing"

The emergence of the Republic of Texas as a focal point of the foreign slave trade set the stage for a vigorous political assault from abolitionists. Among the outspoken voices influencing opinions regarding the subject were scores of descendants of Africans living in America. Taking their appeal to end the illicit distribution of slaves to cities, towns, and villages, crusaders such as Reverend Peter Williams Jr., Nathaniel Paul, James McCune Smith, Robert Purvis, Moses Roper (in the 1830s), Charles Lenox Remond, J. W. C. Pennington, Frederick Douglass, William Wells Brown, Henry Highland Garnet, and Alexander Crummell (in the 1840s), established a foundation for expanding the resistance movement. As admirable as their antislavery endeavors were, one of their greatest contributions was their willingness to embark upon countless trips to England, despite the peril that they and most persons of African descent faced at the hands of unprincipled mariners who made sport and profit out of random enslavment.[43]

Free and enslaved black preachers were particularly important forces in the struggle to abolish the foreign slave trade. They personified the zeal, rationale, leadership, and perseverance that helped shape much of the abolitionist campaign. While those from the south were sponsored and hence closely supervised by white clergy and churchgoers, black ministers in the north exercised more freedom in their sermons, which they used to candidly and publicly articulate their ideas and attitudes. As far back as New Year's Day, 1808, at New York City's African Church, Reverend Peter Williams Jr., son of the founder of the African Methodist Episcopal Zion Church, exhorted his congregants in a powerful and impassioned sermon. Williams encouraged his followers to "rejoice" at the "enchanting sounds" of the "glorious days" the upcoming year was to bring. The "brilliant rays" of "future prosperity" for the descendants of Africa living in the United States, the minister assured his parishioners, would be realized in due time. Williams had devoted much of his adult life and ministerial career in active dissent against the foreign slave trade. He used his oratorical skills and pulpit to give a clear picture of his position on the practice. His keen awareness of the trade reflected his concern about its effect upon the entire country. When he composed a eulogy on the life and death of the great antislavery crusader Paul Cuffe before the New York African Institution in October 1817, Williams took the opportunity to lament the "degraded, destitute, and miserable condition," which the descendants of Africa suffered. Three years following Cuffe's death, Williams was ordained a deacon in New York's St. Philip's Church and six years later he entered the priesthood.[44]

As Williams embarked upon a new phase of his calling, he continued his advocacy for racial justice and equality. Through his legendary sermons Reverend Williams raised the level of resistance against the importation of slave labor. In Williams's case, it was an issue close to his heart. As the keynote speaker at St. Philip's Church in New York City on July 4, 1830, he made several references to and offered examples of contradictions between the principles of the American Declaration of Independence and the plight of African descendants in the United States. He spelled out his opposition toward plans to resettle free Africans and escaped slaves into Canada. The best course of action for Africans to advance their own cause, Williams suggested, was for them to gain full equality within the borders of America. His ardent resistance to colonization led to his resignation from the American Anti-Slavery Society, an organization he had served for several years. Williams had left a great legacy for his successors after his death in 1840, the most profound of which included his fight to rid African descendants of the hideous threat that the foreign movement of slaves posed to their freedom. His objectives fell in line with antislave-trade ideals and those of other abolitionist organizations of the day. Total suppression, however, was a task that had been larger than the capabilities of his resources.[45]

Slave smugglers and traffickers sent an unmistakable message about abolitionists, abolitionism, and the foreign slave trade. They brazenly disregarded the liberties of free Africans as they sought out slaves to sell on the market. In 1834 an anti-abolitionist mob in New York City destroyed the home of Reverend Williams. Known for his unyielding stand against slavery and the illegal distribution of bondsmen, Williams, as did other free and enslaved Africans, faced day-to-day danger from white antagonists who used tactics of gross intimidation to abduct them. Because the market value of slaves exceeded what many white workers could earn in a year, a large number of free Africans risked being kidnapped as much for economic reasons as they were for political ones. "Negro stealing" had become widespread. Following British West Indian emancipation in 1838, African mariners also became favorite targets of smugglers who were intent upon stealing them at any opportunity. When the steamboat *Athenian,* traveling from Balize, Louisiana, arrived in New Orleans in July 1840 with a white man named Bailey and a slave named Gustave, Louisiana authorities picked up the two and transported them to prison until ownership of Gustave could be determined. The *New Orleans Bee* also recorded incidents of slave abductions in Savannah, Georgia, where nearby slave ships customarily absconded with slaves stolen from local plantations. During the 1840s, Mississippi River pilots practiced slave stealing on a grand scale. Large ships at New Orleans often deceived African sailors with promises of wage employment only to force them into slavery after gaining their confidence. In his memoirs of living in the South, Reverend John H. Aughey recalled meeting a man who "was guilty of hiring a colored crew at Boston and then coolly selling them at Galveston in the Republic of Texas as slaves."[46]

"Negro stealing" became a nuisance for smugglers and slave holders. While many stolen slaves ended up on the domestic market, some were transported into Mexico, although numerous attempts to transport them across borders failed. Jourdan, a Mexican slave stealer, was captured and hanged in the city of Texana in the Republic of Texas for allegedly attempting to run off to Mexico with a local slave girl. Jourdan was subdued near Lavaca and killed by a group of local citizens. Another Mexican was arrested and his ears severed for stealing slaves away from several plantations near San Felipe. Two young African boys belonging to General J. W. Gordon of Wharton, Texas, were stolen from a camp near Egypt, three miles east of the Brazos River, by two men riding a donkey and a horse. After paying an inflated price for the bondsmen, the purchasers later learned the slaves had been stolen. One slaveholder in Robertson County placed an advertisement in the *Houston Telegraph* and then hired several bounty hunters to locate the perpetrators who ran off with his slaves toward Mexico.[47]

The *Amistad* case of 1839, in which several Africans had been illegally abducted from their homeland by Portuguese slave smugglers and transported to Cuba, reflected perhaps the most high-profile case of slave abductions. It was in Cuba where they were sold to two Spanish slave dealers. When the *Amistad* was rescued in American waters in August 1839, following a mutiny by the Africans on board, the two Spaniards, who had purchased the slaves, were detained, arrested, and prosecuted for violating American antislave-trade laws. The case went to trial in September, at which time the federal district court ruled that the Africans had been illegally held by the Spaniards and were, therefore, neither responsible nor liable for their acts of violence. The circuit court ultimately upheld the district court decision. The case was appealed to the Supreme Court, where former president John Quincy Adams, who had in the past failed to advance suppression policies, argued the defendants' case. An 1841 Supreme Court ruling sustained the decisions of the lower courts and, in doing so, emboldened the abolitionist cause for years to come.[48]

The founding convention of the Liberty Party at Albany, New York, in April 1840 coincided with the tumultuous *Amistad* trial. Although no formal platform was initially established, the delegates in attendance adopted positions recognizable in the abolitionist agenda of the 1830s. The Liberty Party advocated the termination of the interstate slave trade and, a few weeks later, authorized formal language at its state convention in Massachusetts, which castigated the national government for its refusal to perform more aggressively against the foreign slave trade. British abolitionists observed these actions with great anticipation and interest. The General Anti-Slavery Convention in London urged American abolitionists to put an end to internal slave trading to help facilitate the demise of the external trade.[49]

Abolitionism had gained such social and political momentum in America and England that well-known slave smugglers, in their desperation to evade justice, masqueraded as antislavery crusaders. After being levied a judgment in April 1840 for defrauding his business partner of more than $89,000, the slave smuggler Monroe Edwards escaped from a Brazoria, Texas, jail and fled to Europe where he posed as a wealthy and seasoned abolitionist. He delivered inspirational speeches and published antislavery literature that extolled the virtues of freedom and liberty. He eventually left Europe for the United States after being recognized by Republic of Texas officials stationed in England. Upon his arrival he began publishing written editorials in several American abolitionist newspapers where he bragged about the moral benefits of having manumitted his own slaves. Edwards had actually lost most of his slave property through court-ordered confiscation. He anticipated that his alleged new outlook on slavery would gain the sympathies of abolitionists and divert attention away from his own legal troubles. Despite his self-proclaimed transformation, Edwards continued his criminal ways and orchestrated several large-scale forgery schemes. He was eventually arrested and sentenced to jail in New York's Sing Sing Prison, where he was beaten to death by prison guards for his role in masterminding an escape plot.[50]

The absence of a meaningful and organized abolitionist movement in the Republic of Texas made the enforcement of antislave-trade laws all the more difficult. It did not, however, deter free and enslaved Africans from forming new pockets of resistance. Many were known to camp along the Brazos River where smuggling was evident. Some took part in sporadic outbursts of violence to help slave captives free themselves from smugglers and traffickers. Once they obtained freedom, many joined colonies of other escapees and free persons who had formed communities along the Mexican side of the Rio Grande. There, they were persuaded to help resist the encroachment of the foreign slave trade and the institution of slavery onto Mexican soil. Benjamin Lundy, a northern abolitionist, mentor of William Lloyd Garrison, and founder of the antislavery newspaper, the *Liberator,* had attempted to establish a black colony in Mexico in the early 1830s. Opposition from white Texans, however, derailed his plan before it could materialize. Their reaction reflected the disdain that many held toward antislave-trade crusaders. One Ohio abolitionist was administered one hundred lashes by officials in Lavaca County, Texas, for his part in a plot to help captives cross over into Mexico. A northern preacher was hanged a few miles from Fort Worth, although his colleague successfully fled the country before he could be apprehended. He, too, was eventually captured and hanged for inciting slave revolts. The *Houston Morning Star* characterized this behavior as a "rapidly growing evil." It also warned that there were "some thirty or forty persons" of African decent "within the limits of the Corporation (Houston), prowling about . . . rendering . . . corruption" with the intent of fleeing into Mexico, where they were prone to congregate with likeminded groups. Scores of these free and escaped slaves helped Indians and Mexicans coordinate guerrilla-like warfare against whites in the Republic of Texas.[51]

Texas officials generally relied on intelligence and information from military sources and white vigilante groups to combat abolitionist activities. White Texans often responded by rounding up, whipping, and hanging recalcitrant Africans whom they suspected of taking land, killing whites, conspiring to incite other Africans, or disrupting the flow of slave transhipments. The frequency of these incidents in Louisiana closely resemble those in the Republic of Texas. "The severest punishment which the law prescribes" became part of the social, political, and legal fabric of many Louisiana parishes. Tribunals often sentenced belligerent Africans to public hangings for their part in instigating the movement of slaves to Mexico. Though sheriffs, bounty hunters, slave stealers, smugglers, and traffickers occasionally took Africans into custody, runaway and free Africans had gained such a reputation for fierce fighting that they oftentimes roamed the wilderness for several years with little interference from the groups that hunted them.[52]

Smugglers and traffickers cringed at the idea of a frontier where free Africans and escaped slaves openly waged resistance. They were equally concerned about the random seizure of Africans by abolitionist collaborators or renegade slave traffickers who had migrated into the Republic of Texas. A Mr. Phelps took legal action to have his slaves returned to his home on the west bank of the Brazos after a foreigner named Hall inexplicably confiscated each one and transported them to huts near the Rio Grande.[53]

Seminole Indians helped African escapees improvise strategies of resistance against the schemes of smugglers, stealers, and traffickers. Prior to their intrusive role against the foreign slave trade, black Seminoles had emerged as a distinct ethnic group in seventeenth-century Florida. During this time, the Spanish crown, which controlled Florida, had ceded land to a group of Creek natives to establish a buffer zone between themselves and the English settlers in Georgia and the Carolinas. Over time, the Creeks amalgamated with other bands of Native Americans, such as the Mikasukis and the Apalachicolas. By 1822 they had adopted the uniform name Seminole and numbered close to five thousand. Throughout the history of Spanish Florida, the crown had also offered asylum to runaway slaves. Although Spain's first tenure over the Florida province ended in 1763, the area's reputation as a sanctuary for subterfuge persisted. It forced many runaways and free Africans to turn to the Seminoles for protection. Seminole culture was largely a mixture of African, some white, and its own customs. The maroon (military) camps they formed allowed blacks to own weapons and to exercise autonomy over their labor. The American Indian Removal policy of the 1830s precipitated the displacement of black Seminoles from the Old South and facilitated the establishment of new relations with free and enslaved Africans in Oklahoma, Mexico, and the Republic of Texas. As troublesome as the African-Seminole mergers were, the greatest fear among Anglos was the reputation that black Seminoles had earned as fierce fighters, which they used to protect the series of small communities they had established near the Republic of Texas-Mexico border.[54]

Republic of Texas policy regarding the foreign slave trade helped solidify the links between Africans, Indians, and Mexicans. By 1841 the Mexican border had become a logical place for them to congregate but also an equally natural location for slave smugglers to set up camp. By now, a prime male slave could be purchased in Cuba for $400, sold in New Orleans for $1,250, and by the time he arrived in the Republic of Texas, the price would have escalated even higher.[55]

Slave smugglers and their cohorts assumed a central role in the proliferation and perpetuation of the Republic of Texas foreign slave trade. They competed against the forces committed to its eradication; exploited the deficiencies of the newly formed nation; emboldened those elements dedicated to the survival of slave transshipments; and enjoyed the benefits provided to them by corrupt government officials, favorable judicial mandates, and influential citizenry.[56]

Economic and geographical expansion exposed the inner workings of the foreign slave trade and revealed the political tensions between England, the United States, Mexico, and the Republic of Texas. During the 1830s and early 1840s the economic and political interests of these nations regarding the international distribution of slaves clashed. Each held its own opinion about the prosecution of the Abolition Act and differed in their approaches to suppression. Expansion and conflict necessarily required each to reassess their policies and to reevaluate their role in eradicating the practice. Their laws for suppression conflicted with the economic and political vision of white immigrants in the Republic of Texas. There, the illicit activities of port officials, a chaotic frontier culture, and a small but annoying abolitionist movement comprised of mostly northern whites, free and escaped Africans, and black Seminoles threatened to derail the trade. Participants in the foreign slave trade and their adherents, however, learned to adjust their strategies to accommodate the practice in the face of shifting borders, political disputes, and increased pressures from their opponents.

Seated next to his second wife, Emma Hortense Mortimore, Jean Laffite was one of the most well known slave smugglers following passage of the Abolition Act of 1808. Black and white photograph made from 1844 daguerreotype. Courtesy of the Sam Houston Regional Library and Research Center, Liberty, Texas.

The Laffites used their blacksmith shop in New Orleans as a headquarters for the foreign slave trade. Courtesy of The Historic New Orleans Collection, New Orleans, Louisiana.

Slave smugglers and traffickers congregated at Smugglers Row in
New Orleans to discuss and complete foreign slave trade
transactions. Courtesy of The Historic New Orleans
Collection, New Orleans, Louisiana.

By the 1820s Galveston, Texas, had become a key site for the foreign slave trade. Courtesy of the Rosenberg Library, Galveston, Texas.

Black Seminole communities such as Las Moras Village in Texas provided refuge for illegally imported and runaway slaves. Photograph by Ichabod Nelson Hall, ca. 1905. University of Texas at San Antonio's Institute of Texan Cultures, No. 088-0079, courtesy of John Wildenthal Family.

Black Seminole scouts were instrumental in helping illegally imported and runaway slaves escape into a free Mexico. Photograph taken ca. 1885. University of Texas at San Antonio's Institute of Texan Cultures, No. 074-1111, courtesy of Charles G. Downing.

Slave catchers and bounty hunters sought to turn over illegally imported slaves to their nearest United States marshals' office. Cartoon by Peter Kramer, ca. 1851. The Library Company of Philadelphia, Philadelphia, Pennsylvania.

United States Marshals reaped financial rewards through the capture of illegally imported slaves such as those housed in these barracks in Key West, Florida, in 1860. *Harper's Weekly*, June 2, 1860. Provided courtesy of HarpWeek, LLC.

Free and Enslaved Africans worked aboard whale ships that were often
converted into ships used to smuggle slaves. Courtesy of the
New Bedford Whaling Museum, New Bedford, Massachusetts.

Black and white seamen such as these pictured aboard the USS *Miami* were valuable resources for slave smugglers and traffickers. Their skills were later used to defeat the Confederacy during the Civil War. Courtesy of the Naval Historical Center, Washington, D.C.

4

"Difficult to Repress"

NEWSPAPERS, EXPANSION, RUNAWAYS, AND CONSULS

On December 29, 1845, Texas was officially annexed into the United States. The incorporation of the former republic altered the dynamics of the foreign slave trade in many ways. American jurisdiction meant that the introduction of slaves would be legally limited to the domestic trade. The Abolition Act of 1808 would no longer be an abstract issue but rather a law that placed the entire state under a new paradigm as far as suppression was concerned. Under Mexican authority slave smugglers, traffickers, merchants, and planters had dismissed the ban, as Mexico proved unable to enforce it. The Republic of Texas, however, designed new laws to help sustain the trade. By the time Texas became a state, it had emerged as a focal point for the foreign slave trade. Its link to the international movement of slaves was undeniable. The shift from republic to statehood aligned Texas with other states in terms of its obligation to adhere to federal guidelines calling for suppression of foreign transshipments. Such requirements exacerbated border tensions, placed additional burdens on the American central authority, and kept Mexico and the promises that it held for being a nation free of slavery and the trade at the forefront of the debate. A critique of the attention given to the foreign slave trade by regional newspapers and foreign consuls brings to surface the extent to which its continuation galvanized the attention of American citizenry and how it wove itself into a tapestry of other political issues, mainly Texas statehood, runaway slaves, and westward expansion.

There was far more to the post-1808 foreign slave trade than the mere exercise of introducing slaves into the United States or the Republic of Texas. Slave smugglers and traffickers understood the importance of the markets they serviced and the communities that supported their vocation. Newspaper editorials, articles, and advertisements captured, perhaps, the best evidence of connections between incidents in far-flung regions to the foreign slave trade in the United States. These publications kept adherents of the trade apprised of major occurrences. Foreign consuls also provided critical input regarding the activities of slave smugglers as they saw them from an international and institutional perspective. They frequently pointed toward the United States as an instrumental region in slave smuggling. Because expansion, wars, and boundary and border changes kept the country in a state of flux, it could not avoid becoming a target for traffickers. In many respects, the connections between the United States and the post-1808 foreign slave trade were very visible in its political and social response to Texas statehood and the California gold rush. As American borders and boundaries were reconfigured by these developments, Mexico, once again, emerged as a force in the suppression campaign and as a place of refuge for slaves hemmed in between the United States and the brutal terrain that separated them from freedom.

Newspapers and the Foreign Slave Trade

During the 1840s, newspapers scrutinized more closely the activities related to the distribution of slaves between Africa, the Caribbean, and the United States. They revealed a slave trade in which the equivalent of one in five bondsmen in New Orleans was sold annually. Most of the transactions were auctions occasioned by a legal procedure, and most sales were of broken lots of slaves rather than complete slave families. Newspapers also identified large numbers of runaways. Although they offered limited details and less-than-pinpoint accuracy regarding departure dates, ports of disembarkation, legitimacy of foreign slave transshipments, or the number of slaves shipped, most newspapers demonstrated that issues regarding the practice were relevant to the life-world of those it effected. Newspapers vigilantly gauged the frequency of slave ship seizures, catastrophes, mutinies, and massacres. Such information helped monitor the state of the foreign slave trade and its influence on the economic and political life of the United States. During the 1840s, slave smugglers and traffickers learned from newspaper articles and editorials about the physical limitations of naval squadrons and of the inability of central authorities to probe every suspected slave vessel for illegal activities. They also discovered from local publications the difficulties that bureaucrats encountered in their attempts to substantiate and document cases of misconduct.[1]

The *New Orleans Picayune* displayed great interest in the slave trading ports of Africa. It regularly wrote of attempts to abolish the French-led foreign slave trade on the continent. Since the beginning of French occupation in Algeria in 1830, the subject of banning the African slave trade had created a stir among subjugated Arabs and French emissaries, who contentiously decried any interference with the practice. They were confident that "any meddling in this traffic . . . would endanger French supremacy in Africa" and undermine the economic opportunities of indigenous Arabs, who benefited from the selling and trading of black African slaves. The slave trade played a central role in France's colonial ambitions in North Africa. Slave voyages to France, a country that had reluctantly abolished the slave trade in several of its colonies, helped boost an already reinvigorated foreign slave trade.[2]

The ineffectual suppression of the Algerian slave trade provided the opportunity for traffickers to freely conduct slave voyages between Africa, the Caribbean, and the United States. Some of these voyages originated in New Orleans and involved intermittent trips to France's coastal cities with slaves on board. Most captains pledged that the slaves they transported were not for sale or trade. In January 1844, Richard Keating set out from New Orleans, destined for Marseilles, France, with five mulattos belonging to J. E. Erwin. The two adults, male and female, who accompanied him, were conceivably transported as work hands and body servants. The two- and four-year-old toddlers and the six-year-old child on the vessel were clearly incapable of contributing much to the service of the ship. Perhaps the group indeed represented Erwin's own labor force, or perhaps they were slaves he intended to sell on the overseas slave market.[3]

Of the limited number of American naval squadrons dispatched to the African slave coast to mitigate these voyages, the *Picayune* noted, was that of Matthew C. Perry, who was placed in charge of the frigate *Macedonian,* the sloops *Saratoga* and *Decatur,* and the brig *Porpoise.* By tracing Perry's progress in Africa, the *Picayune,* perhaps unknowingly, conveyed useful information to traffickers about America's suppression strategies. Perry's quartet of ships hardly met the requirement for effectively policing and patrolling the African coastline. The *Picayune* had ample opportunity to expose this point. A January 1843 article illuminated England's successful capture of a slaver carrying three hundred slaves near the Leeward coast while simultaneously pointing out the conspicuous absence of American navy ships during the seizure.[4]

TABLE 2
American Africa Naval Squadron

COMMODORE MATTHEW C. PERRY
(May 1843)

Macedonian (F)—frigate	*Decatur*—3d-class sloop
Saratoga—1st-class sloop	*Porpoise*—brig

COMMODORE CHARLES W. SKINNER
(December 1844)

Jamestown (F)—1st-class sloop	*Yorktown*—3d-class sloop
Decatur—3d-class sloop	*Dolphin*—brig

COMMODORE GEORGE C. READ
(December 1845)

United States (F)—frigate	*Marion*—3d-class sloop
Boxer—brig	*Dolphin*—brig

COMMODORE WILLIAM C. BOLTON
(September 1847)

Jamestown (F)—1st-class sloop	*Dolphin*—brig
Boxer—brig	

COMMODORE BENJAMIN COOPER
(November 1848)

Portsmouth (F)—1st-class sloop	*Yorktown*—3d-class sloop
Porpoise—brig	*Decatur*—3d-class sloop
Bainbridge—brig	

COMMODORE FRANCIS H. GREGORY
(August 1849)

Portsmouth (F)—1st-class sloop	*John Adams*—2d-class sloop
Yorktown—3d-class sloop	*Bainbridge*—brig
Porpoise—brig	*Perry*—brig

COMMODORE ELIE A. F. LAVALLETTE
(May 1851)

Germantown (F)—frigate	*John Adams*—2d-class sloop
Dale—3d-class sloop	*Bainbridge*—brig
Perry—brig	

COMMODORE ISAAC MAYO
(December 1852)

Constitution (F)—1st-class sloop   *John Adams*—2d-class sloop
Dale—3d-class sloop   *Bainbridge*—brig
Perry—brig

COMMODORE THOMAS CRABBE
(April 1855)

Jamestown (F)—1st-class sloop   *St. Louis*—1st-class sloop
Dale—3d-class sloop   *Dolphin*—brig

FLAG OFFICER THOMAS A. CONOVER
(June 1857)

Cumberland (F)—1st-class sloop   *St. Louis*—1st-class sloop
Dale—3d-class sloop

FLAG OPFFICER WILLIAM INMAN
(May 1859)

Constellation (F)—1st-class sloop   *Portsmouth*—1st-class sloop
Vincennes—2d-class sloop   *Marion*—1st-class sloop
San Jacinto—1st-class steam sloop   *Mohican*—2d-class sloop
Mystic—3d-class steamer   *Sumpter*—3d-class steamer

NOTE: The letter "F" denotes the flagship.

SOURCES: House Executive Document 104, 35–2; Senate Executive Document 4, 362; House Executive Document 73, 31–1; Warren S. Howard, *American Slavers and the Federal Law, 1837–1862*, 239–40.

The *Picayune* regularly highlighted the ineptitude of America's Africa squadron. When native Africans captured American navy crews, the newspaper noted that their naval colleagues were generally unable to intercede on their behalf. Little was done to aid the American brig *Carver,* the *Picayune* wrote, whose crew had been kidnapped, robbed, and murdered near the southern cape of Africa. The fact that "Americans have no man-of-war . . . and every other country" has capable ships and crews in the most volatile locations of Africa, an American captain asserted, is what led to the demise of the *Carver* crew. In June 1844 the captain of an English brig offered goods in exchange for the release of American prisoners being held by local residents on the African island of Arguin. A second crew barely escaped from the island after being held against their will. The crew of the brig *Gulnare* suffered a less traumatic experience when a group of Africans kidnapped them, confiscated their ship, and demanded a pay-off from their captain.[5]

While the *Picayune* diligently chronicled events involving the foreign slave trade in Africa, it also devoted a good share of its coverage about the practice in the Caribbean, where the interplay between traffickers, smugglers, and naval squadrons reflected many of the trends common along the African coast. It documented the capture of several suspected slave ships throughout the Caribbean. One case of note involved the seizure of the Portuguese brig *Ulysses* that, reportedly, carried a load of 529 slaves packed into a single compartment. A twelve-hour chase of the ship conducted by British captain Garth of the *Will Watch,* resulted in the confiscation of the vessel but also in the escape of its captain, crew, passengers, and six slaves.[6]

Mass murders, massacres, and catastrophes characterized the harsh realities of life inside the foreign slave trade. The *Niles National Register* reported that a group of smugglers at a depot off the coast of Galinhas, an island in the Bijagós Archipelago of Guinea-Bissau and site of a Portuguese prison and governor's house, made "2000 slaves ready for shipping." Intimidated by a British blockade of the African coastline that impeded their route to overseas slave markets, the flustered and panicked crew, fearful of arrest and confiscation, beheaded the entire cargo before placing their heads on beach poles. The *Houston Morning Star* reported that nearly six hundred captives near Mozambique perished by suffocation when the ship's Spanish captain, battling the force of hurricane winds, ordered his crew to escape-proof the vessel by battening the hatches of the ship, leaving no oxygen for the trapped slaves.[7]

Newspapers provided useful information about the movement of Africans aboard suspicious vessels although some stories begged for verification. The *State Gazette* reported that the ship *Winchester* set out from New Orleans for Liverpool, England, with a large cotton freight and five thousand slaves. The port of Liverpool, from its creation, had been one of England's most profitable. A shift in its economic fortunes, however, brought on by the emergence of New World ports, pushed job seekers away from the area and into various occupations abroad. These economic hardships ushered in an era of debauchery in the city, which elevated the foreign slave trade to an acceptable occupational endeavor among Liverpool's displaced and underemployed population. This, in turn, helped fuel and sustain a popular antislavery and antislave-trade movement among England's working class. The alleged link between Liverpool and the movement of slaves from New Orleans, as reported by the *State Gazette* and other sources, made Liverpool a hotbed of antislavery activism. "In no town in Europe or America," the *Niles National Register* declared, "are anti-slavery meetings more numerous or better attended than in Liverpool." Thus, any transaction involving the sale of slaves aboard ships destined for Liverpool were most likely completed at sea or at one of the many slave harbors en route to England.[8]

Slave smugglers and traffickers were free to devise schemes based upon bits and pieces of information obtained from newspapers. William Del a Rue openly indicated on his United States slave manifest that he intended to ship four adult male slaves directly to Havana, Cuba, from New Orleans on the schooner *Alabama* despite the vigilance of curious newspapers. What Del a Rue failed to reveal was whether or not these slaves would be sold abroad into slavery.[9]

The slave manifest records of the schooner *Alabama* revealed that it was a preferred vessel for Del a Rue and others, most of whom relied on the sea-faring capabilities of H. Windle. Although he operated as an agent for several New Orleans-based slave traders, and his signature appeared on the slave manifests of several ships destined for Cuba, Windle had a special association with the *Alabama*. His popularity as a sea merchant and slaver was highlighted in the local newspapers of New Orleans. They often posted notices of his voyages. One article indicated in October 1844 that Windle's steamship *Alabama* had docked at Charleston, Key West, and Havana before arriving in New Orleans. The *Alabama* had provided a reliable means of transporting slaves between Cuba and the United States. Another snippet appeared several weeks later and asserted that Windle and the *Alabama* had arrived in New Orleans, following a stop in Havana, just days after the slave brig *Titi*, a vessel with known ties to the foreign slave trade, had appeared at the port from Cuba. Windle's uninterrupted movement between the Caribbean and New Orleans raised concerns about his role in slave distributions. Windle's slave cargoes primarily were adult males. In July of 1845 the experienced captain transported four male slaves into Port Aransas in the Republic of Texas. This marked the beginning of a succession of monthly voyages into several of the country's coastal towns where he repeatedly used the names of slaves from previous voyages. Windle's July slave manifest, for example, identified Nathan, Bailer, Charles, and Ned as his slave cargo. One month later the same names appeared as a part of his affidavit, in addition to the names of Daniel and Joshua. These names also appeared on his August, September, and October manifests along with a twenty-seven year old slave named David.[10]

Duplication, Customs Agents, and Interrogation

Windle's use and reuse of names on slave manifests can be attributed to several possible factors. First, the slaves he transported into Port Aransas may have made several trips with him. The hiring out of small but much-needed labor groups to prospective employers was one way to satisfy lapses in the Republic of Texas labor supply. Perhaps the most logical explanation, however, is that slave smugglers and traffickers exploited the ambivalent and inept United

States and Republic of Texas enforcement agencies and surrendered faulty paperwork that was rarely verified. The use of deceptive or fraudulent documents to government agents who had no formal policy for conducting background checks on shippers or on the slaves they transported spared traffickers from the time-consuming task of authenticating the legal status of every cargo. For example, the USS *Vincennes* intercepted the *Isles of Pines,* a Spanish slave ship, in the Gulf of Mexico. Following a cursory search of the vessel and a brief interrogation of its sailors, the ship was released to Spanish customhouse officers after its crew presented Spanish documents that United States officers could only accept as legitimate. As soon as the vessel was declared free, one newspaper reported, the hatches, which had been covered, were thrown open and nearly five hundred slaves confined to a lower deck appeared.[11]

Windle's practice of reusing names was not limited to his trips to Port Aransas. Sailing for William Lockhart of Alabama, he used the steamship *Neptune* to venture into Galveston with seven slaves whose names had been duplicated.[12]

Although Windle enjoyed semi-exclusive sailing privileges into Port Aransas during the 1840s, he had to share the financial blessings that Galveston offered him with other ambitious traffickers who reused the names of slaves. William Rollins, who also used the ship *Neptune,* was one of the more familiar faces to venture into Galveston from New Orleans. Rollins made no fewer than nine trips. The number of slaves he declared on his manifests rarely exceeded three. The same held true for John T. Wright, who agreed to transport slaves to Galveston. In one year alone Wright set out on six journeys for a group of slave owners from Alabama, Arkansas, Kentucky, Lousiana, and Texas. Y. F. Boharmon, F. W. Robertson, G. W. Buford, T. P. Hall, George Eaton, W. L. Haynes, P. L. Croddick, S. Wade, and others, clearly confided in Wright's abilities and trusted his judgment to transport their slaves.[13]

Statehood, Cession, and Trafficking

The Texas Admission Act, which went into effect December 29, 1845, meant changes in the circumstances surrounding suppression. First, the burden of enforcing antislave-trade laws in Texas now rested with the United States. Second, it had a stifling effect on British influence in the region. Matters involving the commercial and economic policies of the Republic of Texas became an American responsibility—something England had dreaded but anticipated for several years. Because American law had banned the foreign slave trade, the legal interstate domestic slave trade quickly became the focal point of Texas's labor needs.

It is no surprise that the New Orleans slave manifests of 1846 reflected a noticeable increase in the number of documented slaves entering Texas from New Orleans following statehood. H. Windle, for example, conveniently added a sizable number of slaves to his tally sheets. Prior to Texas annexation, Windle typically transported a maximum of ten slaves per trip; his count soared following the Republic of Texas incorporation into the United States. On one trip to Galveston in February 1846, Windle hauled thirty-three slaves for James Hamilton, three times more than his customary shipments.[14]

Traffickers used an assortment of vessels, methods, and ship operators to gain access to the bourgeoning coastal cities and towns of Texas following statehood and the legalization of slave movements between it and the United States. H. R. Dobbin from Louisville, Kentucky, concentrated most of his energies on Sabine, Texas, while Rufus Edwards and James Todd focused on Port Caddo. Similarly, Matagorda Bay, Texas, attracted the attention of Joseph Cassinio, John Wilkins, and J. B. Tucker. Port Lavaca, Texas, drew the interest of several ambitious traffickers, none of which holding anything close to a monopoly in slave shipments. Barselli & Co. of New Orleans relied on experienced shippers to transport slaves into Texas after annexation. Some slavers were slower to professionalize their business at the pace that Barselli & Co. did, but were just as dependent on the loyalty of ship operators to complete their slave shipments. William Kay, however, worked independently and personally transported slaves into the new state. Nelson Randle operated in the same vein and accompanied his own slaves to the Texas slave markets.[15]

One of the more glaring changes in the shipping patterns of slavers after Texas statehood was the increase in the number of Atlantic Coast–based ships that transported slaves into Texas through New Orleans. It was no huge secret that numerous slavers had based their trafficking operations at large eastern ports. The bark *Chancellor* of New York operated in the context of this East Coast connection before it was captured by the United States brig *Dolphin* off the coast of Africa and hauled back into the city on suspicion of slave smuggling. Although no captives were found on board, the construction of a slave deck on the ship and an oversupply of water and rice provided adequate circumstantial evidence of illicit activities. The crew of the New York slave schooner *Mary Ann*—which had a history of trouble with the law dating back to 1818, when the United States district attorney of Louisiana, John Dick, arrested William Lee for smuggling forty-five slaves into the Port of New Orleans— elected to wait out an American naval boat patrolling the waters near Monrovia, Liberia. Their five-day stalling tactic was unsuccessful and the vessel was eventually seized and returned to New York for detention.[16]

Although slave ships departing from one United States harbor for another were within their legal rights under American law to do so, it was the shoddy work of government officials and agencies at American ports that helped raise speculation about the intermittent activities of slavers who sailed between the American east coast and the Gulf states. Traffickers were more than capable of engaging in unlawful, undetectable, and unpredictable activities before entering New Orleans and subsequently Texas. Despite United States seizure of the slave brig *Titi* in the Gulf of Mexico in August 1846 on suspicion of slave smuggling, the ship was back in business within a year. By June 1848, the ship's crew was loading slaves at the Port of New Orleans for a trip to Cuba. "It now appears that the suspicious looking vessels that have frequently been seen off the coast of Cuba," the *Democratic Telegraph* reported in 1846, were the schooners of slave traffickers disguised as Mexican privateer boats.[17]

Following admission into the Union, slave trafficking in Texas became a paramount issue in a boundary dispute between the United States and Mexico. This squabble gave rise to armed conflict. Several historical interpretations seek to explain the origins of what was to become the U. S.-Mexican War. One line of reasoning characterized Mexico as a belligerent and irrational nation that failed to act in good faith toward resolving the boundary disagreement and instead resorted to a military solution. To others, preservation of its national sovereignty stand out as Mexico's motivations for war. Failure of the centralist Mexican government to resist the demands of whites regarding contested land meant all-out civil war in Mexico. As for American culpability, the view that President James K. Polk consciously plotted war to satisfy his expansionist supporters is well founded. By the end of the 1840s, Americans were imbued with the spirit of Manifest Destiny; the zeal to annex Texas and, of far greater import, to take California. Some of Polk's most loyal supporters questioned his rationale, as did the literate, educated American public of that day. In 1816, Spain had fixed the boundary of Texas, then a province, at the Nueces River, and by the Adams-Onís Treaty of 1819 the United States boundary with Texas had been established at the Sabine and Nueces Rivers, as is uniformly shown on maps of the period. Such boundaries were accepted by notable political figures including Stephen F. Austin, Andrew Jackson, Martin Van Buren, and John Quincy Adams. Even many Texans were willing to accept the Nueces River as the official line of demarcation—all but the core of Texas's slave interest. By extending the Texas border to the Rio Grande they enhanced their representation and power in the United States Congress. From this premise, the United States instigated the conflict as a means by which to acquire additional Mexican soil in Texas and California. Politics and capitalism were driving forces in this scheme and the continuation of the foreign slave trade was a critical element in that plot.[18]

A full year into the U.S.-Mexican war, slavers were busy plying their trade. Despite wartime issues, Texas continued to play a dominant role in the legal importation of slaves into the United States. Corpus Christi, a southern Texas coastal town, and its cattle industry relied heavily on these slaves who worked as vaqueros (cowboys) on its cattle ranches. Henry Parker, for instance, registered four slaves with customs officials at New Orleans and later transported them to Corpus Christi in June 1852. There, ranchers purchased them for extensive labor assignments. The steamship *Galveston* also supplied Texas with a steady dose of slaves throughout the calendar year of 1850. Its crew routinely imported slaves into Galveston, Port Lavaca, Matagorda Bay, and Indianola. By year's end the *Galveston* had transported nearly two hundred and seventy-five slaves into Texas's most important commercial ports. And an additional fifty-three slaves packed away on the steamship *Meteor* were transported to Galveston by Thomas Forbes, who divided his professional time between the *Meteor* and the steamships *Louisiana* and *Tersereana*. These three vessels were responsible for moving one hundred thirteen slaves into the state between 1850 and 1852. The steamship *Mexico* made its own contribution to the growing pool of slaves shipped into Texas. On its five registered trips to Galveston in 1853, the *Mexico* carried eighty-six slaves. In the same year the steamer *Texas* endowed Galveston with sixty-six slaves ranging from infants to adults. It also shipped fifty-two to Indianola, Texas.[19]

Flight and Recovery

Texas annexation extended legal American slavery. It also reinvigorated the foreign slave trade and energized free and enslaved Africans in their attempts to resist aspects of both. Thus, the runaway slave crisis into Mexico was invariably linked to Texas statehood. Controlling the movement of slaves within the frontier alleviated the pressures of having to sustain a foreign slave trade. Through structured and chaotic runaway systems, however, slaves resorted to flight as a primary strategy of resistance. Their response reflected the maturation of political consciousness. The American slave interest struggled to adjust to the collaboration between free Africans and enslaved captives. These two groups had combined their resources and energies to obtain freedom. Their cooperation created a serious dilemma for Texas slaveholders who found it necessary to wean themselves from the foreign slave trade for political reasons.

An unchecked runaway crisis created unstable and unpredictable circumstances in Texas's labor supply. Galveston slaveholders were alarmed when a group of free Africans from Massachusetts arrived in their county and attempted to rescue slaves from the island. Responding to this conspiracy, Galveston authorities arrested the visitors and later sold them into slavery. Opportunities for escape increased when slaves lived in close proximity to free Africans, rivers, free states and territories, foreign borders of nations that prohibited slavery and the slave trade, or areas where runaways congregated. Of the United States border regions, Mexico posed a greater concern for traffickers and slaveholders than did the Indian Territory or Canada. For several years slaves had found shelter in Mexico. Felix Haywood, a San Antonio slave, found the thought of escaping to Canada an amusing one when Mexico was within walking distance. Haywood's mindset reflected what many in his predicament believed. To many slaves, Mexico was a shining refuge from slavery and the foreign slave trade.

Sam Moore escaped from Alabama to Corpus Christi, Texas, and ultimately made his way into Mexico. He could have stayed there and lived as a free man, but returned to Texas for family reasons. Walter Rimm recalled his father's attempt to transport his family into Mexico and away from slave smugglers in Corpus Christi. "He stays 'way long time de fust time," Rimm declared. "De second time he comes back at night an' tells allus cullud fo'ks to be ready fo' de certain night 'cause he have chartered a boat to picks weuns up an' tooks weuns to Mexico." A group of forty-nine white residents of San Antonio explained to their Bexar County delegation in the General Assembly in Austin that "the insecurity of slave property in this County . . . will at once" require "the necessity of enacting an appropriate remedy" to restrict the free movement of slaves along the Nueces River and into Mexico. The outposts that Texans established along the Guadalupe River and at various points in southern Texas were of little assistance in their attempt to intercept slaves. Their effort to control the refugee flow, one San Antonio observer noted, was a futile one. The virtually unguarded Mexican border and the willingness of Mexicans to assist slaves in their crossing made containing slave departure difficult. The seriousness of the runaway issue was conveyed in one newspaper advertisement submitted by a group of Texans. They threatened to put an end to the exodus through prompt and violent action.[20]

Some runaways depended less on assistance from abolitionists and more on their own attempts to resist recapture. Reuben, a slave who claimed that he had once belonged to President Andrew Jackson, was arrested by a New

Orleans customs house officer who hustled him off to prison. Some runaways confiscated the resources of white residents and lifted whatever items and provisions they could as they made off for freedom. Robert, a slave whom E. P. Shull claimed ownership of, was detained in New Orleans for stealing thirteen barrels of lard and one barrel of pork from the steamer *Wyandotte.* Another runaway committed a daring robbery that terrified the residents of Richmond, Texas, when he entered the chambers of the county clerk, ransacked the room, and slipped away atop one of the best horses in the county with large sums of cash.[21]

Although the sparsely settled frontier appeared to render safe passage, routes into Mexico were at times difficult and hazardous. The journeys across semi-desert regions required courage, perseverance, and navigation skills. It compelled escape parties to carefully counteract the movements of smugglers, traffickers, armed slave-hunting posses, and bounty groups. Escapees also had to deal with inadequate food supply. Julius Frobel told of a horrible scene he and his party witnessed while traveling near Devil's River in west Texas. There they found an abandoned runaway camp littered with skeletal remains. It appeared that a group of runaways had murdered some of its group members to feed themselves after becoming lost and short on food. Three of four slaves from Gaudalupe County, Texas, were caught near Eagle Pass, Texas, while the fourth, the *State Gazette* reported, drowned in the Rio Grande. A slave belonging to the Wallace family of Bexar County met a similar fate when he failed at his attempt to swim across a river.[22]

Other escape parties designed their getaways more meticulously and were careful not to broadcast their plans. Saturday afternoons, Sundays, or holidays were all suitable departure times. They often stowed away on sailing vessels and steamboats. Peter, a slave, was charged in court with assaulting Louis Sourie aboard the steamboat *Port Hudson.* Peter had hoped to avoid being captured by slave smugglers. The captain of the ship *Deucallion* from Liverpool, England, found a slave on his ship and quickly surrendered him at sea to the captain of the *Emporium.* The stowaway was later delivered to the Port of New Orleans. Escapees also packed themselves into the tight quarters of covered wagons, hid away in barns, concealed themselves in outbuildings and abandoned houses, or camped out in the woods, swamps, and remote areas of the frontier. Some jumped nearby trains, while others spirited off on stolen horses. The *Texas National Register* reported that six slaves who were known as Albert, Jack, Rueben, Archy, Paul, and Charles had taken with them four fine-blooded mares, a large pacing horse, and about twenty common horses to Mexico. Other organized groups of slaves carried with them arms and weapons for defense. Such bands were well supplied with multiple items of clothing to avoid detection and to keep warm. Although a large number of slaves fled during periods of cold weather, no set seasonal pattern for flight was ever established. More predictable, however, was their destination. Over-whelmingly, the direction of flight for most slaves along the Texas frontier was Mexico. "Several persons who have lately visited the Mexican towns of Morelos and Presidio for the purpose of re-capturing Africans," the *Houston Telegraph* reported, saw firsthand thousands of escaped captives residing on the Mexican side of the Rio Grande. A party of six slaves, Robert Porter adver-tised in the *Texas National Register,* had run away from him at the "Falls on the Brazos," and all had made their way toward Mexico. One group included the slaves Dave, who fled with twelve dollars; Jim, a hotel waiter; Henry, who was well acquainted with Texas roads; and Davy, who was reportedly accom-panied by a group of whites. In another incident, twenty-five slaves headed for the Rio Grande after securing a few firearms and several of the best mounts in Bastrop, Texas. Five slaves from Bexar County, Texas, were also well sup-plied with "guns and pistols" as they headed for Mexico as bounty hunters pursued them.[23]

Because of the limitation placed upon them by American antislave-trade laws, slave escapes into Mexico aroused the anxieties of Texas's slave interest. The Mexican border represented a beacon of hope for enslaved and free Africans but a nemesis for slaveholders. Some slave smugglers and traffickers initiated their own searches for recalcitrant slaves. Others relied on the work of average citizens. The white citizens of Colorado County, Texas, became suspicious of any movement of Africans, slave or free, after several of them had allegedly conspired to murder the town's entire white population. The locals quickly drew up plans to contain their passage and to recover those that were on the run. After fleeing from Burleson County, Texas, a slave named Lucky was spotted on a rural road. When a stranger and his spouse attempted to secure him, Lucky killed both. The citizens of Travis County eventually captured and hanged Lucky for his offenses.[24]

In view of the frenzied runaway crisis, slave owners and traffickers throughout Texas turned to government officials to help support their cam-paign to extend the life of the foreign slave trade and to aid in the capturing of runaways. In 1847, Washington D. Miller, secretary to Sam Houston, wrote to President James K. Polk requesting that he take action to require the extra-dition of runaway slaves located in Mexico. In Polk, Texans had a sympathetic ear. As an advocate of slavery, the North Carolina-born Polk had demon-strated his support for such law. Polk had endorsed the annexation of Texas and in a message to a joint session of Congress defended the foreign slave trade. To Polk, Texans had as much right to maintain and protect the trade as Californians did to secure their interests in gold mines. Polk's commitment to American guardianship over the foreign slave trade was reflected in March 1847 when he pardoned William Von Pfister and Lorin Larkin, two men who had been convicted of slave smuggling in South Carolina.[25]

A source of opposition to Polk's position on the foreign distribution of slaves came in the form of a movement initiated by the Seminole chief Wild Cat. With a band of two hundred Indians and blacks, Wild Cat announced plans to establish an African colony in Mexico's Santa Rosa Mountains near the town of Piedras Negras. There they hoped to welcome escaped and free Africans from the United States. Accompanied by John Horse, the leader of his own group of former slaves living among the Seminoles, Wild Cat met with Mexican representatives from Coahuila and reached an agreement that allowed North American Indians and free Africans and slaves to settle in the region in exchange for their military service.[26]

Mexico welcomed this African-Indian-Mexican alliance, believing that it discouraged American incursion onto its soil and that it bolstered their abolitionist cause. Their collaboration heightened fears among many Texans. Most were convinced that every free and enslaved African in Texas was poised to join forces with Seminoles and Mexicans and that the life of slavery and the slave trade were doomed unless measures were adopted to stall the exodus of slaves crossing over into Mexico. Slave owners and traffickers scurried to fortify the Texas frontier with their own allies. Texas governor Peter H. Bell appointed Warren Adams, a proven filibuster, to recover escaped slaves and to confiscate free Africans at will. As an experienced "Negro thief," Adams was quite efficient and skillful at his business. His participation in this confiscation plan compelled slave refugees to maintain a constant state of vigilance of his whereabouts.[27]

The Texas Ranger John S. Ford, who united forces with Jose Maria Jesus Carvajal, a well-known military revolutionary, also participated in the hunt for slaves. He established a base camp near the Rio Grande. There, he organized strategies to capture free Africans and runaway slaves from Mexican soil. This was not the first time that members of the Texas Rangers had surfaced in issues regarding the recovery of slaves along the frontier. The Rangers found themselves embroiled in countless confrontations with escapees and antislavery crusaders throughout Texas, Iowa, Nebraska, and Kansas. The soldier and Texas Ranger William "Bigfoot" Wallace commanded a company that encountered border bandits and Indians as he and his mercenaries pursued runaways heading into Mexico. "We had not more than formed in line," Martin Stowell, a devout antislaver, said of his Nebraska abolitionist militia, "when we were attacked by . . . a regiment of Texas Rangers" of which we "killed 65" and upon "surrendering, they threw their arms into the river, declaring they [weapons] should never fall into the hands of Yankees" intent on eradicating the slave trade.[28]

Recovering escaped slaves and confiscating free Africans required diligence, as it took little time and effort for them to assimilate into Mexican border communities. The slaveholder Hugh C. McIntyre was rebuffed by the relatives of a slave who had fled into Mexico by way of El Paso, Texas, and married into a wealthy Mexican family. Had McIntyre not enjoyed the assistance of United States military officers from nearby Fort Duncan, Texas, his attempt to recover his slave might have resulted in his return to Brenham, Texas, empty-handed. It was not uncommon for free Africans and slaves who made it into Mexico to conceal their whereabouts. Still, arriving safely proved to be the most formidable obstacle.[29]

To many Texans, the escape crisis was a "deep and vital" issue as they could not bear both the ending of the foreign slave trade and an exodus of its slave labor to Mexico. In response, local governments began passing laws and ordinances that created daily patrols for runaway slaves and free Africans. Local marshals and their deputies were granted control and supervision over the conduct, demeanor, and deportment of all Africans in their jurisdiction. Some of the laws prohibited whites and Mexicans from establishing intimate social and political relationships with Africans. Municipal judges were given sole discretion to subject free and undocumented Africans to public sale. In certain cases, Texans offered up to six hundred dollars for either, with some payments hinging on their nearness to the Rio Grande at the time of their capture. Civic associations were established and offered rewards ranging from two hundred to five hundred dollars. The white residents of Bexar County, Texas, formed their own security committee to remedy the flight crisis. In addition to establishing a standing two-hundred-dollar reward for their apprehension and delivery, the council also paid five hundred dollars to informants who provided leads that foiled the plots of escape parties or provided information that led to the arrest of co-conspirators.[30]

Slave auctions and bounty hunting played into the interests of slave traffickers and smugglers who counteracted the banning of the foreign slave trade and runaway crisis in Texas by confiscating African sailors. For several years African sailors had enjoyed a measure of modest protection aboard ships and brigs, but the frontier runaway crisis combined with Texas's labor needs made the luxury of sea life more precarious once free African seamen came on shore. Traffickers and slaveholders exerted more energy in their pursuit of runaways, which led them to ports and coastal towns in search of Africans to be sold illegally on the slave market. In Galveston, four free African sailors who were scheduled to work aboard the brig *Billow,* bound for Boston, found themselves being sold "as slaves for life" to the highest bidders. Samuel Qualls purchased the free African sailors Anthony Hays for $325, Levin Smith for $370, and William Brown for $510. John Fordney scrounged $365 to buy the sailor Isaac Thompson. For their own protection, some African sailors were incarcerated during overnight stays at port cities. The United States administrators at Matanzas, Cuba, notified ship captains around the island that their "colored mariners" should "be placed in immediate confinement until the vessels to which they belong are ready to depart." Ship captains often accepted offers to detain and house one another's African sailors. By doing so, they avoided having their crews sold into slavery by white sailors who often shifted their roles and became slave traffickers and bounty hunters when the opportunity presented itself.[31]

Free and escaped Africans counteracted the constraints of the foreign slave trade in their own way. They professed and defended their freedom whenever possible and declared themselves refugees, rather than runaways or fugitives. Claims of freeness, however, meant little to slave traffickers or slave hunters, and even less to local judges and juries. Rather than present herself as a runaway slave to Louisiana authorities, an African woman who went by the name of Isabella claimed to be a free refugee from Texas. She insisted that her status as a free person in Texas during Mexican rule was not automatically forfeited when Texas became a state. Believing, perhaps, that migrating to Louisiana would shield her from the intense smuggling and trafficking culture of Texas, Isabella found out differently when she was confiscated by a Mr. Gates, a Louisiana slave catcher. Gates eventually sold Isabella for cash to satisfy his outstanding financial debt. When Isabella presented her case to the United States District Court in New Orleans, the panel of judges conveniently discredited her claims as well as those of her chief witness, who testified to her freedom as a Mexican resident. Although legally abolished under the Mexican constitution, the court concluded, slavery had thrived in the Texas province, making it difficult to discern free persons from slaves, particularly in the absence of documentation validating one's manumission or emancipation.[32]

By the end of the 1840s, Mexico's continued colonization policies had created opportunities for more organized attempts to offset the illegal distribution of slaves and to abet their movement into Mexico. This effort ultimately integrated itself into the Underground Railroad movement of the 1840s and 1850s. Although it encompassed a wide range of experiences, all connected by the need to resist and abolish slavery and the foreign slave trade, the maturation process of the Underground Railroad phenomenon occurred over an extended period, and it covered a vast amount of territory. The movement itself was predicated on the crossing of borders and boundaries from oppression to freedom, and its meaning and salience is often skewed when considered solely within the narrow context of domestic slavery and the United States history.

The free states of the North and Canada have long been recognized as the primary destinations for slaves fleeing the oppression of southern slavery. The Underground Railroad was the locus of this activity. The elaborate network of abolitionist stations and outposts birthed from this process corresponded with the heroic works and efforts of African descendants such as Harriet Tubman, John Mercer Langston, and others, and is borne out in the historical discussions on the resettlement of slaves in areas north of slavery. Several Canadian towns also served as terminals for this network, which enabled thousands of slaves to enjoy unhindered freedom on the soil of a new country. Escaping from bondage, liberated slaves from the United States found friends, freedom, and protection under the British flag. While on vacation with his family in Niagara Falls, Canada, James S. Evans of New Orleans discovered the pervasive nature of border crossings by runaways. Evans lost possession of a slave girl after he instructed her to procure milk from the kitchen staff of the Cataract Hotel. Evans reported that the girl had been persuaded by a group of African hotel workers to abandon the family before she could be taken back into the United States. Evans hastily formed a three-person search team and successfully traced her to a small Canadian village. There, his group of pursuers was "surrounded . . . in great numbers" by a group of Africans that adamantly refused Evans's request to have the girl returned. It was clear to Evans that this determined "set of free Negroes" had established a pattern of spiriting slaves away from their American captors and owners with the full knowledge and approval of their hotel managers.[33]

Unlike the shuffling of slaves from the Deep South into Canada, the movement of slaves out of the Western Gulf South states was linked almost exclusively to Mexico, where flight across the border was initiated primarily by the escapees themselves and with limited help from northern abolitionists or antislavery sympathizers. Nonetheless, both escapees and abolitionists formulated their own version of trafficking, one that focused on freedom as opposed to profit and one that competed against the foreign slave trade.[34]

Although Benjamin Lundy had introduced the idea of establishing an African colony in Mexico, the project was defeated by the agitation of white settlers in Texas. Yet, a few white abolitionists refused to abandon the vision. William Neale, a white frontier businessman, along with several members of his family, helped to locate escapees and began transporting them into Mexico. With long-standing frontier connections, John Short also supported an underground railroad for escapees into Mexico. By repeatedly reselling slaves to abolitionists at intervals along routes leading into Mexico, Short was able to secure their passage out of the United States. Although his counter-trafficking scheme was measurably successful, his cattle theft ring and counterfeiting operation ended his career as an abolitionist. Short and his son were executed in a public hanging while his son-in-law, William Greenbury Sansom, was sentenced to prison for his misdeeds.[35]

Westward Expansion, Territorial Organization, and Gold

Despite the volatile and unstable conditions brought on by the runaway slave crisis, slave smugglers and traffickers reconstituted themselves to regain a measure of control over the foreign movement of slaves. As the United States expanded geographically, they sought new opportunities to promote the trade.[36]

The outward movement of slaves from the United States into new economies enjoyed a boost when the Treaty of Guadalupe Hidalgo ended the U.S.-Mexican War. The treaty granted the United States title to the disputed border region of Texas, and conceded jurisdiction of New Mexico, Utah, California, Arizona, Nevada, and Colorado (Mexican Cession) to the American government. The agreement also gave rise to a new set of issues involving the legality of foreign slave transshipments within the boundaries and borders of this newly acquired territory. Most specifically, the jurisdiction of American laws remained unclear. By now, most abolitionists and antislavers were convinced that the supporters of the foreign slave trade had finally achieved their long-held objective of expanding the practice. They assumed that those who advocated extending the trade also envisioned it stretching from Africa to the Pacific Ocean. Even the wealthy *criollos* class of Cuba, which had relied heavily on the foreign slave trade, had begun to think of Cuban annexation into the United States as the best way to preserve the practice and to fend off the growing nuisance of abolitionism on their island.[37]

American slave interest had already identified areas of the Mexican Cession as suitable locations to introduce foreign slaves prior to the ratification of the Treaty of Guadalupe Hidalgo. The extent to which New Mexico had emerged as a vital commercial location, and the prominent role that Texans played in the attempt to introduce slavery into the region during Mexican rule, reflected its importance. New Mexicans had debated the African slave trade but found it to be unsuitable. The 1822 opening of the Santa Fe Trail, which stretched from Santa Fe, New Mexico, to Missouri, established a vital link between American business people and those residing in far-flung frontier societies. By the late 1840s, the trail had become linked to the slave trade. Although the Indian slave trade in the region had been banned in 1812 for fear that the practice would provoke warfare between Indian nations, lack of enforcement combined with the high demand for labor kept traffickers of Indian slaves in business. As the market for Indian slave labor declined, traffickers turned to African slaves to satisfy the labor needs of New Mexico. The fertile Mesilla Valley had become the principle agricultural and population center for New Mexico and was settled mostly by Texans predisposed to the foreign slave trade. Gaining control of the rich resources of gold and silver in the area was also an important factor in the aspirations of the slave interest, and it affected the course of affairs. The Texas-Santa Fe Expedition of 1841, a disastrous plan devised by Mirabeau Lamar, president of the Republic of Texas, to seize control of the trade caravans along the Santa-Fe Trail and to have them placed under his jurisdiction, intended to take firm command of New Mexico's agricultural and mining economies. The scheme was foiled when New Mexico forces captured the remnants of Lamar's militia and sent the perpetrators (those who were not executed beforehand) to Mexico City in chains. One faction of prominent New Mexicans went on record in opposition of the slave trade. Acting upon a suggestion made by Senator Thomas Hart Benton of Missouri, they submitted a proposal to the United States Congress in 1848 and requested a territorial government that would protect New Mexico from the foreign importation of slaves.[38]

Until the American acquisition of California, Texas was believed to be the last bastion for the foreign slave trade in the United States. California, however, figured prominently in the extension of the practice well into the late 1840s. The true economic and political intentions of the United States in California were apparent several years prior to the signing of the Treaty of Guadalupe Hidalgo. Reacting to erroneous information that fighting had erupted between the Republic of Texas and Mexico in 1842, Thomas C. Jones, an American commander for the United States naval squadron anchored off the coast of California, seized the port at Monterey. It turned out that Jones had moved prematurely. He later learned that fighting had not occurred, offered an apology to the Mexican central authority, and returned the port back to Mexican officials.[39]

By the late 1840s, a steady flow of American immigrants, some accompanied by slaves, streamed into California in search of gold and other economic opportunities. In his December 1848 State of the Union address, President Polk broadcast the discovery of gold in California. Numerous individuals and investment groups were spurred to travel westward to the region. Some arrived by sea. The business of transporting these prosperity seekers rested with passenger steamship companies that planned and carried out several hundred voyages, resulting in large financial returns for their efforts despite a plethora of obstacles.[40]

The movement of Africans, free and enslaved, into California was also augmented by the gold rush and carried out, in part, by these commercial ships. Charley and Primus, two Africans who had agreed to work as restaurant waiters aboard the New York–based steamship *Pacific* in exchange for a cost-free trip to the West Coast, a region thought to be relatively free of slavery, found themselves embroiled in an intense feud to retain their freedom. The ship's captain accused the pair of loafing on the job. A series of verbal insults was followed by brutal floggings and threats to enslave the pair.[41]

Although commercial voyages emerged as a key method of transporting Africans from the United States into California, certain evidence exists that suggests Africans had also arrived directly from Africa. Some appeared between the Abolition Act of 1808 and the gold rush. Several had claimed Africa as their place of birth. By 1849, any African under the age of forty-one who made such an assertion may have represented those imported into California in violation of the 1808 ban. Many Africans from the Gold Coast of Africa were captured and sold in the Americas. Some were found among runaway slaves. These runaway slave communities emerged as early as the 1530s near Cartagena de Indias. Columbia was an extremely rich gold-mining area and was settled very early by gold-seeking immigrants who introduced African slaves from the Gold Coast of Africa into the New World. American colonists in California relied on the assistance of Africans knowledgeable about various techniques for panning, digging, and processing gold. John Johnson of El Dorado, California, was one such African-born person residing on the California coast. William Marshall of San Francisco, Eman Rodricks of Placer, and Charles Wilkerson of Los Angeles all claimed African nativity. One unidentified resident of California reported that the influence of Africans could be gleaned in part by the African names that appeared during the gold rush.[42]

The influx of many Africans into California before statehood can be traced to the Port of New Orleans, where traffickers continued to profit from existing and emerging slave markets. By the end of the 1840s New Orleans had become a commercial epicenter for commerce and trade in the Western Hemisphere. As merchants flocked to the port in order to ship their goods to developing economies, traffickers continued to embrace the harbor as their link to distant slave markets. Many displayed flagrant disregard for—and rendered unimportant—the antislave-trade laws, and carried on a profitable foreign slave trade between Louisiana, Central and South America, and California.

The commodification of the African population had for several decades infused economic life into the United States economy, and the slave link between the United States and Central and South America, had become a critical component in providing much-needed labor for the rapidly expanding gold-rush economy of California. Discrepancies involving the distribution of slaves between the United States and Brazil emerged during the late 1840s. In 1849, before docking at New Orleans, the captain of the slave vessel *Ohio* offered no justification for the visits he made to Brazil with slaves in tow. He did, however, eagerly assert his legal right to transport slaves from one United States port to another. In the summer of 1849 John Thompson, operator of the brig *Octavia,* also set his eyes on South America with the intent of transporting slaves from New Orleans to New Granada.[43] In H. Windle's case, Panama became a convenient rest station for his California voyages. H. O. Rogers also found Panama to be a suitable temporary layover for the steamship *Falcon,* which recorded its own movement of slaves between Louisiana and the Pacific Ocean. Similarly, the steamship *Philadelphia* noted California trips that established a sailing pattern that included pauses in Panama.[44]

The crisis of territorial organization had a noticeable effect on the behavior of slave traffickers. As emigrants arrived to the gold rush, the military governor of California beseeched the federal government of the United States to establish a suitable territorial government as soon as possible. A bitterly divided Congress struggled to remedy the nagging problem of an unorganized Mexican Cession and California territory. At the core of this quandary was the introduction of foreign slaves. While the Manifest Destiny principle had for many years united the major political forces in the country, the stalemate over the Mexican Cession exposed one issue that exacerbated sectional conflicts. The culmination of a series of resolutions introduced by Henry Clay and Stephen Douglas, which became known as the California Compromise, reflected attempts to remedy the crisis. When the bill became law, California was annexed into the Union as a free state, and New Mexico and Utah were granted territorial status.

Only one of Clay's and Douglas's many resolutions was beneficial for slavers. This was the creation of the Fugitive Slave Law. Its purpose was to return runaway slaves to the jurisdiction of their alleged owners. The act, in part, spoke to fears over the redirection of the foreign slave trade into the developing regions of the Western Hemisphere. Southerners interpreted the inability or unwillingness of California officials to challenge slaveholders, who continued to traffick slaves into the region until the outbreak of the Civil War, as tacit support for the trade. Robert Givens admitted as much when he wrote from California to his father in Kentucky. Givens considered the transshipment of slaves into California a minimally risky proposition since government officials there, he surmised, spent little time investigating such conduct.[45]

Regular shipments of slaves from New Orleans to California were as important to the early establishment of slave labor in the region before passage of the California Compromise in September 1850 as was the immigration of free Africans.[46] Central and South American ports served as a thoroughfare for slave ships bound from New Orleans to the American West Coast, where San Francisco was a principle market for slave labor. T. B. Halfrey and Joseph E. Carson used the schooners *Heroin* and *Florida* in the spring of 1850 to conduct transshipments from Louisiana to the West Coast. C. Stoddard relied on the steamer *Crescent City* for two voyages to San Francisco, while H. J. Hartstine guided the ship *Falcon* and ten slaves on four separate trips to the bay area between January and May 1850. In the same year, the steamship *Ohio* and its master, James F. Schenck, made five voyages with slaves to the gold-mining regions of California. H. Windle, the well-traveled slave trafficker who made his mark as a leading courier of slaves into Texas, extended his commitment to sustaining and expanding the foreign slave trade by introducing slaves into California. He joined a group of traffickers who led convoys of slaves from Havana to California by way of New Orleans.[47]

The California gold rush inspired a group of New York financiers to construct a rail line connecting the Atlantic and Pacific Coasts of Panama. Acting as chief engineers, George M. Totten and John C. Trautwine endured several years of delays and obstructions before they were able to nurse the project to completion. The large number of travelers crossing the Panama Isthmus on their way to California gold mines often drained the country of its local and slave labor. The opening of the Panama Railroad to commercial traffic in 1855 became an important milestone for Pacific-bound cargo. Both Panamanians and Californians recruited outside labor to bolster their economic ambitions, and the foreign slave trade played a vital role for each.[48]

By 1850 slave-trafficking water routes to California went by way of Central and South America; much of this traffic was carried out by American slavers, or those who fronted as Americans. Most either secured fraudulent registrations or hoisted bogus flags atop their vessels in order to deceive the navy crews ordered to suppress their business. Some Portuguese and Spanish captains used other ploys. The "Equipment Clause" of 1839, a bilateral treaty between these two nations, identified specific items that slave traffickers and smugglers commonly used on their ships. The agreement granted each authority to impound the other's vessels when contraband items or undocumented slaves were found. Because of this Joaquim Antonio Ferreira, Joaquim Ferreira dos Santos, Miguel Ferreira Gomes, and others refrained from making direct shipments of slaves into Rio de Janeiro or Bahia, two of the more prominent slave harbors in Brazil, for fear of reprisal from Portuguese and Spanish naval authorities. Instead, they unloaded their cargos a comfortable distance away.[49]

Foreign Consuls

The letters, eyewitness accounts, conversations, correspondence, communications, interrogations, and in some cases, independent investigations of foreign consuls provide clearer images of this ubiquitous foreign slave trade.

American foreign consuls were subject to weak oversight by their superiors, which made them vulnerable to the temptations of the foreign slave trade. One noteworthy example is that of Nicholas Trist, who served as United States consul to Havana in 1841. Trist was implicated in several plots to help slave smugglers transport slaves between Africa, Cuba, and the United States. Born into an aristocratic Virginia family in 1800, Trist grew up in Louisiana during a time when its settlers defined their own rules and established their own unique political, social, and economic cultures. Trist returned to Virginia to practice law. With a granddaughter of Thomas Jefferson as his bride, Trist earned a reputation as an erudite man of principle. He entered government service in 1828 as a clerk in the State Department before becoming President Andrew Jackson's private secretary. He went to Cuba in 1833 to serve as United States consul. It was there that his fortunes changed and his reputation was placed under scrutiny. Trist became very unpopular with New England ship captains, who believed that he was more interested in maintaining cordial relations with Cuban authorities than in defending American interests. Captains and merchants insisted that Trist be removed from his post. British commissioner Dr. Richard R. Madden wrote to United States abolitionists about Trist's involvement in promoting the slave trade through the use of fraudulent documents. Trist earned handsome payoffs by falsifying birth certificates to make it appear as though African natives were Cuban born. The Trist scandal broke just months before the *Amistad* affair, when Africans illegally sold on the Cuban slave market instigated a mutiny on a ship, seized control of it, and attempted to sail for Africa. It was through Madden's testimony in the *Amistad* case that light was shed on the plot. Although Trist vehemently denied accepting financial bribes in exchange for ensuring safe passage for slave smugglers, and had criticized the foreign slave trade as "a pursuit denounced in every way by the law," he found himself embroiled in a scandal that through the complaints of ship captains and a congressional investigation led to his recall.[50]

Crippled by a lack of adequate resources to effectively interdict American involvement in the foreign slave trade, Henry A. Wise, United States minister to Rio de Janeiro, reported in 1847 that the smuggling of slaves was on the increase within his geographical assignment. He specifically pointed out that the slave schooner *Enterprise,* which had been condemned at the Brooklyn, New York, naval yard two years earlier, had made three successful round-trip voyages from Brazil to Africa in pursuit of slaves and was preparing for a fourth journey. Despite the frequent complaints of Gorham Parks—who assumed the duties of United States consul in Rio in 1848—regarding the inadequacies of America's campaign to suppress the foreign slave trade, he and his colleagues struggled to contain the practice along the Brazilian coast.

Parks often complained to his superiors about the difficulties of preventing American vessels from recklessly engaging in the business. He felt helpless in his efforts to rid the Brazilian coast of ships transporting slaves under the American banner. One of his grievances concerned the *Enterprise,* which had joined up with at least three other high-powered and large-sized slave steamers outfitted at Bahia. Each steamer sported 200- to 360-horse-power engines, and one of the three ships, the *Niles National Register* reported, had already conducted a voyage to West Africa, where it allegedly loaded nine hundred slaves and then escaped from the American brig of war *Sea Lark* by simply out-racing the slower military vessel once the two ships reached calmer waters.[51]

British consuls stationed in the United States also played an active part in monitoring the foreign slave trade. These agents were sent to administer diplomatic agendas and to offer opinions and information regarding slave transshipments. The consensus among most British consuls was that the perpetuation of the post-1808 foreign slave trade undermined suppression and was injurious to its political and economic interests. British foreign consuls played an especially critical role in disseminating messages about the precarious state of the trade along the principal slave-smuggling ports of the United States.

Some of these British consuls exposed the international link between America and slave-smuggling activities abroad. Their records offer keen insight and make it possible to reconstruct these events in the United States. Subdued discussions by the American slave interest about the continuation of the foreign slave trade, wrote Arthur T. Lynn, British consul at Galveston, Texas, constituted an acknowledgment of their uncompromising desire to sustain it. In 1851 the British consul in Virginia reported that the slaves of British subjects had been kidnapped and taken to the West Indies, while others were abducted and spirited off aboard one of the numerous New Orleans–based slave ships. British consul Henry G. Kuper of Baltimore gave assurances that the foreign slave trade was being extensively conducted by Americans. His colleague, Consul Edward W. Mark, wrote from Baltimore that at any moment twenty vessels or so might be found under construction at the city's harbor, being admirably built for the foreign slave trade.[52]

British foreign consuls were instrumental in monitoring Mexico's role in mitigating slave transshipments. Britain established formal diplomatic relations with Mexico in 1825. Because British capital and commerce were preeminent in important sectors of the Mexican economy, and commercial interests in Mexico often affected the British economy, the Texas war for independence from Mexico in 1836 demanded an effort by the British Foreign Ministry Office to maintain vigilance over the conflict. British consuls in Mexico were required to inform the Foreign Office about slave-trading activities in the region. The newly formed Republic of Texas had opened a new legal market for foreign slaves, which required intervention that Mexico, the British minister to Mexico reported, was "wholly incapable of checking."[53]

One strategy used by the British Foreign Office to offset the transshipment of slaves was to pressure the Mexican government to sign on to the Anglo-Spanish Treaty of 1835. Under this agreement, enforcement of the British version of the Abolition Act was tightened. British cruisers were authorized to arrest suspected Spanish slavers and to bring them before mixed commissions established at Sierra Leone and Havana. Under this agreement vessels carrying specified "equipment articles" (extra mess gear, lumber, foodstuffs) were declared slave ships.[54]

The British Mixed Court Tribunals that were established in Sierra Leone and Cuba were points of contention for Mexican authorities. Having suffered a major political setback with regard to Texas independence, the Mixed Courts were only useful to Mexico if tribunals were held on its own soil and, if arrested, slave smugglers and their confiscated vessels were brought to Mexico for prosecution. Because Texas was a refuge for slave smugglers, their apprehension, detention, and prosecution were central to Mexico's attempt to restore political credibility. Under the proposed British Treaty, seized slave vessels would be tried within the jurisdiction of the detaining cruiser and then before an assigned tribunal. Mexico's meager resources and preoccupation with the Texas crisis hardly afforded it the luxury of chasing down slave vessels or prosecuting slave smugglers. Mexico also felt obliged to reject the stipulation by which the cases of slave smugglers would be decided without appeal. This clause generated feelings of uneasiness among Mexican federal agents. Thus, it was "in the highest degree improbable," Richard Pakenham insisted, that Mexican naval forces would pursue slave vessels under the conditions of the proposed treaty.[55]

For Mexico, the idea of empowering England to search and seize suspected slave ships in the Gulf region required thoughtful and deliberate consideration, even though the abolition of slavery and suppression of the foreign slave trade had always been key components of its public and foreign policy. National sovereignty and rightful jurisdiction trumped the bold objectives of the Anglo-Spanish Treaty. "Although the wishes of the Mexican government," José Maria Ortiz wrote to Richard Pakenham, "conform most strictly to those of his Majesty with respect to the abolition of the slave trade, as proved by the several laws which have been issued in the Republick [Mexico] it is nevertheless necessary that they should attentively examine the basis of the Treaty" before a final decision could be made.[56]

The feeling of Britain's Foreign Office toward Texas independence and the foreign slave trade was a construct of its own political and economic interests. In 1837, British foreign secretary Lord Palmerston summarized Britain's attitude toward the newly independent Republic of Texas: "We must see whether the band of outlaws who occupy Texas will be able to constitute themselves into . . . a community[,] as it would be decent for us to make a Treaty with a self-denominated State, till events had proved that such a state could permanently maintain its independence." By 1840, Palmerston had decided that it was in Britain's best interest to recognize Texas, although he was not convinced that commercial treaties with the republic would necessarily guarantee smooth diplomatic relations or prevent the annexation of Texas into the United States. Because Britain's 1837 invitation to the United States to create an international patrol to interdict the foreign slave trade was rejected by the Americans, Palmerston had no legitimate reason to believe that recognition of Texas would end its participation in the foreign slave trade. Making allowances for Texas exports, some conservatives recommended, promoted better relations in general, and more successful negotiations on the slave trade. Palmerston argued that cordial relations with Texas would "have the effect of mitigating rather than aggravating the evils" arising out of the legal existence of the slave trade.[57]

Slave trading between Cuba and the Republic of Texas constituted a major concern for the British Foreign Office. Its agents deliberated, contemplated, and kept "watchful attention" on the slave trade between the two. In May 1837 they identified cargoes of slaves on board American schooners bound for Texas. The master of a Mexican vessel stationed at Havana witnessed "forty Negro slaves destined for Texas." He reported this to Mexican officials upon his arrival at Veracruz, Mexico. British agents gathered "many indications of the existence" of illegal slave traffic to Texas and also communicated their findings to the American consul in Mexico. They compiled the names of vessels equipped for the transshipment of slaves.[58]

The British Foreign Office was beset by allegations and rumors that many of its own agents, as well as those of other European governments, were engaged in slave-smuggling enterprises. Although the office offered few specifics regarding these claims, the notion that its consuls made a habit of engaging in slave traffic for financial gain placed the agency in a less-than-optimum position. The actions of the British functionaries in question gave circuitous validation to the foreign slave trade. In Venezuela, for instance, British subjects who resided in the interior of the country owned sizable tracts of land and depended on adequate supplies of slave labor to survive, although British law restricted their participation in the trade. "An estate situated in the Province of Caracas, upon which there are numerous slaves," Bedford Wilson wrote to Lord Aberdeen, "is the property of British subjects or of a British firm established in London."[59]

Mexican agents and consuls presented yet another dilemma for the British Foreign Office. The Mexican government, despite its antislavery and antislave-trade policies, was unable to effectively discourage its consuls from submitting to the financial lure of the trade. Their actions were particularly disconcerting for the Mexican government, but its officials felt no particular obligation to satisfy British requests to monitor its agents more carefully. The inevitability of British recognition of the Republic of Texas, "where a vast colony of slaves" had been settled and slave "traffic" was a daily activity, England's foreign office concluded, hindered Mexican efforts to earnestly cooperate with England in its suppression campaign.[60]

The British Foreign Office also collaborated with American abolitionists as it sought to remedy the foreign slave-trade dilemma. In 1843 Arthur and Lewis Tappan, two venerable abolitionists, were contacted by England's foreign ministry and asked to offer their services toward eradicating the foreign slave trade. Born in Northampton, Massachusetts, in the 1780s, the Tappan brothers became successful businessmen and later used their connections to bolster their abolitionist ambitions. By 1833 they had become involved with the American Anti-Slavery Society and by the 1840s co-founded the American and Foreign Anti-Slavery Society. The Tappans represented an alternative to the American central authority, which had offered measured responses and limited assistance in the campaign to suppress foreign slave transshipments. Operating from their New England offices, the Tappans empathized with the British cause but suffered from their own struggles to make the eradication of the foreign slave trade a central theme in the American political discourse.[61]

The inadequate responses of the American and Mexican governments toward the suppression of the foreign slave trade compelled the British Foreign Office to embark upon more assertive strategies. One included issuing several warrants to its British Admiralty of the Royal Navy instructing it to execute the plans and objectives of the British Abolition Act. British ships were dispatched along the slave coasts of Africa, the Caribbean, and the Gulf of Mexico to enforce relevant antislave-trade treaties. The Foreign Office also informed its foreign agents of its intent to confiscate slaves found aboard slave ships and to transport them to Trinidad or Demerara or to the nearest British settlement.[62]

British foreign agents observed slave transshipments almost daily and assessed information regarding slave-smuggling activities. Consul Robert Bunch of Charleston reported that the *Lydia Gibbs,* a large vessel, was outfitted at that city's port and sailed for Havana under the command of an Irish Scotchman named Watson, a naturalized American citizen, who sold the ship for profit in Cuba and then agreed to an additional six-thousand-dollar advance to sail the brig to Africa to obtain slaves. He earned another six thousand dollars and a portion of the slaves after agreeing to successfully land the cargo in Cuba. The *Lydia Gibbs* was joined in the Charleston-Cuba-Africa connection by the slave ship *Echo,* which had been seized and condemned for slave smuggling. A South Carolina grand jury in Columbia, Consul Bunch conveyed, paid little attention to evidence that the ship's crew was plentifully supplied and heavily funded by financial sources and support groups in Cuba.[63]

British consuls provided additional information detailing the existence of a foreign slave trade within the United States throughout the 1850s. In 1859

Consul Bunch noted that several slave vessels had been outfitted in New York. Consulate reports regarding such activities in other states were voluminous and lengthy. By the late 1850s, Consul Edward W. Mark reported that vessels might be found under construction in Baltimore being adapted specifically for the slave trade by "respectable houses," which executed the orders without entering the trade under their name. British consuls at Mobile issued reports that reinforced many of the concerns their colleagues had also written about. Consul Charles Tulin wrote that there was much excitement over the foreign slave trade. In March 1859 he discovered twenty African slaves in Mobile that could not utter a word of English but rather relied solely on their native African dialect. Later that year he reported that a vessel of six hundred slaves was unloaded near Smyrna, Florida, and another boatload was dropped along the Alabama River.[64]

Most British consuls generally shared a critical and not-so-friendly attitude toward the United States. They challenged census reports, which they thought were very inaccurate in their counting of the influx of foreign slaves. G. P. R. James, upon his arrival in Norfolk, Virginia, following a trip to New England, was ostracized by white Virginians for a poem he had written years earlier and for his defense of several slaves that had been kidnapped from the West Indies. James was not surprised by his observation of slaves being bound together and shipped off to distant slave markets. In 1851 the British consul in Virginia reported that the slaves of British subjects had been kidnapped and taken to the Caribbean.[65]

Some consuls resented their assignments in the United States. They complained of high living costs, debilitating heat and humidity, and expensive vacations that became their only escape, aside from a job transfer. One of the most difficult adjustments, however, was assimilating into a social system of which many of them disapproved. The injurious effects of slavery upon Virginia's economic development stood out in Consul James's view of the state. He wrote with enthusiasm of the great resources Virginia had and of its ambitions for a railroad system that would link its major cities to the West and Northwest and make Richmond and Norfolk rivals of New York. James, however, was disenchanted about Virginia's relationship with adherents of the foreign slave trade. The selling of free blacks at the port of Norfolk was an almost daily occurrence, James wrote. Southern states used public and private jails to house free blacks kidnapped by agents and natives of foreign lands employed to receive and send them outside of the country. These "dens of horror," which kept no registers, made it difficult to track cases of kidnapping and foreign transshipments. In 1851 James's predecessor, Consul F. Waring, reported he had been informed that several free British persons of color had been transported into Virginia against their will and forced to board a New Orleans slave packet. His efforts to curtail these activities were futile. "Frightfully," Waring wrote in 1855, the state district attorney for East Virginia "believed that during the previous year, over two hundred British blacks in the West Indies, employed there as sailors, had been kidnapped and sold in the United States."[66]

British consuls in South Carolina encountered similar circumstances as those in Virginia. They, too, found few kind remarks to bestow upon supporters of the foreign slave trade. In 1850 Consuls Mathew and Bunch wielded their influence and prodded South Carolina's state legislature to pass laws protecting the liberties of free African sailors from a party of "slave traders" headed by the state's own governor, John H. Adams. Bunch expected that South Carolinians would ultimately become reconciled to the foreign slave trade and accept it as the most feasible solution to their slavery dilemma.[67] Bunch had much to say about the foreign slave trade in South Carolina. As long as he was willing to investigate slave smuggling, he seemed to find an incident to report. He wrote that the brig *Frances Ellen* had cleared from Charleston for Africa, to purchase and capture slaves through the Spanish slave-trading firm of Ponjand and Lalas with the express purpose of delivering them to the United States. In 1858 he told the story of a Charleston mercantile house, E. Lafitte and Company, which proposed to send the ship *Richard Cobden,* on a voyage to Africa to bring "free emigrants" to a United States port. The collector of Charleston's port successfully disrupted this plot, and the scheme was eventually abandoned.[68]

British consuls were fully aware that not all efforts to interdict South Carolina's involvement in the foreign slave trade were as successful as the *Richard Cobden* incident. In January 1859 the crew of the ship *Brothers* was captured off the slave coast of Africa and put on trial in South Carolina, where Judge Andrew G. Magrath and a grand jury exonerated the defendants. The brig *Bonita,* Bunch indicated in his writings, was detained in Charleston harbor just after South Carolina's Ordinance of Secession was passed, leaving the legal disposition of the crew and ship unresolved.[69]

Of all the states, Louisiana, by reputation and geography, posed the greatest opportunities for the foreign slave trade in the United States. For this reason the British consul at New Orleans treated most rumors of slave smuggling as if they were episodes of truth. The Mexican consul at New Orleans was forced to put to rest British concerns that the Mexican government, through its Vera Cruz customs office, had furnished "letters of marque" under the Mexican flag to vessels engaged in the foreign slave trade. Despite a history of slave-trade corruption along Mexican coastlines and within its customhouses, the Mexican consul made assurances to the British Foreign Office that there was no collaboration between the Mexican government and slave smugglers.[70]

While Mexico opposed the foreign slave trade in policy, the practical application of its opposition was tenuous. As far back as 1817 "pirate boats" were "very numerous" around Mexico where they committed their "depredations" from "Cape Catouche to La Vera Cruz without respect to flag or nation to smuggle slaves."[71]

William Mure compiled demographic information regarding slave transshipments into New Orleans. His office was particularly interested in "the number of whites, and of coloured people forming that population, distinguishing males from females, and free people from slaves."[72] Mure also wrote about slave vessels clearing the port of New Orleans but admitted that it was difficult to discern their specific destination. He reported that merchants and shipmasters frequently complained about biased treatment and unjust detention of free and enslaved sailors. Under the Negro Seamen's Acts, some were kept in New Orleans jails for up to three months. Africans who were part of shipwrecked vessels were also detained. In some instances, they were left behind and reduced to slavery when their captains were unable to pay the heavy fees required to obtain their release. One form of relief occurred when Mure used his influence to help secure the enactment of a new Louisiana law that softened the stringent requirements of the Negro Seamen's Acts. His efforts held up until 1859, when the state legislature renewed the act "in a worst form." His antislave-trade work in Louisiana encountered yet another special challenge after the state's legislature passed a bill in its lower house authorizing and sanctioning an existing company that had been set up to import twenty-five hundred slaves from abroad. Although the bill was supported by a very small but influential group of "ultra-southern" folk, it nearly won passage in the entire legislature.[73]

This so-called Louisiana apprentice program did not deceive British consuls. They viewed it as a less-than-clever scheme to evade the laws of the country by importing African slaves as indentured servants. Several Louisianans advocated the procurement and employment of these slaves from Africa, Jamaica, and St. Domingo to work on the state's sugar plantations and estates. This "voluntary immigration" was to allow free Africans to enter Louisiana under no compulsion and to choose their own masters, provided they submitted to no less than fifteen years of labor. There was little doubt among British consuls that the measure was the equivalent of legalizing the foreign slave trade because it provided "a stimulus to native African chiefs to embark in new wars for the purpose of getting captives to become emigrants." British consul Arthur T. Lynn of Galveston reported on a similar act passed in the Texas legislature in 1858. This bill sanctioned the importation of Africans under the guise of an apprentice program that allowed free Africans to be enslaved once they arrived on Texas soil. Lynn was skeptical of the law from the onset. The idea of any free person of color entering Texas under the pretense of an apprenticeship, Lynn lamented, was an illusion of the greatest measure, and constituted an illegal act. The Texas "apprentice program" gave validity to a rumor that Lynn wrote of in an 1860 report, one that was confirmed by a Louisiana planter traveling from Louisiana to Indianola, Texas. In this correspondence with the Foreign Office Lynn voiced his worries about African slaves from several foreign ports being secretly landed on the Texas coast.[74]

The suspicions of British consuls that slaves were being introduced into the United States in violation of American and British law were confirmed in May 1860 when two slave ships were captured off the coast of Cuba. The incidents demonstrated that the foreign slave trade into the United States was far from extinct. For the British Foreign Office and its consuls, the confiscation validated many of the claims and assertions found in their field reports. The American slave ship *Wildfire* was captured and seized with over five hundred slaves (mostly children) on board and taken to Key West, Florida, for interrogation. The United States Navy steamer *Mohawk* had patrolled the northern coast of Cuba for several weeks and had encountered numerous innocent merchant vessels before confronting the crew of the *Wildfire*. This case, in particular, revealed the connective links of the American slave-smuggling industry. The *Wildfire* had originally sailed from New York in December 1859 and headed for St. Thomas in the Caribbean. The stopover lasted eight days. From there, the ship was steered to the Congo River in Africa where it took on nearly six hundred slaves and sailed for Cuba. The *Wildfire* episode shared many similarities to the seizure of a French slave ship by Lieutenant John N. Maffitt of the American navy. It too had been located off the Cuban coast with a sizable number of slaves on board. The crew of the bark surrendered to American officers after first flaunting French banners and papers. The slaves they turned over were transported to Key West to be housed and fed.[75]

British consuls also circulated reports of African slaves being smuggled into Galveston, Texas, in 1860. These accounts were based upon "indefinite assertions" that transshipments occurred with the *Thomas Watson* and *Lucerne* vessels. Hunch-backed camels provided the pretext for the *Thomas Watson* to conceal the slaves it brought into Texas. Tom Watson, the ship's owner, had established a place of residence along the Texas coast for the express purpose of carrying out his foreign slave transactions. His activities, however, were well publicized and provided corroborating evidence for the British Foreign Office that "African Negroes" were being introduced onto Texas soil. Word of Watson's undertakings reached as far north as Rochester, New York, where a visitor from Texas revealed his personal knowledge of witnessing "not less than nine hundred native Africans, all of whom were disposed of to planters residing in the interior of the state," and that Watson's business was "transacted as if it was of a perfectly legitimate character."[76]

British anxieties about American response to the foreign slave trade in the United States were further fueled by the prospects of southern secession. As southerners voiced their desire to break from the Union and to prolong the practice, British consuls copiously documented the development of their campaign to separate from the Union and weighed the potential effects on its own suppression campaign. Although American internal political matters were outside of the general purview of British consuls, many seized the opportunity to volunteer their observations and opinions on the sectional crisis. The abhorrence of South Carolinians toward the North and its antislavery policies, Consul Bunch elaborated in a letter, had grown steadily ever since it had become evident that the power of the South had vanished as the superior region, and the enlightenment of the free states emerged. Bunch was deeply impressed by the remarkable unanimity of South Carolinians, including some from the "most respectable classes," who in 1832 and 1852 had opposed secession.[77]

Consul Mathew arrived in South Carolina in 1850, just as the state was beginning to seriously debate secession. The people of this state, Mathew contended, demonstrated hatred of the North and the federal government. A curious feature he found was the pro-secessionist sentiment among clergy and women within the state. Mathew was not the only consul to treat the secession issue with seriousness. G. P. R. James in Virginia approached the debate with keen interest and was convinced that the South was "ripe for a radical political change that would prolong the foreign slave trade." James was persuaded that the determination of Virginians, as well as other southerners, to secede from the United States in the face of opposition was entirely logical from their point of view.[78]

British consuls observed similar trends of secession throughout the South. Some were surprised to find such favorable secessionist sentiment. Conservative views were usually met with able and zealous advocates of Union patriotism, but that trend had given way to antipathy and hostility toward the northern and western states and a more radical discourse designed to spare the foreign slave trade emerged. These secessionist types, William Mure contended, were comprised of politicians, disappointed office seekers, ultra-southerners, and a large class of slave owners.[79]

Adherents of the foreign slave trade sought to satisfy market demand by adjusting their smuggling and trafficking schemes to accommodate westward expansion, changes in territorial jurisdiction, and rises in political tension. Few issues diverted their attention away from this cause. During the 1850s the foreign slave trade was a noticeably relevant issue. As smugglers and traffickers found creative ways to promote the trade, their supporters exhausted their energies to locate sanctuaries from which to continue the foreign distribution of bondsmen.

5

"A Great Frontier Movement"

SANCTUARIES FOR THE
FOREIGN SLAVE TRADE

Several factors helped sustain the foreign slave trade in the United States during the 1850s. One was the highly organized filibuster communities. These expeditions of conquest overcame legal and political attacks and penetrated foreign borders with the intention of toppling governments and reintroducing the foreign slave trade through law, policy, and practice. Using filibusters, whale ships, and recycled vessels, slave traffickers and smugglers shared in this objective. They too worked to locate a safe haven for their vocation. By the end of the 1850s their common interests had converged with those of American slaveholders. By then, the idea of legally reopening the foreign slave trade in the United States had become a principle topic of conversation at southern commercial and economic conventions and conferences. It generated spirited debates that persisted up to the Civil War.

No matter how much borders and boundaries changed and central authorities may or may not have suppressed the foreign slave trade, in the end, participants in and supporters of the practice always searched for ways and places to advance the practice. By the 1850s the trade bound together the interests of the United States with a range of nations, territories, and colonies and its adherents fueled many of the contentious issues that shaped the political and economic context of remote and border regions. Smugglers and traffickers were rarely short of supporters, collaborators, or resources. They sought out locations where they could implant their business. Evidence of the help they received could be seen in the actions and activities of filibusters, who orchestrated plans to establish slaveholding republics that would be sustained through the foreign slave trade, and provided capital for purchase or renovation of otherwise dormant or useless ships. During the 1850s the foreign slave trade was widely recognized as a vital component of America's slave economy, and those who were most convinced of this made their feelings known and their voices heard to have the practice legally reinstated and sustained.

Filibusters and Foreign Invasion Plots

Filibuster campaigns and the foreign slave trade brought to surface many of the latent issues that helped expose the necessity of ratcheting up antislavetrade campaigns. When the interests of slave traffickers and smugglers converged with foreign invasion plots (sometimes referred to as "Aaron Burr schemes" or "buffalo hunts") designed to overthrow existing governments and to install political systems that favored their goals, their activities were met with intense scrutiny.

Derived from the Dutch term *vrijbuiter*, a filibuster in English usage refers to a freebooter. During the seventeenth century, "filibuster" originally referred to English buccaneers or maritime pirates who roamed the Caribbean in search of Spanish quarry. By the 1840s and 1850s, it more often applied to virtual armies of adventurers from the United States and to individuals who joined their ranks. Almost without exception, filibusters preferred Latin America. They mixed political and pecuniary motives, pursued territorial conquests through intervention in the domestic affairs of foreign countries in which the United States was a neutral party, and demonstrated fearless devotion to their cause. Filibustering was viewed by southern planters as necessary to defend and maintain slavery abroad. The object was to enlarge American territory and to influence and expand slavery through the continuation of the foreign slave trade. Revolution, political grievances, liberation, promises of available land, and the desire to control and dominate commercial trade and certain commodities, inspired their actions. Although filibuster expeditions violated the United States Neutrality Act of 1818, which prohibited private warfare by American citizens in foreign lands, thousands joined as recruits or provided material and financial support. Filibusters established their own patterns of conduct and often launched their escapades from American soil by winning the trust of wealthy Americans, politicians, journalists, lawyers, doctors, authors, overseers, immigrants, and the unattached and unencumbered. Viewed by many as heroes, filibusters epitomized the spirit of the frontier. "Conquest and transformation" was their manifesto. Their private military expeditions gave rise to several disputatious issues and to numerous widely publicized controversies. Many of these disputes were tied directly to the foreign slave trade.[1]

"Annexationism" in Cuba coincided with the expansionist or Manifest Destiny movement in the United States. As Americans were on the brink of acquiring the Mexican Cession, some lawmakers formulated ideas of making Cuba an integral part of their vision, not only to preserve and extend the foreign slave trade but to sanctify it. By the time the Cuban annexation movement had matured, slaveholders, slave traffickers, and smugglers had mounted a calculated campaign to increase their representation in Congress and to establish independent slaveholding states in Cuba and Central America. With the help of Texas lawmakers who held public meetings and raised funds to subsidize the cause, the filibuster General William Walker worked in cahoots with American slave traffickers and the Venezuelan native General Narcisso Lopez to establish Nicaragua as a way station for the foreign slave trade. The pair formed an expeditionary army at the ports of Galveston and Corpus Christi to carry out their plan to invade Cuba.[2]

Filibusters collaborated with American and foreign slave smugglers to preserve the foreign slave trade through the invasion and conquest of foreign lands. Uncovering their conspiracies required government intrusion into their affairs. Following an American interrogation, it was discovered that the French adventurer Count Gaston de Raousset-Boulbon had led hundreds of Frenchmen residing in California on several expeditions into Mexican Sonora between 1852 and 1854. Around the same time, a party of five filibusters sailing on a ship bearing English credentials escaped from Mexican sailors by leaping onto a British navy ship called the *Dido,* which had been sent to investigate suspicious activities in the Gulf of Mexico. Filibusters were less fearful of British reaction to their schemes, provided that no link between their operations and those of the foreign slave trade could be established, than they were of American responses. Laurence Oliphant, son of the chief justice for Britain's colony of Ceylon, journeyed all the way to Nicaragua in 1856 to talk the famous filibuster William Walker into opening his venture to British subjects. Mexican attempts to foil Walker's invasion plot had led to the arrest of his expeditionary band in 1854. Suspicious of his political motives, Mexico had refused Walker a land grant for fear he would use the land to establish a military colony. Recruits from all regions of the United States had flocked to join Walker's operation and to cash in on the venture by invading the most vulnerable parts of Mexico. Recognized as one of the leading filibusters of his day, Walker had, in fact, envisioned a slaveholding Mexican society near the American border that would preserve the foreign slave trade and some day be annexed into the United States.[3]

Filibusters channeled a large share of their energies toward colonizing Mexico and certain regions of Central and South America. Their intention of sustaining the foreign slave trade was evident in their response to the crisis of slave escapes. The flight of slaves into Mexico made that country a target for filibusters. One source placed the number of runaways at three thousand in 1851. John "Rip" Ford, a well-known Texas Ranger, estimated that approximately four thousand of these refugees, with a market value of more than three million dollars, had made their way across the Rio Grande by 1855.[4]

Although Walker was twice arrested and prosecuted for his role in spearheading invasions into Mexico and Nicaragua, he successfully recruited willing participants. He dispatched several of his agents to the Isthmus of Tehuantepec in southern Mexico, with supplies and equipment in advance of his own arrival. He procured funding and much-needed resources from wealthy Americans and foreigners. Walker used bonds to subsidize his plan to establish the Republic of Sonora. Each bond carried a stipulation that the buyer would receive a square league of land located on the public domain of the new country. Ship owners in the United States covered much of Walker's transportation costs during his filibustering career. Julius Hessee and Company, a shipping firm organized by the local merchants of Mobile, Alabama, announced the creation of the Mobile and Nicaragua Steamship Company, which relied on the *Fashion* to make scheduled surveillance trips from southern Alabama to Central America. It was aboard this vessel that Walker and two hundred of his associates traveled from New Orleans to Mobile and then on to Nicaragua, where they hoped to topple the country's government and set up their own administration to establish a slave state sustained through the foreign slave trade.[5]

Williams's plot to seize Mexico was met with mixed reaction among Americans. Some welcomed the opportunity to expand slavery and the slave trade. Others were unconvinced that the establishment of a new republic under Walker's control ensured slaveholders any real relief. Texans clamored almost uncontrollably for a resolution to the refugee crisis into Mexico and demanded the extradition of escaped slaves. Sam Houston, who himself suffered the loss of two slaves to Mexico, broached the subject before Congress in 1850. In Texas, the state legislature passed a joint resolution endorsing extradition, and delegates from the Southern Commercial Convention debated the issue at its 1855 New Orleans convention. Presidents James K. Polk, Zachary Taylor, Franklin Pierce, and James Buchanan all attempted to resolve the dilemma in their own way, but Mexican officials refused to accept any proposal that advocated returning escaped slaves to the United States. Instead, it appointed military commander Edvard Emil Langberg and others to discourage filibuster schemes and resist American encroachment onto Mexican soil.[6]

Promises to expand and control the foreign slave trade were prerequisites for most filibuster expeditions. Many American expansionists were reluctant to rally behind filibustering schemes unless guarantees could be made. The expedition plans of José María Jesús Carbajal to invade Mexico during the early 1850s gained impetus once Carbajal made it clear that he intended to allow bounty hunters entry into Mexico to pursue slaves. During Carbajal's 1851 expedition, the slave hunter Warren Adams coordinated an unsuccessful mission to confiscate free and enslaved Africans. His excursion netted the seizure of one African family, which he snatched from an African-Seminole maroon colony at Monclava in Coahuila.[7]

James H. Callahan's filibustering expedition into Mexico provided indisputable evidence of the strident attempts made by proponents of the foreign slave trade to support invasion plots. Callahan's mission enjoyed the financial, political, and sentimental blessings of American slaveholders who feared that the increased number of free and enslaved Africans fleeing into Mexico legitimized the country as a land of freedom for runaways. In July 1855, Texas governor Elisha M. Pease authorized Callahan to organize a force to disrupt the alliance between marauding Indians, Mexicans, and Africans who attacked whites throughout the Texas frontier. Their assaults on the white population increased when three thousand United States troops from Texas were sent to Kansas to quell violence that had erupted following passage of the Kansas-Nebraska Act. At public meetings in San Antonio, Seguin, Gonzales, and Bastrop, Texas, residents spoke out about the urgent need to finance Callahan's Mexican expedition. They promised to cover the cost of rewards for any captured free African or runaway slave. Their monetary and moral support allowed Callahan to cross from Eagle Pass, Texas, into Mexico. Marching westward with a military contingent, Callahan took possession of Piedras

Negras, a town well known for harboring runaways, and ordered it looted and burned. Having failed to satisfactorily recover an adequate number of Africans before returning to Texas, he lobbied for additional funds for a second incursion. Callahan's death in April 1856 ended the invasion plan.[8]

The 1850s witnessed several filibuster campaigns. The targets included Cuba, Nicaragua, and other parts of Central America. Support for these adventures was less a function of hegemony among America's slave interests and more a reflection of self-serving agendas. An expanding Texas planting economy during the 1850s, in particular, offered unprecedented potential for the accumulation of wealth and for the establishment of independent republics that could offer access to the foreign slave trade. Participants in filibuster movements consisted of patriots who collaborated with cross-sections of the American population to also reestablish themselves as political and economic forces.

With promises of a foreign slave trade, large land grants, and political clout, Texans were often enticed by the invasion schemes of filibusters. The *Quitman Free Press* reported that leading figures in Galveston supported filibuster campaigns only because they promised to set up bases for the foreign introduction of slaves. "If you agree to slavery," wrote the editor of the *Galveston News,* "you must agree to the trade, for they are one. Those who are not for us must be against us. Those who deny . . . the slave-trade are enemies." Francis Lubbock also articulated what some Texans felt about the foreign slave trade when he addressed a group of Galvestonians at a public meeting. Lubbock spoke to the unwavering support that Texans had for strengthening and maintaining the practice. They had learned "how to acquire foreign "territory by cheap and facile method" and delighted in opportunities to conquer Nicaragua and Cuba. In March 1856, E. H. Cushing, the influential editor and publisher of the *Houston Telegraph* newspaper and ardent supporter of William Walker, reported that Archibald Wynns had left Galveston to inspect Nicaragua for a possible invasion. This "clever, high-toned gentleman of solid information and close observation," Cushing wrote, compiled several reports concerning opportunities to seize new land.[9]

Filibusters organized many of their invasion plots at public gatherings. In July 1850, Texas governor Peter Hansborough Bell delivered a speech that expressly defended the invasion and annexation of Cuba. The following year, Sam Houston addressed a mass meeting in New Orleans and spoke of plans to execute this mission. During his talk, Houston laid out methods and strategies for acquiring the resources and materials to implement the invasion. In April 1856, Dr. R. J. Swearinger of Chapel Hill, Texas, addressed a well-attended

meeting at a Galveston courthouse and provided vivid details about his rec-
onnaissance filibuster trip to Nicaragua. Swearinger provided valuable information about the prospects for a safe settlement and a prosperous foreign
slave trade. Additional meetings were held in Galveston "for the purpose of
giving expression to views" concerning the importance of providing aid to
local filibuster plots. Present at these meetings were prominent political and
public figures. Judge David G. Burnet, ex-president of the former Republic of
Texas, presided over an assembly that residents had organized to discuss their
invasion strategies. General Sidney Sherman, General G. D. McLeod, John
Henry Brown, Dr. William Carper, Oscar Farish, and Professor Caleb G.
Forshey, director of Rutersville Military Institute, all participated. They recommended that aid be given to the "patriots of Nicaragua," referring to con-
tributors to the Nicaragua plot. They also formed a committee to arrange
transportation for Cuban and Nicaraguan emigrants from Galveston. Fermin
Ferrer, a transportation agent for William Walker, contracted William L.
Cazneau of Texas to provide one thousand able-bodied men to accompany
Walker's Nicaraguan expedition.[10]

Filibuster campaigns relied on the financial blessings of its citizens and
community organizations. Money was collected on a weekly basis in Houston
and Galveston in support of the movement. Some paid as little as $35 per per-
son to secure a spot on the *Charles Morgan* ship, which arrived at Galveston
harbor every eighteen days for voyages bound for Nicaragua. At a meeting in
Galveston, eleven new recruits volunteered for the venture and $475 was
raised for the cause. In July 1856, P. R. Edwards acknowledged the receipt
of monies from a Galveston church that had been donated to aid William
Walker's campaign.[11]

With slavery and the foreign slave trade foremost in their minds, filibusters justified their plans for conquest and regarded them as an opportunity to extend their beliefs, objectives, and ideals. But their overseas military
defeats and their failure to secure the political support of federal officials hindered most of their efforts to seize or colonize foreign lands. In 1855, filibusters assembled a militia of six hundred in Galveston for a Cuban invasion,
only to have their hopes dashed when the administration of President Franklin
Pierce failed to produce the necessary political support for the scheme.
Although Cuba was considered by many in Washington to be the "Pearl of
the Antilles" to be conquered by sword or by purse, the United States minister to Spain was unsuccessful in securing an acceptable endorsement from
the Spanish government, which would have allowed the invasions to continue without American or Spanish interruption or denunciation. Although

the armed invasions of foreign countries often occurred with full knowledge of American officials and in clear violation of United States neutrality laws, the American central authority displayed little outward or noticeable public support of or opposition to filibusters. This ambivalence allowed many expeditions to proceed with confidence. The United States secretary of the treasury for President James Buchanan, Howell Cobb, upon whose office rested the responsibility to enforce laws regarding illicit activities between borders, dispatched instructions to Hamilton Stuart, the collector of customs at Galveston in 1857. Cobb insisted that Stuart "keep a sharp look out" for steamers transporting filibuster militias from Galveston to Nicaragua, though he offered no specific plan for curtailing their activities.[12]

Prosecutions and Invasion Plots

The interplay between the foreign slave trade and nineteenth-century filibuster campaigns revealed the conspiratorial nature of each. The criminal prosecutions of filibusters illustrated the difficult task of securing convictions against them. The federal trial of Mississippi governor John A. Quitman was one such example. A native New Yorker, Quitman settled in Natchez, Mississippi, at a young age. He was later implicated in a Cuban filibuster scheme in which he and his cohorts, mainly General Narciso Lopez, a native Venezuelan and longtime resident of Cuba, conspired to invade and seize control of the island. Had the invasion succeeded, it would have won them control of its slave trade.[13]

Committed to overthrowing Spanish rule in Cuba with the help of influential Americans such as Quitman, Lopez had narrowly escaped arrest on the island before arriving in Bristol, Rhode Island, in July 1848. There, he wasted little time organizing an American military expedition. Using New York City as his home base, Lopez was in the company of several East Coast slave-trade syndicates. While in New York he collaborated with numerous slave traffickers. He also consorted with several Cuban exiles who comprised the Cuban Council, an offshoot of the Havana Club, an organization that coordinated the international movement of slaves for profit. The non-English–speaking Lopez relied on bilingual Cubans to handle his English transactions and many of his financial concerns when he interacted with American filibusters and slave traffickers.[14]

Lopez and his loyal followers believed that they, along with the visionary Quitman and his supporters, were to become saviors of the foreign slave trade. Their three-tiered plan called for the disruption of Spain's control of Cuba, and in the process they hoped to "Africanize" the island through the international transshipment of slaves. The first phase required a preemptive assault and seizure of the island before emancipation could be implemented. The second step was to proclaim Cuba an independent republic and to ensure a constitutional continuance of the foreign slave trade. The final ploy was to annex Cuba into the United States as a slave state, exempting it from American antislave-trade laws. One of Quitman's plantation overseers announced the need to raise an army of filibusters to accomplish their goals. Felix Huston, a Louisiana planter, pledged to raise a contingency of three thousand persons for the Cuban expedition and to initiate a marketing campaign to sell bonds that would finance the operation.[15]

The *New Orleans Picayune* documented Quitman's campaign. Because of the "strictest secrecy" surrounding the expedition, the newspaper relied on government insiders for information. Sketchy details regarding this invasion plot often appeared in other local and regional newspapers. One such article referenced America's attempt to mitigate the conspiracy when it dispatched the sloop-of-war *Jamestown* to troll, "without delay," the waters of Cuba in search of Lopez and Quitman.[16]

Suspicion about Quitman's early involvement in the Cuban filibuster scheme had surfaced upon his return to Mississippi from a military stint during the United States-Mexican War of 1848. Quitman had served under General Winfield Scott in the Victoria, Texas, campaign. There, he observed the foreign slave trade in action. These slave transshipments posed little hindrance to Scott's military maneuvers or his troop's occupation of Victoria; they did, however, raise Quitman's curiosity about the possibilities of the trade. With his earnings from a local law firm and through the introduction of foreign slaves, Quitman developed four prosperous plantations, one located on the Mississippi River about nine miles from his home ("Monmouth") just outside Natchez; Palmyra, another Mississippi plantation (Warren County), in which he gained by marrying Eliza Turner in 1824; Live Oaks, in Terrebonne Parish, Louisiana, near the town of Houma, which he started developing in the mid-1830s; and Belen, on Bee Lake (near the Yazoo River) in Holmes County, Mississippi, which he did not develop into a plantation until the mid-1850s. Quitman often justified his participation in the foreign slave trade, and on one occasion suggested that the transferring of "the Negro" from the "cruel and despotic" environments of Africa into the United States was a virtuous and worthy endeavor.[17]

Quitman used his public popularity and political influence to secure the financial blessings of aristocrats to help finance his campaign. Some investors sank their life's savings into his invasion plots. Most, however, resorted to classic capitalist strategies: the issuance of stocks and bonds. Some issued two-thousand-dollar bonds, endorsed by Narciso Lopez, Ambrosio Gonzales, Jose Maria Sanchez Iznaga, and Cotesworth Pickney Smith, a Mississippi Supreme Court judge. The bonds promised a 6 percent return to each investor payable in five annual installments, and were backed by Cuba's public lands, fiscal resources, and the people and government of the island. Samuel R. Walker, a Louisiana sugar planter and friend of Quitman, articulated his belief that the annexation of Cuba would best enhance the movement of slaves between the United States and the emerging slave markets of the Western Hemisphere. Walker rounded up monetary and political support for Quitman from Americans across the country, and he personally arranged the room and board for filibuster recruits.[18]

Quitman's federal trial in which he faced charges of slave smuggling and filibustering exhibited the classic signs of a predictable outcome. The manner in which inquests concerned themselves with the question of the foreign slave trade reflected the basic nature of the American judicial system. Upon leaving his bond hearing at the United States District Court in New Orleans, Quitman was met at his hotel by a multitude of supporters who greeted him with chants and songs of encouragement. These admirers, as did most residents living in slaveholding regions, believed it their civic duty to protect advocates of the foreign slave trade and their adherents. To condemn Quitman was to condemn themselves and their interests. The support Quitman received from the New Orleans public contributed significantly to his acquittal.[19]

Establishing personal and business relations with persons of influence during the filibuster craze of the 1850s helped advance the foreign slave trade. Access to bona fide legal services and prominent lawyers, in particular, allowed slave smugglers and traffickers to avoid heavy-handed punishments. Many freebooters retained the services of William Pitt Ballinger. Born in Barbourville, Kentucky, Ballinger, upon completing his college education, relocated to Galveston, Texas, studied law, and enlisted as a soldier during the U. S.-Mexican War. While in Galveston, Ballinger teamed with Samuel May Williams at an 1856 public meeting, where he denounced the American antislavery campaign and censored others from publicly expressing their opposition to the foreign slave trade. "That your right," Ballinger and his comrade insisted, through "free opinion . . . is fully recognized . . . there is one subject, that of slavery—on which anyone entertaining your views" would be refused permission to speak in a public setting.[20]

Freebooters regularly retained the best legal minds to defend them in judicial proceedings. Through his experience as a United States district attorney in

Texas, Ballinger became intimately acquainted with many of these criminal subjects. Because of their patronage, Ballinger was able to build a successful law practice that litigated the trials of several smugglers. Among his most prestigious clients was Galveston merchant James Merrill, who was charged by the deputy collector of customs, James Cocke, with failing to pay the required duties on specific imported goods, and for smuggling slaves from Cuba into Galveston. Merrill denied all allegations and dismissed them as personal vendettas for nonpayment of a bribe promised to agent Cocke. Merrill's version of events was intended to further besmirch the already tarnished reputation of the United States Customs Agency, which by the 1850s had not fully recovered from its sullen image of previous years. Initially, Ballinger accepted Merrill's claim of a failed bribery scheme. His own investigation, however, revealed no evidence of a sinister plot on Cocke's part. Instead, he discovered that his own client had been less than truthful about his extended role in the smuggling of slaves. Merrill later admitted to his involvement and confessed that he had fabricated his story about Cocke. Because there was "good money to be made on the island selling Negroes," Merrill pleaded, the "$1,000 to $2,000" he earned justified his actions. Despite Merrill's cry of innocence, Collector Cocke confiscated several cases of rum, stashes of cigars, piles of silk fabrics and linens, and ten slaves from his ship. Cocke later sold all the slaves at a public auction—except for the ones he exported to Cuba.[21]

Despite Merrill's confession, Ballinger successfully negotiated a plea bargain. His ties with officials from the federal government paid dividends. An empathetic secretary of the treasury, Robert Walker, who had himself become an impressive Mississippi cotton, land, and slave speculator, who embraced the expansion of the foreign slave trade imposed a two-hundred-dollar fine, although he was well within his legal powers to have ordered Merrill's execution.[22]

Corruption within the foreign slave trade ultimately reached the inner circles of Ballinger's own law firm. It is unclear whether the clandestine participation of his two law partners in the enterprise affected the outcome of the Merrill case—although it did demonstrate that Merrill's escapades were part of a culture that included other prominent Galvestonians who profited from the demand for foreign slaves.[23]

The filibuster court cases of the 1850s defined the legal conditions under which traffickers and smugglers operated. The New Orleans trial of the steamship and ironworks magnate Charles Morgan, who had facilitated and organized transportation for several filibuster groups, garnered as much attention as any other legal proceedings of the day. Morgan, president of the Accessory Transit Company, which dominated intra-Gulf commercial trade, established close relationships with Cornelius K. Garrison, who ran a Pacific Coast operation that carried commercial passengers and filibusters between New York, New Orleans, San Francisco, and Nicaragua. When federal authorities conducted one of their rare raids in the winter of 1856, they deliberately took action against Morgan's shipping fleet. They suspected Morgan had played a key role in the smuggling of slaves and in the organization of filibuster plots. In January 1856, just a few months after United States district attorney John McKeon seized Morgan's *Northern Light,* they apprehended and arrested several suspected filibusters and their accomplices, and ordered Morgan to hand over several known criminals aboard his ship. McKeon issued twelve grand jury indictments to individuals linked to Morgan's transportation empire and filibuster plots, and threatened to seize Morgan's *Star of the West.*[24]

Morgan amassed a thriving inter-port shipping network that was closely linked to filibusters, slave traffickers, and smugglers. His business practices had become connected to William Walker, who had made plans to establish a nation beyond the borders of the United States. By 1856 Walker had established a base of operation at Mobile harbor where Morgan docked and leased several of his vessels. Their relationship did not go unnoticed. In 1856 the United States district attorney for the Eastern District of Louisiana was instructed to disrupt Morgan's operations in the region and to inspect and seize all of his vessels. United States attorney general Jeremiah S. Black ordered his special counsel in Mobile to determine why the filibuster vessel *Susan* had successfully departed from the city's port bound for Nicaragua and to locate government officials who were "in default" of their duties.[25]

The emergence of collaborative relationships between filibusters and slave traffickers complicated the efforts of federal authorities to curtail slave-smuggling schemes during the 1850s. When Secretary of State Daniel Webster warned the New Orleans collector of customs in 1851 that his federal agents would be "held to strict accountability" with regard to the foreign slave trade, his warning reflected one of the many hollow threats central authorities had made throughout the life span of the Abolition Act. Webster's high-sounding rhetoric failed to provide the necessary impetus needed to counteract the federal government's ineffective policing efforts and meager resources for combating the foreign slave trade. "The slave trade at present," officials of the United States Navy revealed, "seems to exist only in very limited sections of the [African] coast." The *True Delta,* however, then wrote of a steady flow of slaves from the Old Continent into the United States. It reported in October 1857 that the American slaver *Mazeppa* was captured en route to New Orleans with fifteen hundred slaves. Sylvia King endured one of these trans-Atlantic journeys during the late 1850s. "I didn't know it then," but "I found out afterwards," she recalled. "It was in New Orleans . . . I was put on a block and sold. I don't know who it was who stole me . . . but I know I was born in Africa . . . and was stolen from my husband . . . three children," and put in "the bottom of a boat."[26]

Pre-Owned Ships

The amalgamation and expansion of the filibustering and slave-smuggling enterprise during the 1850s expanded an old capitalist venture, one that allowed merchants to peddle used slave vessels for profit. Although such transactions were no anomaly, they became very common during the latter part of the decade. Because the New Orleans harbor served as the commercial gateway to the emerging economies of the frontier, traffickers and smugglers found it particularly convenient to purchase pre-owned ships there, rather than from ports along the Atlantic Coast or in the Caribbean. The sale and purchase of the *W. D. Miller* in March of 1856, for instance, reflected a growing trend in which slave ships outfitted at foreign ports ended up in New Orleans, where traffickers negotiated to purchase them at bargain prices. Joseph Villarubia Jr. enjoyed the benefits of owning a used sea-worthy slave vessel that he used to secure over four hundred slaves at Sierra Morena, Cuba. Villarubia's success in transporting foreign slaves using a pre-owned vessel encouraged other traffickers to emulate his actions. One such imitator was Benjamin Tisdale, who purchased the *Ardennes,* a slave ship that had consistently sailed under suspicious circumstances and whose crew was known to swap flags and sailors. In November 1856, the vessel conducted foreign slave voyages despite an ongoing criminal investigation that implicated its captain and crew in several slave-smuggling schemes.[27]

The use of pre-owned slave ships reflected how the foreign slave trade had meshed with the filibuster campaigns of the day. New Orleans was responsible for the dispersal of many of these ships. Between January and December 1857, smugglers and traffickers used several pre-owned ships purchased and sold at the Port of New Orleans. Relying on these old but dependable vessels, slavers set out from the United States for popular slave-trading outposts. Included in these voyages were eleven reputed slave ships. Each had already garnered attention from American officials for their role in the foreign slave trade. John Hinckley sailed on one of these voyages to Amo Bon, Guinea, where he searched for slaves. Ambriz, Angola, the historic cen-

TABLE 3
Slave Ships Purchased at New Orleans, 1856–1860

Ship	Date	Purchaser	Disposition
W. D. Miller—brig (175 tons)	3–13–56	Joseph Villarubia Jr.	Outfitted at Havana
Ardennes—bark (231 tons)	11–14–56	Benjamin F. Tisdale	Sold and outfitted at Havana
Mary Elizabeth—brig (150 tons)	12–23–56	James B. McConnell(M)	Outfitted at Havana
Adams Gray—brig (152 tons)	1–31–57	John Henry (M)	Cleared for Cárdenas 2–5–57; captured by HMS *Prometheus* 4–16–57
Jupiter—schooner (167 tons)	2–57	John Gilbert (M)	Cleared for Teneriffe 2–26–57; captured by H. M. S. Antelope 6–29–57 with 70 slaves
William Clark—brig (180 tons).	2–12–57	Francis Ranger (M)	Cleared for Teneriffe 2–26–57; captured by HMS *Firefly* 8–22–57
Splendid—bark (270 tons)	2–12–57	Joseph A. Barbosa	Cleared for Nuevitas 2–12–57; captured by Portuguese cruiser *Cabo Verde* 7–1 7–57 under the assumed name *Velha Anita*
Nancy—brig (219 tons)	2–23–57	Marcus N. Radovich (M)	Cleared for Ambriz 3–7–57; landed slaves in Cuba, late 1857
Wizard—brig (191 tons)	3–20–57	John J. Miller (M)	Cleared for Ambriz 3–26–57; reportedly escaped from Africa with slaves
Charles—ship (381 tons)	3–27–57	John S. Vent (M)	Cleared for Ambriz 3–28–57; driven ashore by HMS *Sappho* 9-18-57, 358 of the Africans aboard being rescued
Vesta—bark (259 tons)	4–26–57	William Smith (M)	Cleared for Ambriz 4–26–57; captured by Spanish cruiser *Isabel Segunda* 10–5–57 with 169 slaves
Lewis McLain—schooner (176 tons)	4–29–57	John H. Hinckley (M)	Cleared for Annobon 5–1–57; captured by HMS *Alecto* 10–15–57

TABLE 3 (continued)

Ship	Date	Purchaser	Disposition
Windward—brig (177 tons)	6–18–57	Charles Rauch (M)	Outfitted at Havana
Putnam—brig (188 tons)	11–7–57	Edward C. Townsend (M)	Captured by USS *Dolphin* 8–21–58 with 318 Africans
J. W. Reed—bark (350 tons)	5–5–58	Frederick B. Sladden (M)	Outfitted at Santiago
Toccoa—brig (227 tons)	11–2–58	Anthony Horta	Outfitted at Havana
William H. Stewart—brig (207 tons)	12–7–58	Salvador Prats	Sold into Chilean registry at Havana 9–59; captured by HMS *Archer* 1–30–60
Brownsville—brig (148 tons)	2–9–59	Salvador Prats	Cleared for Congo River 2–14–59; reportedly landed slaves in Cuba
Rebecca—ship (534 tons)	3–29–59	Salvador Prats	Cleared for Monrovia 4–27–59; reportedly landed slaves in Cuba
Stephen H. Townsend—schooner (182 tons)	4–15–59	Thomas A. Myers (M)	Cleared for St. Thomas 4–16–59; captured by HMS *Archer* 7–23–59
Mary J. Kimball—bark (398 tons)	5–24–59	Five owners	Outfitted at Havana
Triton—brig (208 tons)	8–22–59	John O. Dupeire from Onesime Buijson	Buijson remained as master; captured by USS *Mystic* 7–16–60 and condemned.
William R. Kibby—brig (191 tons)	11–1–59	Ignacio de Ayala	Sold and outfitted at New York
Peter Mowell—schooner (119 tons)	2–6–60	Salvador Prats	Cleared for Monrovia 2–9–60; believed to be a slaver
Nancy—brig (219 tons)	6–9–60	P. Oscar Aleix	Outfitted at Havana
Mexina—bark (208 tons)	11–2–60	Salvador Prats	Outfitted at Havana

NOTE: The letter "M" denotes an owner-master. There was some uncertainty as to whether or not the vessel destroyed by the *Sappho* was the *Charles* (see Napier to Cass, January 7, 1858, Senate Executive Document 49, 35–1, pp. 30–34).

SOURCES: *New Orleans Daily Picayune*, shipping columns; *Work Projects Administration, Ship Registers and Enrollment of New Orleans, Louisiana* (6 vols.; Baton Rouge: Louisiana State University Press, 1942), 5; House Executive Document 7, 36–2; Senate Executive Document 49, 35–1; House of Commons, Papers, 1861, LXIV, 360–61; 1865, LVI, 529; Warren S. Howard, *American Slavers and the Federal Law, 1837–1862*, 253–54.

ter for Brazilian slave traders, also became a favorite location for American slave smugglers who used their New Orleans pre-owned ships to procure slaves. In Ambriz, they packed slaves into the holds of these recycled ships. Marcus Radovich used the ship *Nancy,* which he had obtained at New Orleans in February 1857, to transport slaves from Ambriz. As Radovich made his trek along the African coast, several other traffickers were putting their New Orleans–purchased ships to use for the same purpose. John Miller, sailing the *Wizard,* for instance, fled Ambriz with a collection of slave captives, as did John Vent and William Smith.[28]

Whalers and Whale Ships

To offset impediments that threatened to block their access to emerging slave markets, slave smugglers and traffickers resorted to a variety of strategies to ensure contact. The use of expert whalers and renovated whale ships allowed many of them to achieve their goal. This ploy became most apparent when freebooters began purchasing large merchant vessels that could be disguised as whale ships. There were numerous reasons why whale ships were so useful to slave traffickers. One was size. Also, New and Old World slave harbors and supply stations had become efficient and sophisticated enough to pack the large hold of whaling vessels with slaves in relatively short periods of time. Additionally, most whale ships sported built-in stoves, which could be used to boil large quantities of rice to feed slaves. They also maintained large supplies of water for hydration and transported extra lumber for the construction of slave decks. Most whale ships came equipped with a full set of charts and maps. Moreover, whaling crews were hospitable comrades for slave traffickers. They became logical recruits for slaving firms in search of knowledgeable maritime workers.[29]

Shifts in the economic fortunes of the whaling industry lured some whalers into the foreign slave trade. Slave trafficking opportunities offered them a chance to pay for much-needed ship repairs and to replenish their dwindling assets. Following an arduous and unsuccessful two-year trip at sea in 1846, the whaling bark *Fame* ended up at Rio after it sprung several leaks. Its captain, Anthony Marks, who invested the necessary funds to repair the damages, decided to convert the whale ship into a slave vessel. This type of spontaneous transition from whaling to slaving was both simple and profitable. Although limited evidence exists that converted whale ships played a major role in the practice, the traffic routes of many slave ships placed them in proximity to those of whale ships. In May 1844 Captain John A. Webster of the United States revenue cutter *Forward* of Baltimore, Maryland, reported what he described as a whale boat speeding around Cape Henlopen, Delaware, carrying about fifteen slaves. Giving chase, Webster forced the vessel to shore, where all of its occupants fled on foot into a nearby forest. In another incident the American captain of the whale ship *Herald* changed course after setting sail for the Indian Ocean with his crew in December 1845. Following several days of bad weather and financial catastrophes, the captain decided to head for Rio de Janeiro. There, he consulted with slave traffickers about the economic advantages and benefits of dealing slaves rather than whales. He agreed to outfit his ship to conceal any slaves he intended to transport to market. On his way to Africa, the captain confided to a crew member that he had completed a deal with a Rio firm to sell one of his whale ships for $12,000 and that he had also agreed to conduct three slaving voyages for one of Brazil's largest slave-trafficking companies. The agreement allowed the captain to sail under the Brazilian banner and to change flags at his discretion.[30]

Economic hardships and lapses in pay, combined with their whaling experience, made African whalers willing participants in slave-smuggling schemes. Skilled seamen, aware of whaling's unsavory side, generally avoided employment on whale ships. Whaling merchants had no objection. More inexperienced hands responded better to orders and often worked for less money. Whaling captains seldom exercised full command of their vessels, but relied on racially and ethnically mixed crews to, among other things, juggle the flags and paperwork of these ships. Many of them recruited African whalers into the ubiquitous world of the foreign slave trade. Both enslaved and free Africans had been pushed by their masters and pulled by personal aggrandizement into the strenuous world of whaling. African whalers sought at sea what many of them were denied on land. Whale ship work offered opportunities for responsibility and promotion but kept sailors at sea for years. Some spent more time on water than they did on land. A considerable number of African whalers were transient, homeless, or unemployed, and the turnover among these workers remained quite high during the peak whaling years. Despite dismal pay, African whalers customarily earned wages that equaled those of whites. Pay, in most instances, was determined by job classification. Desperate for cash, free Africans in the northern states abandoned the civilian job market and their farms and opted for the more liberating and adventurous occupation of whaling, which, by the 1840s, accounted for a significant portion of their total earnings. In 1822, Absalom Boston gained notoriety for mastering an all-African crew aboard the whaling schooner *Industry*.[31]

The *Echo* and the *Wanderer*

Although whale ships were irrepressible in the continuation of the foreign slave trade, the capture of two particular slave ships demonstrated that their effective use was just as critical to the trade. The first episode involved the American seizure of the slave ship *Echo* off the coast of Cuba in 1858. The *Echo* had disembarked from New Orleans with a Portuguese and Spanish crew. It set sail for Cabenda on the Loango Coast of West Central Africa, where it loaded 470 Africans before setting out on its return trip to Cuba. Before the *Echo* was intercepted by the USS *Dolphin* and hauled into Charleston, South Carolina, one-third of its captives had perished. An additional thirty-eight died in captivity at the unfinished Fort Sumter complex in the state. The fate of the crew and the remaining slaves became the responsibility of a South Carolina grand jury and a federal circuit court in Charleston. Under the United States law of 1820, which declared slave smuggling a capital offense punishable by death, the prosecution in the *Echo* trial clamored for conviction and execution of the captain and crew. The grand jury, however, expressed an unwillingness to undermine slavery or the foreign slave trade. They conveyed concern about their economy and the role each played in its survival. Predictably, the captain and the crew of the *Echo* were acquitted in both state and federal courts. Despite the efforts of South Carolina senator Robert Barnwell Rhett to have the captives sold into slavery, President James Buchanan intervened and ordered them deported.[32]

As the *Echo* episode reached its conclusion, a new dilemma involving another slave ship had emerged. The slave vessel *Wanderer,* built at Long Island, New York, in 1857, had sailed to Charleston, South Carolina. There, William C. Corrie outfitted the ship for a group of loyal Georgia slave traders who set their sights on Africa. The *Wanderer*'s public reputation as an illegal slave ship prevented Corrie from concealing the intentions of the crew. Federal marshals in Savannah, Georgia, capitalized on this liability and seized the *Wanderer.* They launched an investigation into the affairs of the ship's captain and crew but were unsuccessful in their attempt to obtain a criminal conviction. Southern legal precedent held to form. A Charleston grand jury refused to indict Corrie for slave smuggling. The jurors recanted on a previous conviction, dismissed charges against all parties in the case, and protested for the return of the *Wanderer* to its owner. Motivated by the "grandeur" of the foreign slave trade and inspired by "the dollars," it was not until Corrie was cleared of all charges that he confessed his role in plotting a slave-smuggling scheme.[33]

The capture of the *Echo* and the *Wanderer* reverberated throughout the country. Slaveholders commented on the events and expressed concern about the effect of these two cases on their livelihood. Ben Stuart, an editor for the *Galveston News* and well known for his historical sketches of life on the frontier, highlighted the seizure of the two ships in an essay that focused on the global realities of the foreign slave trade. Stuart's reconstruction of these events provided detailed accounts of both. Advocates and detractors used Stuart's editorials to support their divergent positions on a growing sentiment to reopen the foreign slave trade.[34]

Southern Commercial Conventions and the Reopening Debate

By the 1850s, the foreign slave trade was a highly debated topic that emanated from an elite minority and yeoman majority. Sentiments and opinions regarding the legal reopening of the foreign slave trade were mixed. Many complained that filibusters and freebooters had effectively cornered the international market in slaves and that this had unfairly inflated prices. Some upstart plantation owners and domestic slave traders felt alienated from the marketplace due to financially endowed slave syndicates that determined the flow of foreign slaves. Others held that the ban of 1808 was directly responsible for over-priced slaves and that only the repeal of the abolition acts could restore marketplace integrity. A commonly held view was that the foreign slave trade was of far greater importance to certain regions of the country than it was to others. Southerners relied more on the internal replenishment of slaves to adequately supply them with the labor needed to sustain their economies. Fearful of competitive and emergent frontier economies, some southerners resisted legal efforts to restore the legal foreign slave trade, citing the usurpation of their standing and clout within the slave-trade market. Some predicted that the reproduction rate of the domestic slave population would more than satisfy the labor needs of the slave region well into the twentieth century. Therefore, the legal reopening of the foreign slave trade amounted to an "impossible" and needless "experiment."[35]

The foreign slave trade was an indispensable part of slave distributions in the United States. In 1854 the first attempts to legally reopen it came from two South Carolina grand juries that urged its supporters to defend the trade by "active aggression." These two judicial bodies, one from Richland, South Carolina, and the other from the Williamsburg district of the state submitted an expressed opinion that the practice "would confer a blessing on the African race" as well as one for Americans. In newspapers, magazines, letters, speeches, public meetings, election campaigns, state legislatures, and political conventions, advocates of the commerce argued in its defense. The African Labor Supply Association and the African Labor Immigration Company proposed to purge federal, state, and local laws that stigmatized the industry. The friends and supporters of the trade collated facts to demonstrate its necessity. One factor they relied upon in their arguments was the inflated price of slave labor in both the domestic and foreign markets. The increased demand and cost for slaves, combined with the expense of maintaining and rearing them, was to some slaveholders incontestable evidence that justified the reinstatement of the foreign slave trade. Its legal continuation would increase the labor supply and relieve buyers from exorbitant prices and owners from the painstaking financial upkeep of a limited number of slaves.[36]

The radicalizing of the Southern Commercial Convention in the late 1850s represented one of the most organized attempts to protect the foreign slave trade. Early meetings of the Southern Commercial Conventions initially sought to defend the South's economic orientation within the context of American unity. During the 1840s its members focused primarily on commercial issues affecting the construction of the Pacific railroad, the exportation of cotton, federal assistance to build levees along the Mississippi River, direct trade and steamship communication to remote markets, the use of slaves as factory workers, and the role of manufacturing in the South. Though their commercial interests in its early years of existence were linked to slavery, southern economic and political autonomy occupied a significant place at the annual conferences. George McDuffie of South Carolina called for direct trade between the South and Europe during the 1837 meeting held in Augusta, Georgia. He also insisted that the South, in reaction to the growing sectional tension with the North, establish a foreign commerce of its own. The Charleston Convention of 1839 recommended support for the *Southern Review*, a magazine dedicated to southern interests. The conventions at Baltimore in 1852 and Memphis in 1853 urged southerners to educate their children in southern schools with southern teachers and southern textbooks.[37]

By the last half of the 1850s, the convention experienced a radical transformation. The organization became noticeably less commercial and Unionist and more political and nationalistic. Its conventions of the 1850s displayed a sharp difference between the interests and purposes of the foreign slave trade than did its early conferences. The intensification of its regional agenda was evident. Its political pronouncements at public gatherings reflected a rekindled commitment to the enterprise. The editor of the *New Orleans Picayune* intimated that the Southern Commercial Convention had abandoned its original mission and degenerated into a radical political assembly that increasingly placed an emphasis on the foreign slave trade.[38]

The shifting ideological focus of the Southern Commercial Conventions was due primarily to the changing composition of its delegates. The early, commercially focused meetings were attended by politicians, editors, business people, merchants, bankers, manufacturers, and railroad and steamship promoters. These delegates were appointed by state governors, city councils, mayors, chambers of commerce, citizen groups, and agricultural associations. Unlike the earlier conventions, the gatherings of the late 1850s were dominated by southern politicians who craved votes, power, and the dissolution of the Union, rather than by business folk who would have reveled at the prospects of southern commercial and manufacturing development. "Extremist politicians," the editor of the *New Orleans Picayune* expressed in an 1859 article, had co-opted the convention and, in the process, maneuvered the proceedings toward discussions regarding the legitimization and expansion of the foreign slave trade. They had transformed the conventions into sanctuaries for those who defended the commerce.[39]

The debate over the proposed legalization of the foreign slave trade was forceful and confrontational. At the epicenter of the polemics were three firebrands from Louisiana. Henry St. Paul, Edward Delony, and James Brigham all engaged in daring and radical efforts to evade federal laws that regulated the foreign importation of slaves. The trio had devised numerous schemes to meet the frontier's demand for labor. The African Apprentice Bill of 1858 reflected their intention to supplement slave labor in Louisiana through "apprentices," which the *New Orleans Daily Delta* reported as "the boldest stoke of policy known in the annals of Southern legislation." It was designed to arrest the monopolization of slave labor in the country. Brigham was determined to preserve Louisiana's role in introducing foreign slaves into the United States. His house bill authorized the importation of twenty-five hundred "free" Africans to be employed as indentured workers for a fifteen-year period. Despite having the classical features of an indentured servant system, which spelled out a distinct contractual agreement between employer and worker, opponents of the apprentice bill, as the *Baton Rouge Advocate* pointed out, made it clear that under Brigham's plan Africans would be subjected to the domestic slave market and could be sold into "servitude for life at $500 per head." The Virginian and venerable supporter of the foreign slave trade, Edwin Ruffin, concluded that the apprentice bill amounted to a reauthorization of the foreign slave trade. His declaration raised the anxieties of the bill's opponents, who characterized the legislation as an obstruction to southern industrial development, an impediment to modernization and an indictment of American antislave-trade laws.[40]

While some debated the apprentice issue, others were engaged in their own acrimonious and contentious feud over the re-legalization of the foreign slave trade. The issue bitterly divided Texas citizenry. Various opinions on the topic emerged from a cross-section of its population. Two rather important and distinct institutions that championed the campaign to reopen the trade were the state's Methodist and Presbyterian churches. In the late 1850s, Presbyterian leaders made their views on the issue public knowledge. The church argued for and rationalized what it considered to be an opportunity to civilize Africans. Congregants of the Methodist Church shared similar views but suffered from a schism that divided its membership into opposing factions. The Methodist Episcopal Church in America, having begun its life in 1784 as an antislavery church, later found it expedient to compromise its standards. By 1800 the church had all but abandoned its efforts to eradicate slavery. In the "Pastoral Address" of 1836 it indicated that it had no "right, wish, or intention to interfere in the civil and political relation as it exists between master and slave in the slaveholding states." Their perspective allowed southern Methodists to live comfortably within the national church. But when antislavery agitation aroused northern Methodists in 1844, they demanded that the strict interpretation and enforcement of the long-standing but dormant rules and guidelines regarding slavery, including the tradition against slaveholding bishops be upheld. Adherents of slavery and the slave trade reacted by withdrawing from the church and organizing one that would serve their specific needs. For instance, the Methodist Episcopal Church South, which was centered in the Houston-Galveston area, supported the foreign slave trade. Their stand clashed with the Methodist Episcopal Church North, of Dallas-Fort Worth, which struggled to eradicate it. In their resolve to reopen the foreign slave trade, members of the Methodist Church South delivered an ultimatum giving "all persons connected with the Church North 60 days to leave the state." They followed up their directive by hanging Anthony Brewley, a Fort Worth abolitionist Methodist minister.[41]

Those who supported the revocation of any and all antislave-trade laws competed against their detractors for public support. In February 1859 Willard Richardson, editor of the *Galveston News,* warned that "the public mind of the country was not prepared for a measure" that would legally reopen the foreign slave trade. Others felt obliged to follow this point and emphasized their opposition to the idea as well. Hardin Runnels, one of Richardson's contemporaries, recognized the political risks associated with the reopening issue.

During his 1859 Texas gubernatorial campaign, Runnels attempted to defuse the intense reopening debate that threatened to alienate Texas voters one way or the other. Standing in opposition to Runnels were Sam Houston and his supporters. Houston and his followers successfully exploited the controversy and skillfully linked Runnels to southern and frontier schemes to circumvent state and federal laws that prohibited the trade. Houston and his organizers orchestrated a successful strategy that united an array of groups against anti-Union politics and the reopening of the foreign slave trade. Included in Houston's coalition were the Know-Nothings (a conservative anti-immigrant political organization), unionists, National Democrats, non-slaveholders, and Protestant immigrants. Houston's one-sided gubernatorial victory over Runnels marked the beginning of several months of political wrangling over the future of slavery and the foreign introduction of slaves.[42]

Although the proposal to reopen the foreign slave trade was a widely discussed topic, it was not a major part of the political platform of any national party or a primary issue in most state-level political campaigns during the late 1850s. Sam Houston's victory demonstrated that those willing to support the issue through public policy were far fewer in number than those who refused to back it. "It was generally supposed throughout the South," Eli Shorter of South Carolina asserted, "that Texas desired the reopening of the trade, but the recent elections of Sam Houston for Governor over Runnels settles that question."[43]

Filibuster episodes, the prosecution of slave smugglers and traffickers, and the reopening debate legitimized the political and economic significance of the foreign slave trade. Many viewed the enterprise within the context of certain regional, class, and political issues rather than on purely ideological grounds. By the late 1850s the trade affected economies from New York to California in one form or another. Although support for it weakened by the early 1860s, the life of the commerce was sustained by a group of determined investors who, despite increased efforts by the federal government to facilitate its complete demise, struggled to maintain its existence.

6

"No Argument Could Be Made"

THE POLITICS OF SUPPRESSION

From his prison cell in New Orleans a convicted slave smuggler, prior to being pardoned for his offense, boasted that New York City had the reputation among slave smugglers and traffickers of being a "chief port" for the foreign slave trade, and that foreign consuls and federal agents were well served to begin directing their attention there as well as the Western Gulf South. "Neither in Cuba or in Brazil," he also asserted, "is it carried on so extensively." He later bragged that New York City had, in fact, become the primary "headquarters" for the trade. By the 1850s it had indeed become an important center in the organizational structure of the trade. British consul Henry G. Kuper of Baltimore gave assurances that Americans, especially in New York and some southern states, were extensively involved in the foreign slave trade with assistance from Spanish authorities in Cuba, where many of the cargoes were originally loaded. Consul Edward W. Mark wrote from Baltimore that on any given day one could observe slave ships being prepared for the trade, and that the practice in "New York and the eastern parts of the Union" had fallen into the hands of firms who collaborated with American slave smugglers to carry out their mission. Ports along the East Coast had played an important role in the foreign slave trade since the Revolutionary period, and most smugglers and traffickers recognized their value. A unique grouping of these slavers were located in New York City's central business district where they exerted noticeable influence over the trade. Using American capital and the investments of joint stock companies to fund their enterprise, the "Spanish Company" and the "Portuguese Company"—two renowned slaving firms comprised primarily of Brazilian immigrants— merged into a single pseudo-corporation. The group functioned under the name "Portuguese Company," a generic term that New Yorkers used to describe both firms after the consolidation. Jose da Costa Lima Viana and Manoel Basilio da Cuhna Reis began their careers with the Portuguese Company as clerks. John A. Machado, a naturalized Azorean, had vacated Rio de Janeiro and joined up after England intensified its attempts to disrupt the foreign slave trade in Brazil. Although the Portuguese Company was not a company in the formal sense, it operated one of the more successful slave-smuggling businesses in the United States by the 1850s. The Portuguese Company professionalized the art of selling slaves imported from abroad with American capital.[1]

During the late 1850s, numerous reports surfaced alleging that foreign slaves were being introduced into New York and other parts of the United States. In April 1859 the citizens of Matagorda, Texas, passed a resolution affirming their intent to obtain slaves "from some foreign country" and recommended that their efforts be conducted under the supervision and protection of the state. The *Richmond* (Texas) *Reporter* also published advertisements seeking newly imported African slaves. In June 1859 the newspaper alerted residents to an upcoming sale that involved four hundred Africans "lately landed upon the coast of Texas." In 1860, the British consul at Galveston wrote of a plot to land foreign slaves onto the Texas coast and also broadcasted to his government that a Louisiana planter had revealed to him that he [the planter] was on a trip to Indianola, Texas, "to buy Africans."[2]

The sectional crisis between the North and the South made it difficult at times to detect the extent of the foreign slave trade. Once secession was declared and the Confederacy was established, jurisdiction over the trade became an uncertain issue. Although documented evidence of the practice decreased in the South during secession and the Civil War, except for the reports of the British Foreign Office, evidence of it in the North was visible and proof of its existence was recorded in court dockets, slave ship sales, ship seizures, and newspaper coverage. Evidence of the trade demonstrated that it had survived suppression and continued to function. It became a noticeable distraction in New York where it attracted the type of attention that one would expect in a leading commercial center. Studying the foreign slave trade through the framework of the political responses of government authorities during secession and the Civil War offers insight and perspective on the attempts made to maintain it and to the efforts designed to bring about its demise.

Some of the most profound reactions to the foreign slave trade during the 1850s and early 1860s came from influential political figures. Presidential politics figured prominently in the campaign to interdict the movement of slaves from foreign ports and into the United States. As the force of the trade resurfaced in the American North, two presidential administrations reenergized the call for more effective suppression. Each declared that the political cost of an ambivalent suppression policy gave impetus to the trade and emboldened its adherents. The full force of suppression came into play after abolitionists gained control of the federal government through the Republican Party. The execution of a single slave smuggler, combined with other political and military maneuvers, wrote the final chapter in the history of the foreign slave trade in the United States.

The *Clotilde*

The difficulties associated with purchasing affordable domestic slaves compelled slaveholders to seek alternative solutions. Left with few choices, small southern planters and farmers turned to the foreign slave trade. The *Vicksburg Sun* printed a brief advertisement in April 1859 indicating that "any person by visiting the slave depot on Mulberry Street in this city can get a sight at some of the latest importations of Congo Negroes." Eighteen slaveholders from Enterprise, Mississippi, pledged to purchase up to one thousand slaves, with the stipulation that they be brought directly from Africa. Several "Negroes who never learned to talk English" and were hidden in the "piney woods" of Mississippi, the *Mobile Mercury* reported, may have been part of this planned transshipment.[3]

One ship that raised suspicion about its participation in the continuing foreign slave trade during the late 1850s was the *Clotilde*. Public interest in the *Clotilde* during the fall of 1859 reflected the extent to which the introduction of foreign slaves had become a key issue in many parts of the country. The *Clotilde* was the personal ship of Bill Foster. He purchased the vessel for $35,000 and instructed Captain Timothy Meaher, a successful steamboat operator, to overhaul the ship and outfit it for the African slave trade. Meaher had earned a reputation for being one of the more seasoned and successful ship captains in the region. His maritime experience brought him into close contact with a range of personalities, including groups and individuals who often expressed their opinions about the African slave trade. It was through these conversations that Meaher and Foster were able to gauge public sentiment regarding the practice. This allowed the pair to plan a course of action for introducing slaves into the country. Meaher's confidence in the foreign slave trade was demonstrated by his willingness to wager a $100,000 bet with one Alabama visitor. Meaher was unconcerned about finding suitable slaves across the Atlantic. Southern newspapers kept him informed on political and social conditions throughout the African West Coast with up-to-date reports and editorials. "The quarreling of the tribes on Sierra Leone River," as reported by the *Mobile Press Register,* convinced Meaher that the region offered good opportunities for successful captures and purchases. There, his seamen rounded up over one hundred slaves, whom they transported to the Mobile port.[4]

The *Clotilde* was believed by many to be the "last slave ship from Africa" to arrive in the United States. This of course raises important questions and some level of doubt, since several alleged instances of foreign slave importations were observed during the late 1850s and early 1860s. One such example involved a shipment of camels to Indianola, Texas. The cargo turned out to be a consignment of slaves. Records indicating the presence of a sustained foreign slave trade during secession and the Civil War from the Confederate side was more problematic than that of evidence from the Union side. From the Union perspective, documentation exists that suggests northern states grappled with the trade well into the war years.[5]

James Buchanan

Evidence of a foreign slave trade caught the attention of the James Buchanan administration during the late 1850s. Described by many as "indecisive" and "weak," Buchanan, who was elected president in 1856 and held the office until the election of Abraham Lincoln, had expressed regret that slavery existed and he viewed the institution as wrong and immoral. He demonstrated, however, few outward signs of indignation against it or sympathy for its slave victims. His profound political and emotional attachment to slavery and the South calls into question the sincerity of his attempts to suppress the foreign slave trade. On more than one occasion Buchanan undermined attempts to limit the expansion of the institution and defended the right of slavery to exist. Buchanan allowed for postmasters to monitor and censor the language of abolitionist antislavery literature and mailings. As a Jacksonian,

Buchanan supported the annexation of Texas as a slave state. During the 1856 presidential campaign he had run as the candidate who could defeat the Republicans, whom he later blamed for the Civil War.[6]

Despite his attitude toward the antislave-trade campaign, some credited Buchanan with initiating a formidable response to the foreign slave trade. Antislave-trade legislation promulgated during his presidential years helped fuel the abolitionist movement and marked a significant turning point in the history of the foreign movement of slaves. By spring 1859 Buchanan's administration had succeeded in bringing about several changes in the antislave-trade cause. The first was to transfer responsibility for suppressing the foreign slave trade from the Department of the Treasury to the Department of the Interior. The intention was to shift the concentration of authority and the execution of the laws regarding the practice away from the military and the Department of the Treasury, which were burdened with tactical issues at sea and laden with financial and revenue concerns respectively, to the Interior, which played a more comprehensive role in affairs involving American commerce and trade. The second was to aggressively enforce the Act of 1820, which broadly defined slave trafficking and smuggling and made participation in the foreign slave trade a capital offense.

Buchanan supported increasing funding to combat slave smuggling. Of the $75,000 approved by Congress in March 1859, $45,000 was used to subsidize and maintain the American naval fleet off the coast of Africa. Prior to 1859 the number of government vessels deployed by the Department of the Navy to suppress the foreign slave trade never surpassed six, and even fewer were sent to the Caribbean and the Gulf of Mexico. In the period between June 1857 and May 1859 the African squadron consisted of only three vessels: the *Cumberland,* the *Dale,* and the *St. Louis.* Five steamers purchased to intercept filibustering expeditions into Central and South America were later ordered to join up with the United States' African coast fleet. By November 1859 eight American navy ships roamed the African coast, and five cruised the waters of the Caribbean. Monies were also used to provide sustenance for illegally captured Africans held in American custody. A good portion of these funds were allocated to the American Colonization Society, which had entered into a secret agreement with the Buchanan team to oversee the care, shelter, provisioning, and resettlement of Africans imported illegally.[7]

Buchanan followers viewed these new changes as progressive steps toward the elimination of the foreign slave trade. Those who lauded this progress pointed to government records to support their case. The data showed that prior to the Buchanan presidency the number of vessels seized by American squadrons for violating antislave-trade laws were few in number. By the beginning of 1857 government documents, mainly naval and congressional, indicated an increase in activities to interdict them. By 1860, United States naval squadrons had made a total of eighteen arrests, of which twelve were prosecuted.[8]

The underlying motivations behind Buchanan's policy shift can be traced to the rising strength and visibility of the Republican Party. The new party posed a grave threat to the future of the Democratic Party. It was during the political and social turmoil of the mid-1850s that the Republican Party took shape. It emerged out of a response to the hostile conditions that flared over the Kansas-Nebraska crisis. Democrats had given Kansas and Nebraska immigrants the right "to form and regulate their domestic institutions in their own way." Consequently, the principle of popular sovereignty opened the way for slavery to flourish in a part of the public domain where it had previously been restricted. It was this dynamic that spurred opponents of the Democratic Party to form a national organization and to convene a meeting at Pittsburgh in February 1856. The gathering was intended to prepare its constituents for future presidential elections. This new coalition was comprised of fragments from the northern Whigs, whose national identity had taken a political beating from the Democrats. It also consisted of angry "anti-Nebraska" Democrats who rejected the repeal of the Missouri Compromise; Free-Soil partisans who demanded federal legislation to exclude slavery from the territories; abolitionists from the Liberty Party; and a sizable number of northern anti-Catholic nativists.[9]

Slavery and the foreign slave trade were among the greatest concerns for Republicans. To most of their followers the *Dred Scott* decision was the culmination of a series of sinister events that had emboldened the Slave Power regime. The *Scott* case reinforced the property rights of slaveholders, denied the humanity of slaves, and declared that a slave was the property of his or her master. Although the court's ruling applied primarily to legal domestic slavery, slave traffickers had reason to celebrate after United States attorney general Caleb Cushing publicly praised the Supreme Court and Chief Justice Roger B. Taney's majority opinion. "The very incarnation of judicial purity, integrity, science and wisdom," is how Caleb described the actions of Taney and his consenting colleagues. The *Scott* decision was rendered soon after Buchanan's inauguration. It spoke to the collaborative relationship between the president and Chief Justice Taney which, some charged, was evidence that the Supreme Court had joined the administration in a conspiracy to re-empower the power of slaveholders and to yield to their every demand.[10]

New York

The *Scott* decision occurred at a time when many Republicans realized that the formalization of a well-integrated foreign slave trade within New York would have profound effects on and implications for the nation's economy and politics. For one, it served notice that the foreign slave trade had emerged as a formidable threat to the ideals of modernity and to the prospects of a free labor society in a state with a longstanding history of antislave trade activity. As early as 1788, New York had enacted a law making it clear that "if any person shall sell as a slave within this state any Negro or other person who has been imported or brought into this state, after the 1st June, 1785, he shall be deemed guilty of a public offence and forfeit 100 pounds and the person so imported or brought into this state, shall be free." Nonetheless, several legal disputes regarding the foreign slave trade surfaced within the state in the years following passage of this statute, exposing the presence of an illegal trade. One incident occurred in June 1839 when Her Majesty's brig *Buzzard,* commanded by Lieutenant Charles Fitzgerald, escorted two American slave ships into New York. The crew of the brig *Eagle* and the schooner *Clara* were handed over to a United States marshal. The *Clara* had once been condemned in the district court of the United States in Louisiana, where the defendants asserted that they had operated the ship at the request of its owners and were not liable for the financial penalty set by the court. The defendants refused to pay and the plaintiff (collector of the port at New Orleans) never secured the reward.[11]

New York became Britain's preferred point of destination following its captures of suspected American slave ships. The drama of British ships seen escorting slave ships into American harbors provided the publicity England had always sought to promote suppression. It was a measure of embarrassment for American authorities who had failed to effectively interdict the trade over time. More drama played out when the schooners *Wyoming, Butterfly,* and *Catharine* were also seized and brought into New York harbor by the British navy. The *Catharine* was an American-registered vessel, built and owned in Baltimore but later sold to an American citizen named Tyng, a shipbroker. The ship's captain evaded British detection long enough to hoist an American flag. He confused his interrogators when he conveniently replaced the paperwork for his American crewmen with documents that gave them Spanish and Portuguese status. Nevertheless, handcuffs, ropes, shackles, and other material and items generally associated with transatlantic slave voyages found on the ship tainted the crew's alibi of being a vessel engaged in legitimate enterprise. Ship documents exposed the sailing pattern of the *Butterfly,* which had sailed from Havana to the West Indian islands and finally to Africa.

A dual set of documents provided details about the ship's cargo, crew list, and passenger history. Its slave decks were most compelling and supplied British officials with the circumstantial evidence needed to justify seizure. These ship captures demonstrated that England had detected a trend in slave movements between Africa and New York. Some of these vessels and crews were taken to Sierra Leone to stand trial before the Anglo-Spanish mixed commission. Because many of the ships sailed under an American banner but presented both American and Spanish documents, the commission was left confused about its own jurisdiction and authority. With the mixed commission refusing to act, and because there was a scarcity of American warships available for interdiction, British officers had little choice but to escort suspected slave ships to the United States and to present them for trial.[12]

British suppression conflicted with the goals and objectives of New York slave smugglers and traffickers. Periodic ship seizures, however, failed to discourage their participation in the trade. When the ship *Kate* arrived at New York harbor in May 1860 from Havana, it was part of a pattern in which captured slave ship crews were presented before federal judges and subjected to mild prosecutions. Ownership of the *Kate* had changed hands on several occasions; its captain at the time of confiscation had been granted clearance to sail to the slave coast of Africa by New York customs agent Smith, who had a history of dispensing such documents to ships engaged in the foreign slave trade. The bark was "found fitted out with arrangements designed" for the practice, and all its cargo was either adapted or capable of being adapted for the same. The crew, which included one slave smuggler named DaCosta who "had, some four years before, been indicted for slave trading," appeared to have made an unhindered departure but was quickly detained a few miles out at sea and escorted back to harbor and charged in court. A small fine was paid, and shortly thereafter a new clearance was granted by the same customs agent. After a second seizure, articles relevant to the slave trade and not reported to customs were found aboard the vessel. Iron pots, furnaces, stockpiles of rice, and a crew list that included a first mate who had sailed to Africa several times to secure slaves were inventoried. The *Kate* commonly carried sets of manacles, dismantled slave decks, and extraordinary quantities of provisions, medicine, and equipment used especially in the foreign slave trade. The *Kate* would often appear at port as a lawful trading ship, before being converted to a slave vessel.[13]

The acts of omission and commission by customs officials at New York gave permission to the activities of freebooters. One individual, who had been in the customs house at New York for seven years, testified that he had noticed vessels being designed for the foreign slave trade. Many were sold two or three times before going into service. The ship *Sarah* contained the usual items found on vessels normally condemned as slavers, and was prepared to set sail from New York to Africa where the captain and his crew were to go "black-binding." The bark, however, was seized by a United States marshal. His investigation uncovered a plot involving several persons who had gathered to prepare the ship for a slave venture.[14]

Customs agents at the New York port also allowed the *Weathergage* to sail for Ambriz, Angola, under the pretense of being a legitimate merchant vessel bound for Hong Kong. Federal court judges were not persuaded by the story. The presence of slave-trading equipment and a plan to also sail the ship to Ambriz raised enough suspicion to have the vessel impounded.[15]

American judicial limits regarding the foreign slave trade were evident in New York. During the trials of the *Eagle* and the *Clara,* United States district attorney Benjamin F. Butler floundered through the cases. Questions regarding American jurisdiction over ships that presented Spanish documents complicated trial proceedings. Butler dismissed all charges against the two vessels and ordered the ships escorted to the British vice-admiralty courts. There, the judge refused to prosecute non-British vessels arrested in non-British waters. The mixed court at Sierra Leone provided no clear solution to the issue either. It had adopted a new policy that discouraged the prosecution of American vessels unless clear, reliable, and uncompromised evidence was presented.[16]

The New York–based link to the foreign slave trade aroused the attention of several national figures during the late 1850s and early 1860s. While laying the groundwork for his political future, Stephen A. Douglass, the Illinois senator who represented a new generation of politicians emerging from frontier states, demonstrated the growing anxiety over the foreign slave trade when he made an unsubstantiated claim that in excess of fifteen thousand African slaves had been illegally imported into the country in 1859. Contributing to this uncorroborated activity were eighty-five slave ships that were outfitted at New York harbor and twelve additional slave vessels loaded with three thousand or more slaves.[17]

The presence of New York–based slave-trafficking firms, the sight of work crews outfitting slave ships in nearby harbors, and the capture of slave vessels along the East Coast bound for Africa, the Caribbean, and the Gulf of Mexico also supported Douglas's claim. The British consul at New York estimated that "of the 170 slave-trading expeditions fitted out in little more than three years preceding 1862, no fewer than 74 were known or believed to have sailed from New York, 43 from other American ports, 40 from ports in Cuba," and the rest from European ports. During this period, the *New York Journal of Commerce* observed that few of its readers were "aware of the extent to which this traffic is carried on in close alliance with" the "legitimate trade; and that down-town merchants of wealth and respectability are extensively engaged in buying and selling African Negroes, and have been for an indefinite number of years." In May 1858 a *New York Herald* correspondent stated that a number of slaves were being smuggled into the interior of the country from Africa. In August 1860 the same newspaper reported that by the late 1840s and early 1850s, slave traffickers had infiltrated New York City's business establishment and had routinely coordinated illegal slave transactions. The *Herald* noted that the profits from these sales were used to finance the political campaigns of New York and New Jersey politicians who supported the agendas of slave traffickers. At no other moment, the *New York Times* concluded, had "the traffic been as actively and successfully prosecuted as at present." Most of this activity, it emphasized, involved the illegal slave transactions of New York–based slavers. Under the pretense of the legal slave trade, they often gained clearance from New York's Custom House, "bringing all the appliances of the [slave] trade with them." They maneuvered along "the whole slave coast of Africa" in search of slaves they could snare for profit. The *New York Evening Post* published its own list of "eighty-five vessels fitted out in New York, from February 1859, to July 1860" for the foreign slave trade.[18]

The *New York Evening Post* gave its readership a perspective on the foreign slave trade debate that its rival newspapers failed to provide. William Cullen Bryant had been its editor for several years and had become a public figure whose prestige and influence surpassed most of his contemporaries. Bryant had acquired extensive first-hand knowledge of the slave trade through slow, arduous travel. In addition to his journey through the South, Bryant printed articles and commentaries regarding abolitionism and the consequences of Texas annexation. He also sailed to Cuba, where he witnessed the island's economic activities. Although it generally supported the right of abolitionists to speak out against slavery, the *Evening Post* did not cover antislavery activities in the North or the resurgence of the foreign slave trade in New York in great detail. On a few occasions the newspaper did acknowledge antislavery in the North. One instance followed the passage of the Fugitive Slave Law. Another example was the publication of *Uncle Tom's Cabin,* which it defended against attacks from rival publications.[19]

The *Evening Post* displayed equal ambivalence toward the clandestine work of the New York–based Portuguese Company. By the late 1850s the

Portuguese Company had active members in Spain, Portugal, and the United States. The New York offices of the company were spread between Manhattan and Brooklyn. With obscurity and secrecy as their hallmark, they set up dummy businesses as fronts for their illegal slaving activities. The recruits they seduced and trained included ship fitters, deputy marshals, district attorneys, customs agents, and just about anyone they could swear into a life of loyalty.[20]

The relationship between New York city dwellers and the Portuguese Company offers a limited explanation for the comfort that New York's circle of slave traffickers enjoyed. The preferential treatment they received from customs agents, federal judges, and local juries explains why some perceived the city as the northern capital for the foreign slave trade. Slavery flourished in New York during the eighteenth century, a time when the city consistently recorded a higher proportion of African residents than any other colony north of Delaware. Although slavery was legally abolished in the state with a general emancipation in 1827, city merchants and slave smugglers continued to finance the burgeoning southern and Western Gulf South economies.[21]

New York businesspeople and slave dealers were not the only supporters of the foreign slave trade. On the eve of the 1860 presidential election, the *New York Times* identified a prominent local white minister and politician as a staunch advocate of the practice. Most had perceived Brooklyn native Moses F. Odell as a God-fearing man entirely devoted to his Christian faith. But it was rarely mentioned that this Democratic candidate for Congress from the Second District of New York City had used his political clout, community connections, and position as naval officer for the Port of New York to help facilitate and perpetuate international slave transshipments. Odell was a cog in a wheel of well organized groups who persistently agitated for the disestablishment of governmental controls and restrictions on the international distribution of slaves.[22]

New York's free African community did its part to help place pressure on folks such as Odell. After Reverend Peter Williams's death in 1840, African civic leaders used financial, social, and political resources to counteract the resurgent foreign slave trade and were not restrained in their efforts to obtain fair and just treatment. During the mid-1840s the New York Vigilance Committee was committed to advancing racial equality. Benevolent organizations, literary societies, institutional mechanisms such as black newspapers (mainly *Freedom's Journal, Rights of All,* and the *Colored American*), mutual aid societies, political parties, campaigns, conventions, and churches united militantly around the cause of resistance. At the center of much of this agitation was William Powell. As a New York delegate to the American Reform Board of Disfranchised Commissioners, Powell and others sought to secure immediate suffrage for African residents as early as 1840. In 1850 Powell, founder and keeper of the city's Colored Sailor's Home, which assisted destitute and homeless sailors, expressed his sentiments regarding local race relations in a letter to the editor of the *National Anti-Slavery Standard*. Referring to an occasion when Frederick Douglass, the famous black abolitionist, was assaulted while walking in the company of two white women, Powell noted that he, like Douglass, would have stood his ground in the face of this mob action. Powell also led a mass meeting of freemen in New York who had gathered to angrily protest passage of the Fugitive Slave Law. Speaking before a jammed-packed Zion Church in October 1850, Powell stated, without contradiction, that attempts to disrupt the lives of African citizens in New York City would be met with physical and armed resistance. This type of open activism often resulted in sporadic acts of violence against Powell from irate white citizens. Powell's own Globe Hotel was targeted by some of these agitators. They lurked around the hotel premises hoping to nab free Africans that they could sell on the slave market. Powell had, however, outwitted most of them. He devised a secret escape route, which began at his hotel and ended with a boat ride to Bedford, Massachusetts.[23]

New York's antislavery campaign reached fever pitch in the late 1850s. The formation of the Abolition Society of New York City and Vicinity openly declared that the foreign slave trade and all its components were contrary to the core principles of the United States Constitution. Its defiance was driven partly by the presence of numerous slave ships or "blackbirders," as they were so often called, in New York harbor between 1857 and 1860. As in the New Orleans pre-owned ship business, slave traffickers in New York had capitalized on this emerging commerce. From 1857 to 1860 at least twenty-nine of these used vessels were outfitted, bought, sold, and captured for their participation in the foreign slave trade. In 1857 thirteen of them changed ownership at least twice. A portion was sold in New York but outfitted in Cuba. In February 1857 Jose A. Mora bought a 308-ton slave ship that was overhauled in Havana. Nicholas Danese's *Clara B. Williams,* John Weeks's *Braman,* William Thompson's *Lyra,* George Brown's *C. Perkins,* Adam Smalley's *Cortez,* and William Scranton's *Tavernier* were all reconfigured in Cuba.[24]

New York–purchased slave ships were also modified in other parts of the Caribbean. Pierre L. Pearce had the *Wildfire* altered on the island of St. Thomas in the Danish West Indies. The ship was later captured at sea by the USS *Mohawk* with 530 slaves. Seafaring vessels were likewise converted into useful slave ships at European cities. The ship *Haidee,* for instance, which Emilio Sanchez y Dolz purchased at New York in January 1858 and used to transport 903 slaves to Cardenas, Cuba, was outfitted for the slave trade in Cardi, Spain. Ships restructured for the slave trade also appeared in Charleston, South Carolina, and in New Orleans. The slave schooner *Wanderer,* purchased by William C. Corrie, was overhauled in Charleston in 1857 and later set out for Africa to collect slaves. After deceiving British naval squadrons, its crew loaded nearly 500 Africans and transported them to Brunswick, Georgia, for the slave market. New York buyer Oneseme Buijson purchased the 208-ton *Triton,* which had been reconfigured in New Orleans. Although Buijson remained as the ship's master, he sold the vessel two months later to John Dupeire. A year after that, the vessel was seized by the USS *Mystic* and later condemned for participating in the foreign slave trade.[25]

The renovation of New York–purchased vessels meant traffickers could make effective use of space and load their ships to capacity. Concealment of their cargoes often enabled them to avoid detection. The slave ship *Charlotte,* which Guilheme F. de la Figaniere purchased in New York and later sold along the Congo River, served the new buyer well as it allowed him and his crew to escape from Africa with 500 slaves. Samuel Curry utilized the space aboard the *Harris* to squeeze 500 Africans into its quarters for their journey into slavery. Thomas Morgan gained ownership of the *Orion* and found a way to situate 888 slaves on it. Lima Viana acquired legal access to the *William G. Lewis* in December 1859 and almost immediately sold the vessel to Francis Rivery. He then set sail for the Congo River. There, he loaded 300 Africans onto the ship. Charles Smith also sailed along the Congo River aboard the *William Kibby,* which he purchased in New York from Jonathan Dobson, he did not enjoy the same success as Rivery. Smith was only able to secure 3 slaves, whom he transported to Cuba. In November 1857 Edward C. Townsend was able to cram 318 slaves onto the *Putnam;* in August 1858 his vessel was captured by the USS *Dolphin.* Townsend was among several traffickers to have their New York–purchased vessels impounded and their cargoes confiscated. John P. Weeks purchased the *Ellen* in April 1857, and Thomas Carlin obtained the *Merchant* in the same month of the same year. Federal officers seized both ships. Frances M. Chase's plans to transport 385 slaves aboard the ship *Paez,* which he had purchased in New York, were interrupted in March 1857 when that vessel was also seized.[26]

New York slave ships were often passed from one owner to the next even after being seized by federal authorities. When John Weeks's legal ordeal involving the *Ellen* ended in his favor, the way was cleared for him to sell the slave ship. Weeks was among a select number of slave traffickers who commonly made multiple purchases of used slave ships. In 1857 Weeks had negotiated the purchase of three pre-owned vessels. By February 1858 Joseph Santos was in possession of the *Ellen,* and four months later Augiolo Dello Astrologo had claimed ownership. Astrologo used the ship to transport slaves.[27]

Pre-owned and resold New York slave ships were often disguised as whalers to elude federal agents. These bogus whale ships played a significant role in the foreign slave trade. Robert McCormick registered his New York–purchased ship *Atlantic* as a whale ship, but used the vessel to land several slaves in Cuba in December 1860. Similarly, Mary Jane Watson camouflaged the *Thomas Watson* as a whale ship and also used it to transport slaves to Cuba. William Sharpe, John Wilson, and John Pringle pooled their financial resources to purchase the *Montauk,* which cleared New York in April 1860 as a whale ship. At the time of its capture in December 1860, the *Montauk* was sailing under the assumed name *Lesbia* and surrendered 916 slaves. It was the opinion of the United States federal court in New York that the *Augusta,* which had been fitted out at Long Island, was also intended for the foreign slave trade. The court rejected the captain's claim that the ship was nothing more than a whaling ship. Because the renovation of the ship occurred at a port where whaling had been abandoned; the ship was much larger than typical whaling vessels; the provisions on board exceeded what was necessary for average whaling voyages; and the crew members were not experienced whalers, the court concluded that the ship had been prepared for the foreign slave trade.[28]

By the early 1860s, the link between slave traffickers, New York slave ship sales, and the foreign slave trade was pronounced and visible. As ship purchases abounded, slave traffickers traversed the waters to promote their practice.[29] A familiar feature of this process was the frequency of criminal prosecutions against New York freebooters. One pressing dilemma for the courts was the predisposition of New York–based slave traffickers to skip bail once they were released from detention. Freebooters often faded into obscurity after posting bond for their release. The case of William Tyson and the *de Zaldo* went unaddressed after he had disappeared and failed to show up for his trial. In 1850 Captain Henry Merrill was arrested at sea for illegally introducing Africans into the slave trade from the ship *Martha.* Merrill was released at New York after satisfying a $3,000 surety bond but failed to fully satisfy his legal obligations. Before his court date had arrived, Merrill and his bond agent had both vanished. Benjamin B. Naylor also skipped bail after charges were filed against him for violating antislave-trade laws while commanding the *Panchita*. William C. Carter held little regard for the judicial system and demonstrated his contempt by refusing to honor the bond he posted for the trafficking charges filed against him. By the time New York prosecutors were prepared to present their case against Carter, he was nowhere to be found.[30]

It was not uncommon for traffickers to receive pardons after serving little to no jail time. Some often anticipated early release from prison, even when posting bond was not an option. Henry Merrill's shipmate Henry Johnson challenged the charges brought against him but failed to convince a federal court of his innocence. Johnson's two-year sentence was commuted after he was granted a full pardon for his crimes.[31]

New York juries that failed to acquit slave smugglers did them no harm if they were unsuccessful in reaching a verdict. When the jury in the trial of the ship *Nightingale,* a vessel that had sailed from Liverpool, England, to the slave coast of Africa and loaded eight hundred slaves, could not reach a consensus, one American citizen avoided jail time for his role in the plot.[32]

Acquittals often factored into the legal drama of New York slave-smuggling cases. Several were the result of superior legal defenses, while others were the direct outcome of juries and judges who advocated for the accused. Several cases on the docket ended up with traffickers walking free. One instance involved Rudolph E. Lasala, owner of the brig *Horatio.* In June 1856 twelve jurors were selected to consider Lasala's case. Lasala made a direct payment to a stevedore who equipped the ship with water casks, firewood, and other items necessary for the transshipment of slaves. This alone did not implicate him in the foreign slave trade but supplemented the evidence that United States district attorney John McKeon had collected against him. McKeon secured a damning handwritten note from Lasala that suggested the trafficker was in control of the ship during the time slaves were loaded onto the vessel. To present the note as credible evidence to the court, McKeon was compelled to drop charges against Lasala's ship captain in exchange for his supportive testimony. Despite an assortment of circumstances which seemingly pointed toward Lasala's guilt, the presiding federal judge, Samuel R. Betts, offered a peculiar interpretation of the slave-trade act of 1818 which prohibited United States citizens from participating in the foreign slave trade. His jury instructions bound the group to consider a guilty verdict only if it could be determined that Lasala was in control of the ship or supervised its modifications for the slave trade. If not, Betts insisted, the defendant was not in violation of federal law. Obeying Betts's guidelines, the jury acquitted Lasala of his crimes.[33]

The Lasala trial established legal precedent for several New York–based slave-trafficking cases. Joachim Jose Lopez, Casper M. Cunha Antonio, and nine others from the crew of the schooner *Falmouth* were arrested and charged with violating antislave-trade laws. Their acquittal followed a pattern by which other alleged smugglers profited. In 1856 Josefi Pedro da Cunha, Placido de Castro, Augustine C. de Mesquita, John P. Weeks, Benjamin F. Wenburg, M. B. da Cunha Reis, Louis Brown, J. H. Hinckley, Juan B. Larrusca, John Freddell, Richard T. Bates, and others benefited from loose legal interpretations of the country's antislave-trade laws.[34]

Lincoln

New York slave-smuggling trials emerged as significant public issues just as the foreign slave trade had become central to the nation's political discourse. Key to this dialogue was Abraham Lincoln, who had for several years offered opinion, commentary, and speeches on the foreign movement of slaves. Lincoln had emerged as a formidable figure within the newly formed Republican Party, and quickly rose in stature by virtue of his oratorical skills and candid viewpoints. In October 1854 Lincoln alerted a Peoria, Illinois, audience about the increased momentum among segments of the population to revive the foreign slave trade. He also reminded the group that illegal acts of slave trading carried the punishment of death upon conviction, and reiterated the legal restrictions Congress had placed upon the practice. How can one, Lincoln surmised, justify or rationalize prohibiting the importation of slaves from foreign countries while allowing for their introduction into the territories, as some had advocated for Kansas and Nebraska? For Lincoln, there was no distinction between the two. "No argument could be made," he insisted, "in favor of a man's right to take slaves to Nebraska, which could not be equally well made in favor of his right to bring them from the coast of Africa." The only means of securing the territories from slavery, Lincoln claimed, was to enforce the country's laws against the foreign slave trade.[35]

Lincoln's clever tactic of linking slavery to the foreign slave trade generated widespread interest throughout the country. It drew great attention among abolitionists, who began to place the commerce at the center of their critique. The foreign slave trade represented an opportunity for its opponents to establish transnational political links and relationships. Abolitionists promoted Lincoln as a symbol for their campaign. Crusaders such as William Lloyd Garrison, J. W. C. Pennington, Benjamin Lundy, Charles Weld, Frederick Law Olmsted, and Lewis and Arthur Tappan helped elevate Lincoln as they articulated the indispensable association between the foreign and internal distribution of slaves.[36]

The abolitionists' assault on the foreign slave trade enjoyed a significant boost in 1860 when Lincoln was elected president. By mid-September of that year it had become fairly clear that Lincoln had enough states to win the November election. Consequently, the last few months of the presidential campaign had less to do with selecting a president than with deciding the political future of the country and the international movement of bondsmen. Secessionists pounced on the opportunity to confront voters and politicians with the question of how slave economics could be preserved and maintained without at least a modicum of slave transshipments from abroad. Lincoln's victory gave impetus to these queries. Taking a cue from South Carolina secession elections, states throughout the South chose delegates that would decide whether or not to leave the Union.[37]

When word of Lincoln's victory circulated, pundits and critics elevated their discourse. According to Louisiana press reports, the election-night atmosphere within its state was full of "gloom." News of the outcome "cast a pall over the city," and the minds of all parties, regardless of past differences and bitterness, were filled with "deep anxiety and forebodings." Once Lincoln's victory was fully realized, groups emerged and warned of their intent to stoke the flames of opposition to Republican rule. During the late summer and early fall of 1860, the debate over secession represented a political touchstone, and the results of the 1860 presidential election raised the rhetoric on secession even higher.[38]

Although intensely parochial, the subject of secession confronted voters with questions and issues of momentous regional and national significance. The official parish-by-parish Louisiana presidential election returns for 1860 offer a glimpse into the political psyche of southern voters. Analysis of the election returns reveals that Lincoln was not a factor, as the 50,510 presidential votes cast were shared primarily between John C. Breckinridge (22,681), John Bell (20,204), and Stephen A. Douglas (7,625). The Breckinridge candidacy drew support from voters who no longer held "tender regard" for northern prejudices, support for compromise, or deference toward abolitionism. They avowed a need for radical and hostile groups to secure the reins of government. Breckinridge supporters organized political clubs and held meetings, rallies, processions, and oratorical programs in their efforts to restore harmony within the Democratic ranks and to become a symbol of strength throughout the South. They reasoned that a Lincoln presidency was a great danger to the union and an even greater peril to the distribution of slave labor. These same elements made Louisiana, especially New Orleans—a city with significant interests in the transshipment of slaves—a formidable part of the secessionist movement. As early as May 1860, representatives of the city's commercial, industrial, and slave interests designated themselves as principle figures in the cause for disunion. New Orleans's entire state senate delegation, and sixteen of its twenty state house representatives, were elected to the state's secession convention.[39]

Unlike Louisiana, secession in Texas rolled in like a sudden storm in November 1860. No widespread call for secession existed in Texas prior to the presidential election. But with news of Lincoln's victory came increased rhetoric and conversation regarding Texas's role in the Union. Within days of the election returns, modest efforts to organize a secessionist movement began. Initially, public meetings were called to discuss the implications of a Lincoln administration, and proposals were made for the state legislation to meet in special session to resist "Black Republican Rule." For Texas disunionists, the only logical alternative was separation. By the end of 1860 the Texas secessionist movement had gained momentum, as demonstrated by secessionists hoisting the Lone Star Flag in Galveston. As a port town, Galveston had supplied much of the state's foreign slave labor. The great planters of Texas enthusiastically endorsed secession with their time, money, and votes. Their interest in the campaign stemmed from the accepted belief that control over the slave population and over the mechanisms that controlled the foreign distribution of slave labor was essential to the survival of their economy. The ultimate success of Texas's secessionists resulted from a disorganized unionist community that relied on political canvasses and high-profile personalities to argue their case, while secessionists had organizational ties to the Democratic Party and statewide officeholders to help assist and legitimize their cause.[40]

As early as his first inaugural address, Lincoln openly expressed repudiation of the foreign slave trade and assailed the practice as a nuisance to American modernity. He reiterated a theme evident in most of his discourse on the foreign distribution of slaves. He reminded members of Congress and other dignitaries in March 1861 that there could be no practical solution to the slavery question until the "imperfectly suppressed" foreign slave trade was eradicated.[41]

Lincoln used the celebrated slave-smuggling case of Captain Nathaniel "Nat" Gordon as an opportunity to demonstrate his intention to put an end to foreign transshipments. Although Gordon and his cohorts had been arrested at sea aboard the ship *Erie* a month before the 1860 presidential election, Lincoln skillfully used Gordon's conviction to promote suppression. In December 1861, a few weeks following the Gordon verdict, Lincoln took the time to laud the work of federal antislave-trade agencies that participated in the confiscation of his slave vessels. In his annual message to Congress the first-term president boasted that the seizure and condemnation of "five vessels being fitted out for the slave trade" indicated that the "execution of the laws for the suppression of the African slave trade" was attended with "unusual success." Two crew members, Lincoln pointed out, were subject to the death penalty as mandated by federal law. He made no reference to Gordon by name, but few cases other than his had generated as much interest.[42]

The Execution of Captain Nathaniel Gordon

The trial, conviction, and execution of Captain Nathaniel "Nat" Gordon represented a watershed in the suppression of the foreign slave trade. Gordon's journey to the hanging scaffold in New York City was preceded by a lengthy slave-smuggling career that stretched back to his seafaring years in Portland, Maine, and reached as far away as Brazil. Born in 1826, Gordon hailed from a Maine family of mariners which was often referred to by newspapers as "respectable." A certain Nathaniel Gordon, however, perhaps the father of the younger Gordon, was linked to the brig *Dunlap* of Portland, Maine. He was charged in the circuit court of the Southern District of New York in 1838 with importing "with force and arms" slaves from Guadeloupe into the United States. Although records do not disclose the final disposition of this case, the elder Gordon clearly occupied a place within the circles of the foreign slave trade. A decade after the first Gordon episode, Captain Nathaniel Gordon fell under suspicion for engaging in the illicit practice in Rio de Janeiro. There, Lieutenant Commander William W. Hunter of the USS *Alleghany* detected fittings and configurations on Gordon's ship, the *Juliet,* that were consistent with those of vessels engaged in slave smuggling. In Rio, the gossip had reached the office and ears of United States consul Gorham Parks alleging that Gordon had sailed there with the intent of transporting slaves between South America, Cuba, and the United States.[43]

If Gordon was operating as a legitimate shipper, his actions and suspicious conduct suggested otherwise. As American officials intensified their pursuit of the mariner, Gordon resorted to practices common among smugglers. Despite having passed an eleven-hour inspection of the *Juliet* by an American search team, Gordon placed the vessel in the hands of a Brazilian crew. Weeks later, Rio was once again abuzz that the *Juliet* had returned with a cargo of slaves.

Three years later, Captain Gordon reemerged in Brazil commanding the *Camaro,* a ship that he guided to the Cape of Good Hope after remaining in Rio for several months. By now, Gordon was back in charge of both the *Juliet* and the *Camaro,* and he ordered each ship to the African coast. There, in the words of the United States Brazilian consul who relied on the testimony of captured crew members, Gordon took the ships to "an unoccupied spot," loaded "about five hundred Negroes, with water, etc.," and "succeeded in reaching the Brazilian coast about two hundred miles south of this port" where they "landed safely." Soon after, the crew abandoned the vessels and set them ablaze. Captain Gordon then set sail for the states.[44]

By the 1860s, federal authorities had identified Gordon as one of the more active freebooters in the country. Much of the distrust and curiosity surrounding his activities stemmed from his reputation as a slave smuggler. Captain Gordon had demonstrated measured ambivalence toward antislave-trade laws and sober indifference for its supporters. Early in 1860 he had commanded a New York–registered ship that came under suspicion in Cuba. When he applied for his clearance papers at Havana, the American consul, C. H. Helm, detained his ship for two days. There was no clear evidence that the vessel was engaged in the illicit distribution of slaves, but it was outfitted and laden with supplies and equipment (150 or more hogshead of liquor, barrels of pork and beef, bags of beans, barrels of bread and rice, 250 bundles of staves, and many hoops for making barrels or casks) often used in the trade. Helm was "morally convinced this vessel, if not taken," would bring a cargo of African Negroes to Cuba."[45]

The federal government's heightened surveillance of Gordon's activities was matched by his own zeal to undermine their attempts to suppress his business. Gordon's predisposition for smuggling made him a target for United States naval forces. By August 1860 he had entered the Congo River, dropping his anchor some forty-five miles upriver. With his mate and crew at his side, he proceeded to load several hundred slaves brought in from *barracoons* (large holding depots for slaves brought from the interior) onto his vessel. He compensated his sailors one dollar for each captured African. Within twenty-four hours from the time he had loaded his ship with slaves, the U.S. Navy ship *Mohican* penned Gordon's vessel along the coast. Packed tightly beneath the deck of the ship were several slaves.[46]

Gordon's arrest and the confiscation of his property fell squarely within the most critical time period of the 1860 election. By August 1860 Gordon and his shipmates, William Warren and David Hale, were taken into custody, and by October of the same year Gordon's ship was condemned and sold for

$7,823.25. The three suspects were hauled into a New York court and placed in the city prison without bail. A victory by the old guard of the Democratic Party (John C. Breckinridge) in the 1860 election, rather than the one by the more progressive branch (Stephen A. Douglas) of the party or by the Republican Party (Abraham Lincoln), would have perhaps increased Gordon's chances for acquittal or a presidential pardon. Forty years had elapsed since the foreign slave trade had been declared a capital crime in 1820. Although many had participated in the practice, none had suffered execution as allowed by law. Gordon could take solace from the 1854 slave-smuggling case of Captain James Smith, who, despite being found guilty, was spared the death penalty and later pardoned in 1857 by President James Buchanan.[47]

By the early 1860s, New York City had become a base to outfit illegal slave ships but also a difficult place to prosecute slave smugglers. This was reflected in Gordon's initial trial when several witnesses refused to appear and testify on behalf of the prosecution. Finally, a divided jury deliberated for several days in June 1861 but failed to arrive at a consensus on the mariner's guilt or innocence.[48]

Lincoln's election and his subsequent presidential appointments altered the temperament of the central authority and the manner in which federal prosecutions approached slave-smuggling cases. One such change involved the replacement of a Democratic United States district attorney for the Southern District of New York with E. Delafield Smith, a Republican intent upon fulfilling the political objectives of his party as it related to the antislave-trade laws. It was Smith who refused to accept confessions from Gordon and his co-defendants in exchange for prosecutorial leniency. Smith had played an active role in New York's Republican Central Committee and was a protégé of United States secretary of state William H. Seward. The *New York Tribune* commented that Smith "is still one of the younger members of his profession, and has not achieved its highest distinctions; but he has talents and a spotless reputation."[49]

Smith began fulfilling many of the expectations placed upon him by his colleagues and friends when he presented a forceful second prosecution against Nathaniel Gordon and his crew. For Captain Gordon, this meant facing the prospect of a rigorous retrial and the unlikely chance of a presidential pardon. By November the second trial was underway—this time with key witnesses who provided damaging testimony. The prosecution's case was simple—to decide whether the prisoner was "guilty or not of forcibly confining or detaining the negroes on board this vessel in the Congo River, with the intent of making them slaves." Smith methodically traced the history of

Gordon's *Erie* ship and stressed the inhumane manner in which slaves in the past had been packed onto the vessel. He pointed out that several naval officers were unsuccessful in repacking them into their original spots once they had been removed for examination. The prosecution turned Gordon's own crew and sailors against him. Each told of their confrontation with Gordon and insisted that it was not until the vessel had arrived at the Congo River that many of the crew learned of his intended purpose. They were adamant that Gordon had remained in command of the ship even after the captives were taken out to sea, and that he had offered each sailor one dollar for every slave they could land in Cuba. Prosecutors ignored Gordon's claims of foreign citizenship and gave no credence to his assertion that the *Erie* had been sold to a Portuguese firm (perhaps referring to the "Portuguese Company") prior to his capture.[50]

Gordon presented a formidable defense and resorted to every conceivable legal tactic that he could reasonably offer. Justice Samuel Nelson, however, used the latitude of his bench to repudiate many of Gordon's claims of innocence. His commentaries and instructions prompted a swift jury verdict. In less than one-half hour Gordon was found guilty and a sentence of death was pronounced on November 30, 1861. In a stern lecture on the wickedness of the foreign slave trade, Judge William D. Shipman, speaking on behalf of Justice Nelson, declared that one should "not imagine that because others share in the guilt of this enterprise yours is thereby diminished; but remember the awful admonition of your Bible, 'Though hand join in hand, the wicked shall not go unpunished.'" A motion for an appeal and a third trial failed. Gordon's execution was set for February 7, 1862.[51]

Slave smugglers had for many years escaped harsh punishment. In Gordon's case, the intense political climate accompanying slavery and secession minimized the prospects for judicial salvation. Having exhausted his legal options, Gilbert Dean, Gordon's resourceful counsel, hastened to Washington and presented evidence favorable to his client's case to members of Lincoln's inner circle. He urged a pardon or a commutation of the death sentence. Although presidential pardons had worked to the benefit of freebooters and smugglers in the past, the political circumstances confronting the nation during the early 1860s had radically altered the mood of the central authority. By now, a bedrock of its foreign policy was the elimination of the foreign slave trade. Modest hope for Gordon prevailed when Lincoln took the time to consult with his cabinet regarding the situation. Gordon was granted a short reprieve but no pardon. Three days before the scheduled execution, Lincoln, by proclamation, extended Gordon's fate for two weeks, so as to make "the necessary preparation for the awful change which awaits him." Dean used the short stay to present his case for commutation before the United States Supreme Court. Despite his best efforts, Dean's motion was refused.[52]

Gordon met his fate on February 21, 1862, but not before an attempted suicide by strychnine the night prior to his hanging. On the day of his execution hundreds of curious onlookers, city and county officials, lawmakers, and members of the press crowded into the central square of New York's city prison. Hundreds of other spectators found places atop neighboring buildings. Rumors of a final escape attempt circulated throughout the crowd. Such a getaway was next to impossible, considering the complement of United States marshals double-filed with muskets loaded and bayonets fixed. City police maintained guard outside the hanging gallows. Within minutes, Gordon was placed "beneath the fatal beam" and executed. From the gallows a large but somber crowd followed Gordon's coffin to Cypress Hills Cemetery, where the convicted smuggler was laid to rest.[53]

What was the meaning of Nathaniel Gordon's hanging to the foreign slave trade? Although political expediency may have been one motivation for the Republican approach to Gordon's trial, another argument could be made for their sincere desire to once and for all eradicate the foreign slave transshipments of slaves into the United States, and Gordon's trial, conviction, and execution was a major step in that direction. To some, his execution indicated the sincerity and efficiency of Republicans to end the practice. It showed that the approach of the American central authority toward antislave-trade laws had been radically altered after Republicans gained control of the mechanisms of government. Particular credit was given to E. Delafield Smith for his relentlessness, and to Abraham Lincoln for his refusal to adhere to an established pattern of granting pardons to convicted slave smugglers. Democrats, despite a common perception that they offered little help in the way of ending the practice, had also contributed to Gordon's conviction: the mariner had been arrested by a warship assigned to the Congo by Democrats for the purpose of capturing slave smugglers; he entered the judicial process and went to his death under an indictment obtained by a Democratic district attorney; and the presiding judges in Gordon's second trial, Justice Samuel Nelson and William D. Shipman, were avid supporters of the Democratic Party.[54]

The execution of Captain Gordon was followed by the ratification of the Lyons-Seward Treaty of 1862. The need to recall United States navy vessels policing the slave trade for service against the Confederacy compelled American authorities to unite with British officials and make concessions regarding the searches of suspected slave vessels. The treaty provided for three mixed courts—at New York, Sierra Leone, and Cape Town. They were composed of equal numbers of judges from each nation who were given authority to prosecute suspected slave smugglers and traffickers. The mutual cruising areas lay within two hundred miles of the African coast in specified latitudes and within thirty miles of Cuba. The United States Senate unanimously ratified the treaty on April 25, 1862.[55]

Ratification of the Lyons-Seward Treaty marked a significant turning point in the history of the foreign slave trade. British vessels promptly went to work inspecting and searching ships, while the American central authority proceeded to dismantle the vestiges of slavery through the preliminary Emancipation Proclamation in September 1862, the final Emancipation Proclamation in January 1863, and a massive naval blockade in the same year.

The Republican response to the foreign slave trade was felt throughout the country and was reflected in public and private accounts. Abraham Sheppard of Matagorda County, Texas, wrote a rather elaborate and detailed will in September 1863 which voiced concern about the impact that a diminished foreign slave trade would have on the availability of slave labor. He released ninety slaves and a plantation he owned jointly with his sister, "in case the casualties or the results of the present" economic and political conditions "should greatly diminish my estates" by a declining slave population. "If the Yankees invade & overrun Texas," Lizzie Neblett wrote her husband in January 1864, "my negroes will be lost, and then, all will depend upon my exertions; and how shall I meet that emergency?"[56]

Despite the highly publicized execution of Captain Nathaniel Gordon, the issuing of the Emancipation Proclamation, the Union's naval blockade of the South, precarious military conditions, and a ruined southern economy, slave smugglers continued with their activities. Some were motivated by the optimism displayed by their supporters who believed that the foreign slave trade would survive the Civil War. Many estate managers hired out bondsmen in their charge to start out the year in 1865. As late as March 17, 1865, two slaves from the Brazoria County estate of Sidney Phillips were hired out for the remainder of that year. Advertisements for slave purchases appeared in the early months of 1865, and on April 25, less than two months before "Juneteenth," the month when enslaved Africans in Texas received word of their emancipation, a slave was sold at auction on Congress Street in Austin, Texas.[57]

The level of dependency on the foreign slave trade in the United States following the execution of Captain Nathaniel Gordon, and during the travails of secession and the Civil War, is difficult to measure. As the Union applied extreme military pressure, the transshipment of foreign slaves faced a British navy with expanded powers to search and seize vessels and an American sea force intent upon intercepting all forms of commerce between the Confederacy and foreign ports. Thus, the foreign slave trade on which many had relied for over half a century faded into obscurity. Its legacy and impact is one that teaches much about the significance of the practice and about its place in the history of the United States.

Conclusion

Although this study discusses a finite number of foreign slave trading incidents, it nevertheless demonstrates that freebooters established traceable patterns that outline the history of their efforts to maintain the practice from 1808 until the Civil War. Research into customs records, foreign office records, court cases, newspapers, and contemporary observations helps reconstruct a more vivid picture of the trade following passage of the Abolition Act of 1808. In the details of this history are confirmations that the enterprise was an important issue for those who supported its cause. Though contemptible to some, the foreign slave trade lingered as an important topic in the United States during much of the nineteenth century. Pursuing their fantasies of wealth and power, freebooters and smugglers parceled slaves across borders almost at will. Their activities, subversive acts, misdeeds, and intricate and variegated world now serves as a lens through which one can study the anatomy of informal political systems, power arrangements, and the collective-identity formations that emanated from attempts to prolong the trade. For all their subterfuge, slave smugglers and traffickers contributed to the geographical expansion of the foreign slave trade and enabled the institution of slavery to persist beyond 1808. The spectacle of the foreign slave trade after 1808 became a prominent sight around slave-trading ports, plantations, waterways, and hideaways up to the Civil War.

The foreign movement of slaves helped shape the political, social, and economic identities of some communities. By assembling like-minded participants guided by similar sets of values, foreign slave traders grounded and legitimized their activities. The rational core of their culture was fully realized through public recognition. Driven to defiance, they supported their actions by infusing their interest into the complicated web of attitudes, feelings, and personal motivations of the citizenry. They planted their objectives into the social and political order, from which they shaped a collective con-sciousness to extend the life span of their vocation for more than five decades.

Slave smugglers and traffickers approached their business as a necessary methodical and profitable vocation, guided by free discretion and market demand. The freedom to ply their trade unencumbered by legal constraints, government influences, state-controlled trade systems, or public or quasi-public authorities represented an exercise in economic liberty. Their rejection of the legal commands of the Abolition Act of 1808 undermined the politi-cal soundness of the United States government, whose obligation to conserve the integrity of its political economy relied upon the enforcement of its own laws as a principal instrument.

The struggle to maintain the foreign slave trade occurred at a time when frontier and border societies often encouraged the distribution of contraband goods. Remoteness from population centers created a security vacuum. Central authorities often allowed locals significant leeway in establishing and negotiat-ing their own standards of conduct. This made policing the foreign slave trade a complicated endeavor. Consumer needs often outweighed state interests, prompting locals to evade laws that had been established to protect the parent government's control over commerce and the economy. Even when authori-ties tried to enforce regulations, contraband nonetheless flowed with minimal interference. Societies shaped their own informal and illegal economies and exercised wide discretion over them. They repudiated what they believed to be the sinister severities of institutional and legal forms of power, and promoted themselves as primary determining forces, substituting their own limitations. The process of suppression, even as it attempted to regulate and eradicate the foreign slave trade after 1808, served as a form of punishment that ultimately encouraged the very behavior it sought to eliminate. Suppression by its very nature, if unintentionally, produced unexpected outcomes.

To increase the economic value of their society, supporters of the foreign slave trade after 1808 established illicit relations with merchants and dealers from a range of locations and with an assortment of objectives. The policing of their activities was left primarily to national bureaucrats and agents, many of whom possessed indisputable knowledge about, and in some cases vested interests in, the needs of local populations and their illegal business practices.

As significant as the legal slave trade was in the maintenance of slavery, the post-1808 foreign slave trade also played an important role in the per-petuation of the institution.

With some exceptions, previous stories or accounts of the post-1808 foreign slave trade have been relegated to myth, legend, descriptive footnotes, or bibliographical entries, as if documentation and sources on the trade were remote, elusive, or did not exist at all. Instead of looking deeper into the details and nuances of the trade, its relevance in the shaping of American history has been dismissed or minimized. What was the effect of the post-1808 foreign slave trade on American political, economic, and social institutions? Clearly, a consensus on this question has yet to be established. One premise, however, has been set in place in this study: the post-1808 foreign slave trade was an important factor in sustaining slavery in the United States up to the Civil War.

The failure of historians to fully critique the role of foreign slave distribution in the United States after 1808 is due, perhaps, to their reluctance to recognize the practice as a significant force. It is worth noting that the continuation of the trade provided motivation and inspiration for its opponents who used the issue to propel their own antislave-trade movement, thrusting both slavery and the foreign slave trade to the center of their political discussions.

Historians must begin to reassess and reanalyze the political, economic, social, and cultural implications of the post-1808 foreign slave trade. Only by pursuing new questions and theories regarding the practice will its history become more complete. Historians may never fully ascertain the breadth of the trade until they come to terms with the intricate nature of slave smuggling and trafficking in nineteenth-century America. More specialized, detailed, and local studies that examine not only the number of imported slaves after 1808, but also the extent of collaboration between government agents, buyers, sellers, and other operatives around the globe are needed to complete the picture; a task awaiting future generations of historians.

Notes

INTRODUCTION

1. See Joe G. Taylor, "The Foreign Slave Trade in Louisiana after 1808," 36–45; William C. Davis, *Three Roads to the Alamo: The Lives and Fortunes of David Crockett, James Bowie, and William Barret Travis*, 52–54; Fred H. Robbins, "The Origins and Development of the African Slave Trade into Texas, 1816–1860," 51–55. The Bowie quote is found in C. L. Douglas, *James Bowie: The Life of a Bravo*, 24–25.

2. "George Washington Appoints First Marshals, 1789," www.usdoj.gov/ marshals/usmshist.htm. Also see Frederick S. Calhoun, *The Lawmen: The United States Marshals and Their Deputies*.

3. Sam Steer to John Minor, August 3, 1818, William J. Minor and Family Papers (hereafter cited as Minor Papers); Gene A. Smith, "U.S. Navy Gunboats and the Slave Trade in Louisiana Waters," 144.

4. For discussions on the constitutional debate over the African slave trade, see Bernard Bailyn, *The Ideological Origins of the American Revolution*; Richard R. Beeman et al., eds., *Beyond Confederation: Origins of the Constitution and American National Identity*; Ira Berlin and Ronald Hoffman, eds., *Slavery and Freedom in the Age of the American Revolution*; David Brion Davis, *The Problem of Slavery in the Age of Revolution, 1770–1823;* W. E. B. Du Bois, *The Suppression of the African Slave Trade to the United States of America, 1638–1870*; and William M. Wiecek, *The Sources of Antislavery Constitutionalism in America, 1760–1848*.

5. The terms "smugglers" and "traffickers" suggests individuals or groups of individuals who knowingly undermined or circumvented antislave-trade laws. Although "traffickers" sometimes participated in the legal domestic trade, this study uses the term to refer to those who participated in the illegal post-1808 foreign slave trade along with smugglers who only operated in violation of the law.

6. See *London Times*, December 31, 1807; January 2, 1808; January 5, 1808; January 7, 1808; January 8, 1808. Also, Alan L. Karras, "'Custom Has the Force of the Law': Local Officials and Contraband in the Bahamas and the Floridas, 1748–1779," 282–87; Alan L. Karras, "Caribbean Contraband, Slave Property, and the State, 1767–1792," 250–69; G. Earl Sanders, "Counter-Contraband in Spanish America," 60–61, 76–78; John Leedy Phelan, "Authority and Flexibility in the Spanish Imperial Bureaucracy," 47–65; John Caughey, "Bernardo de Galvez and the English Smugglers on the Mississippi,

1777," 46–58; John Howe, *Journal kept by John Howe while he was employed as a British Spy, during the Revolutionary War; also while he was engaged in the Smuggling Business, during the late War,* 28–31. See also John W. Tyler, *Smugglers and Patriots: Boston Merchants and the Advent of the American Revolution;* John Brewer, *The Sinews of Power: War, Money, and the English State, 1688–1783,* 176; Francis Ludlow Holt, *A System of Shipping and Navigation Laws of Great Britain,* 61; and Joseph Allen, *The Navigation Laws of Great Britain: Historically and Practically Considered,* 17–44. For more on the policing of remote harbors and frontiers, see Hugh Thomas, *The Slave Trade,* 672–73.

   7. See James A. McMillin, *The Final Victims: Foreign Slave Trade to North America, 1783–1810,* 6, 36–37, 43–44; Warren S. Howard, *American Slavers and the Federal Law, 1837–1862,* 3. Also, J. D. B. DeBow, *Statistical View of the United States, Embracing Its Territory, Population—White, Free Colored, and Slave—Moral and Social Condition, Industry, Property, and Revenue; The Detailed Statistics of Cities, Towns and Counties: Being a Compendium of the Seventh Census, to which Are Added the Results of Every Previous Census, Beginning with 1790, in Comparative Tables, with explanatory and illustrative notes, Based upon the Schedules and other Official Source of Information,* 63, 82; Robert Fogel and Stanley Engerman, *Time on the Cross: The Economics of American Negro Slavery,* 20–22, 44–49; Gwendolyn Midlo Hall, *Africans in Colonial Louisiana: The Development of Afro-Creole Cultures in the Eighteenth Century,* 280–81; Paul F. LaChance, "The Politics of Fear: French Louisianans and the Slave Trade, 1786–1809," 21; Patrick Riordan, "Finding Freedom in Florida: Native Peoples, African Americans, and Colonists, 1670–1816," 34–40; Edwin L. Williams Jr., "Negro Slavery in Florida," 93–110; Robert H. Gudmestad, *A Troublesome Commerce: The Transformation of the Interstate Slave Trade,* 18–20; Daniel H. Unser Jr., *Indians, Settlers, and Slaves in a Frontier Exchange Economy,* 112–16.

   8. For accounts of the development of the domestic slave trade, see Frederic Bancroft, *Slave Trading in the Old South,* ch. 1–2; Allan Kulikoff, "Uprooted Peoples: Black Migrants in the Age of the American Revolution, 1790–1820," in *Slavery and Freedom in the Age of the American Revolution,* ed. Ira Berlin and Ronald Hoffman, 143–71; Michael Tadman, *Speculators and Slaves: Masters, Traders, and Slaves in the Old South,* 11–21.

   9. See Edward E. Baptist, *Creating an Old South: Middle Florida's Plantation Frontier before the Civil War,* 2–7. For more on frontier analysis, see the classic work of Frederick Jackson Turner, *The Frontier in American History.*

   10. David R. Johnson, *Policing the Urban Underworld: The Impact of Crime on the Development of the American Police, 1800–1887,* 3–13. Examinations on the economic and political benefits of the slave trade tell much about the motives of those engaged in the commerce. See David Eltis and James Walvin, *The Abolition of the Atlantic Slave Trade,* 10–11; Lawrence R. Tenzer, *The Forgotten Cause of the Civil War: A New Look at the Slavery Issue,* 61–68.

11. W. E. B. Du Bois, *Suppression of the African Slave-Trade,* 109–11.

12. Du Bois, *Suppression of the African Slave-Trade,* 109–11.

13. W. E. B. Du Bois, "The Enforcement of the Slave Trade Laws," 163–74; Du Bois, *Suppression of the African Slave-Trade,* 1, 9, 17–18, 197–99.

14. Fogel and Engerman, *Time on the Cross: The Economics of American Negro Slavery,* 20–22, 44–49.

15. See Eltis and Walvin, *The Abolition of the Atlantic Slave Trade,* 12–13; David Eltis, "The British Trans-Atlantic Slave Trade after 1807," 1–11; and David Eltis, "The Traffic in Slaves between the British West Indies Colonies, 1807–1833," 55–64. For Curtin's estimate, see Philip D. Curtin, *The Atlantic Slave Trade: A Census.* J. E. Inikori rejected the validity of Curtin's entire census research and using his own methodology and analysis revised the figure upward by 40 percent. See J. E. Inikori, *Forced Migration: The Impact of the Export Slave Trade on African Societies.* Also, McMillin, *The Final Victims.* Other scholars have offered their own thesis regarding the volume of the post-1808 foreign slave trade. See David Eltis et al., eds., *The Trans-Atlantic Slave Trade: A Database on CD-ROM.*

16. The few works that examine the post-1808 foreign slave trade along the Western Gulf South include Gene A. Smith, "U.S. Navy Gunboats and the Slave Trade in Louisiana Waters," 135–47; Joe G. Taylor, "Foreign Slave Trade," 36–45; Eugene C. Barker, "The African Slave Trade in Texas," 145–58; Eugene C. Barker, "The Influence of Slavery in the Colonization of Texas," 4–5.

17. Charles H. Wesley, "Manifests of Slave Shipments along the Waterways, 1808–1864," 160.

18. Eric Williams's quote is found in Patrick Curtis Kennicott, "Negro Antislavery Speakers in America," 34; Howard, *American Slavers and the Federal Law,* 25–27.

19. Theodore Dwight Weld, *American Slavery as It Is: A Testimony of a Thousand Witnesses,* 139–40.

CHAPTER 1

1. "Extract from the Lists of Passengers Reported at the Mayor's Office by the Captains of Vessels Who Have Come to this Port from the Island of Cuba," July 18, 1809, August 7, 1809, in *Official Letter Books of W. C. C. Claiborne, 1801–1816,* ed. Dunbar Rowland, 4:381–82, 409; Paul F. LaChance, "The 1809 Immigration of Saint-Dominque Refugees to New Orleans: Reception, Integration and Impact," 110–11.

2. McMillin, *The Final Victims,* 6; Jed Handelsman Shugerman, "The Louisiana Purchase and South Carolina's Reopening of the Slave Trade in 1803," 263–90.

3. Sam Brown to William Vernon, April 20 and June 8, 1789, Slavery Papers, Box 1, New York Historical Society, New York City; *Charleston*

Courier, October 28, 1803; Stephen D. Behrendt, "The British Slave Trade, 1785–1807: Volume, Profitability, and Mortality," 31; Julia Ford Smith, *Slavery and Rice Culture in Low Country Georgia, 1750–1860,* 99; McMillin, *The Final Victims,* 36–37, 74, 120, 124–31. According to Behrendt, Liverpool merchants sponsored 111 slave voyages in 1806 and 71 in 1807. McMillin indicates that from 1803 to 1808 nearly 100 slave ships were outfitted in Charleston.

4. Joseph Clay to James Jackson, February 16, 1784, Clay, Telfair and Co. Letter Book 1782–1784, Vol. 1; Elizabeth Donnan, ed., *Documents* 4:630; Clay and Telfair to Nathaniel Hall, March 11, 1784, Telfair and Co. Letter Book, vol. 1, 1782–1784; Clay, Telfair and Co. to James Jackson, March 29, 1784, Clay, Telfair and Co. Letter Book, vol. 1, 1783–1784, Georgia Historical Society, Savannah, Georgia; *Georgia Gazette,* August 12, 27, 1795; Savannah City Council Minutes, September 1802, Georgia Historical Society, Savannah, Georgia; *Charleston Courier,* October 28, 1803; *Providence Gazette,* August 20, 1803; Donald D. Wax, "'New Negroes Are Always in Demand': The Slave Trade in Eighteenth-Century Georgia," 193–220; Du Bois, *Suppression of the African Slave Trade,* 250–60; McMillin, *The Final Victims,* 63; Helen Tunncliff Catterall, ed., *Judicial Cases,* 4:450–51.

5. LaChance, "Politics of Fear," 162–97; Edwin L. Williams Jr., "Negro Slavery in Florida," 93–110; McMillin, *The Final Victims,* 46–48, 65.

6. Gwendolyn Midlo Hall, *Slavery and African Ethnicities in the Americas,* 90–91.

7. Margaret Washington Creel, *"A Peculiar People": Slave Religion and Community-Culture among the Gullahs;* Gwendolyn Midlo Hall, *Slavery and African Ethnicities in the Americas,* 91–94.

8. Hall, *Slavery and African Ethnicities in the Americas,* 92.

9. Hall, *Slavery and African Ethnicities in the Americas,* 92–93. Two slave-trade databases offer the most comprehensive assessment of slave-trade voyages into the United States. See David Eltis, David Richardson, Stephen D. Behrendt, and Herbert S. Klein, eds., *The Trans-Atlantic Slave Trade: A Database on CD-ROM;* and Gwendolyn Midlo Hall, "Louisiana Slave Database, 1719–1820." Also see Douglas B. Chambers, *Jamaican Runaways: A Compilation of Fugitive Slaves, 1718–1817,* CD-ROM (in possession of author).

10. Inward Slave Manifest for the Port of New Orleans, March 9, 1807, RG 36, United States Customs Service Records for the Port of New Orleans, National Archives, Washington, D.C. (hereafter cited as Inward Manifest); D. C. Corbitt, "Shipments of Slaves," 545–46; Shugerman, "The Louisiana Purchase and South Carolina's Reopening of the Slave Trade in 1803," 263–90. For the Louisiana Purchase, see Robert Smith, "Napoleon and Louisiana: Failure of the Proposed Expedition to Occupy and Defend Louisiana, 1801–1803," 21–40. Also, Elijah Wilson Lyon, *Louisiana in French Diplomacy, 1759–1804;* Alexander De Conde, *This Affair of Louisiana;* and Carl A. Brasseaux and Glen Conrad, eds., *The Road to Louisiana: The Saint-*

Domingue Refugees, 1792–1809, 188–89. The most current and thorough assessment on the shifting interpretations of the Louisiana Purchase is "The Purchase and Its Aftermath, 1800–1830," in Delores Egger Labbé, *The Louisiana Purchase Bicentennial Series in Louisiana History,* vol. 3. For additional analysis on the Louisiana Purchase, see Lawrence S. Kaplan, *Thomas Jefferson: Westward the Course of Empire,* 137–39; John Keats, *Eminent Domain: The Louisiana Purchase and the Making of America;* Lyon, *Louisiana in French Diplomacy, 1759–1804;* Donald Barr Chidsey, *Louisiana Purchase;* James Alexander Robertson, *Louisiana under the Rule of Spain, France, and the United States, 1785–1807;* and C. A. Welborn, *The Red River Controversy: The Western Boundary of the Louisiana Purchase.*

11. Jefferson to Senate, January 11, 1803, in Richardson, ed., *Messages and Papers,* 1:338–39; Jefferson to Senate, October 17, 1803, in Richardson, ed., *Messages and Papers,* 1:350; Jefferson to Senate and House, December 3, 1805, in Richardson, ed., *Message and Papers,* 1:371–72; Corbitt, "Shipments of Slaves," 545–49. On Jefferson and the frontier slave trade, see Don E. Fehrenbacher, *The Slaveholding Republic: An Account of the United States Government's Relations to Slavery,* 98–99, 111–12.

12. Fehrenbacher, *The Slaveholding Republic,* 254–62.

13. Hugh Thomas, *Slave Trade,* 548.

14. Quote is found in Eric Williams, "The British West Indian Slave Trade after Its Abolition in 1807," 176–78; David Eltis, "The Traffic in Slaves between the British West Indian Colonies, 1807–1833," 55–64; Eltis and Walvin, *The Abolition of the Atlantic Slave Trade,* 21–63; Suzanne Miers, *Britain and the Ending of the Slave Trade,* 9–33.

15. Catterall, ed., *Judicial Cases,* 5:344–45. See Michael Löffler, *Preussens und Sachsens Beziehungen zu den USA während des Sezessionskrieges,* 1860–1865, 35; Shearer Davis Bowman, *Masters and Lords: Mid-19th-Century U.S. Planters and Prussian Junkers.* See also Georg Norregard, *Danish Settlements in West Africa, 1658–1850;* and *Colloque International sur Ia Traite des Noirs, de la Traite a 1'sclavage; Actes du Colloque International sur la Traite des Noirs, Nantes, 1985;* James Ferguson King, "Latin-American Republics and the Suppression of the Slave Trade," 387–411.

16. Christopher Lloyd, *The Navy and the Slave Trade: The Suppression of the African Slave Trade in the Nineteenth Century,* 41, 61–62.

17. Rosanne Marion Adderley, "'New Negroes from Africa': Culture and Community among Liberated Africans in the Bahamas and Trinidad, 1810 to 1900," 13–15; Peter T. Dalleo, "Africans in the Caribbean: A Preliminary Assessment of Recaptives in the Bahamas, 1811–1860," 15–24; Fehrenbacher, *The Slaveholding Republic,* 144–45; Hugh Thomas, *Slave Trade,* 551–52.

18. Catterall, ed., *Judicial Cases,* 4:426–27, 450–51, 492, 497, 499, 505–6.

19. Lloyd, *The Navy and the Slave Trade,* 61–62; Robert Edgar Conrad, *World of Sorrow: The African Slave Trade to Brazil,* 136–38; Ernest Ekman,

"Sweden, the Slave Trade and Slavery, 1784–1847," 221–31; Catterall, ed., *Judicial Cases,* 3:450; 4:450–51.

20. Eric Williams, "The British West Indian Slave Trade after Its Abolition in 1807," 175–78; David Eltis, "The Traffic in Slaves between the British West Indian Colonies, 1807–1833," 55–64; Gwendolyn Midlo Hall, *Slavery and African Ethnicities in the Americas,* 31–32, 34, 56, 96; Barry Higham, *Slave Populations of the British Caribbean,* 68–69; Herbert S. Klein, *African Slavery in Latin America and the Caribbean,* 94–98; McMillin, *The Final Victims,* 1–3.

21. Peter T. Dalleo, "Africans in the Caribbean," 15–24; Wesley, "Manifests of Slave Shipments," 159–60; Corbitt, "Shipments of Slaves," 549; Joe G. Taylor, "The Foreign Slave Trade," 37; Gene A. Smith, "U.S. Navy Gunboats and the Slave Trade in Louisiana Waters," 135–38; Eric Williams, "The British West Indian Slave Trade after Its Abolition in 1807," 175–78; David Eltis, "The Traffic in Slaves between the British West Indian Colonies, 1807–1833," 55–64; Robbins, "Slave Trade into Texas," 42–51; Gwendolyn Midlo Hall, *Slavery and African Ethnicities in the Americas,* 31–32, 34, 56, 96; Higham, *Slave Populations of the British Caribbean*; McMillin, *The Final Victims,* 1–3; Luis Martinez-Fernandez, *Fighting Slavery in the Caribbean: The Life and Times of a British Family in Nineteenth-Century Havana,* 4–5; Klein, *African Slavery in Latin America and the Caribbean,* 94–98, 246–48; Kenneth F. Kiple, *Blacks in Colonial Cuba, 1774–1899,* 36; Hubert H. S. Aimes, *A History of Slavery in Cuba, 1511–1868,* 33–39.

22. "Extract from the Lists of Passengers Reported at the Mayor's Office by the Captains of Vessels Who Have Come to this Port from the Island of Cuba," July 18, 1809, August 7, 1809, in *Official Letter Books of W. C. C. Claiborne, 1801–1816,* ed. Dunbar Rowland, 4:381–82, 409; LaChance, "The 1809 Immigration of Saint-Dominque Refugees to New Orleans: Reception, Integration and Impact," 110–11. Based on his study of census records, Paul LaChance estimated that several thousand more refugees arrived before 1809 than previously believed. These additional people would increase the number of immigrants to between 13,000 and 15,000 arrivals for the period. See LaChance, "Politics of Fear," 196–97; Paul F. LaChance, "Repercussions of the Haitian Revolution," 209–14. David P. Geggus has done the most recent, careful, and judicious work on the effect of the Haitian Revolution. See David P. Geggus, ed., *The Impact of the Haitian Revolution in the Atlantic World.* For 1809 arrivals, also see Gwendolyn Midlo Hall, *Africans in the Americas: Continuities of Ethnicities and Regions,* ch. 3; Gwendolyn Midlo Hall, *Africans in Colonial Louisiana,* 277–82; Thomas N. Ingersoll, "The Slave Trade of St. Dominique and the Ethnic Diversity of Louisiana's Slave Community," 133–36; Fehrenbacher, *The Slaveholding Republic,* 98–99.

23. David Porter to Secretary of the Navy, January 1, 1810, and May 4, 1810, Letters Received by the Secretary of the Navy from Commanders, 1804–1886, RG 45, Microfilm M147, National Archives (hereafter cited as

Navy Letters Received); David Porter to John Henley, July 2, 1810, John Henley Papers; Michael B. Carroll to John Henley, June 20, 1810, and Michael B. Carroll to Secretary of the Navy, July 5 and 28, 1810, in John Shaw Papers, Naval Historical Foundation, Library of Congress; Henry Demis to District Court of New Orleans, October 9, 1810, Brugman Privateer Papers, The Historic New Orleans Collection; Udolpho Theodore Bradley, "The Contentious Commodore: Thomas ap Catesby Jones of the Old Navy, 1788–1858," 25–26; Jane Lucas DeGrummond, *Baratarians and the Battle of New Orleans,* 12–15.

24. Du Bois, "The Enforcement of the Slave Trade Laws," 173; Du Bois, *Suppression of the African Slave Trade,* 112–30, 142–43; Winfield H. Collins, *The Domestic Slave Trade of the Southern States,* 20; George F. Dow, "Slave Smuggling a Hundred Years Ago," in *Slave Ships and Slaving,* 237–54; Philip D. Curtin, *The Atlantic Slave Trade: A Census,* 74–75; Noel Deerr, *The History of Sugar,* 2:202; Robert William Fogel et al., *Without Consent or Contract: The Rise and Fall of American Slavery: Evidence and Methods,* 50–52.

25. Annals of Congress, 9th Cong., 2nd Sess., 1806–1807, 484, 528–638; *United States Statutes at Large,* II, 429; "Proclamation by the President of the United States," May 20, 1804, in Richardson, ed., *Messages and Papers,* 1:357; Jefferson to the Senate and House of Representatives, November 8, 1804, in Richardson, ed., *Messages and Papers,* 1:357–59; Wesley, "Manifests of Slave Shipments along the Waterways, 1808–1864," 155–57; Fehrenbacher, *The Slaveholding Republic,* 144–45; Hugh Thomas, *Slave Trade,* 551–52.

26. Gudmestad, *A Troublesome Commerce,* 25–26.

27. David L. Lightner, "The Founders and the Interstate Slave Trade," 25–51; William L. Miller, "A Note on the Importance of the Interstate Slave Trade of the Ante Bellum South," 181; Laurence J. Kotlikoff and Sebastian Pinera, "The Old South's Stake in the Inter-Regional Movement of Slaves, 1850–1860," 434–50; Alrutheus A. Taylor, "The Movement of Negroes from the East to the Gulf States from 1830 to 1850," 367–83. Also, see Gudmestad, *A Troublesome Commerce;* and Walter Johnson, *Soul by Soul.*

28. Herman Freudenberger and Jonathan B. Pritchett, "The Domestic United States Slave Trade: New Evidence," 449–50.

29. Gudmestad, *A Troublesome Commerce,* 6–8.

30. Gudmestad, *A Troublesome Commerce,* 15, 22–25.

31. Gene A. Smith, "U.S. Gunboats," 144; DeGrummond, *Renato Beluche,* 12, 38–41; Vincent Nolte, *Fifty Years in Both Hemispheres,* 189, 207; Walter Johnson, *Soul by Soul,* 117–34. Slave price data for a particular time and place have limited value unless it can be compared with price data in other time and places. For the relevance of slave prices, see Gwendolyn Midlo Hall's *Louisiana Slave Database,* www.ibiblio.org, and *Slavery and African Ethnicities in the Americas,* 173–79. Her data contains important price information. Differential prices of slaves over time by origin or ethnicity, racial designation,

gender, age, and skills for Louisiana slaves has been calculated by Professor Hall.

32. "Proclamation by the President of the United States," May 20, 1804, in Richardson, ed., *Messages and Papers,* 1:357; Jefferson to the Senate and House of Representatives, November 8, 1804, in Richardson, ed., *Messages and Papers,* 1:357–59; Hugh Thomas, *Slave Trade,* 672–74.

33. John G. Clark, *New Orleans, 1718–1812,* 297–98, 332, 354.

34. John G. Clark, *New Orleans, 1718–1812,* 275–360; Walter Johnson, *Soul by Soul,* 1.

35. Wesley, "Manifests of Slave Shipments," 159–60; John G. Clark, *New Orleans, 1718–1812,* 270, 274–75, 297, 359; Walter Johnson, *Soul by Soul,* 1–3, 5–7, 47–48; Albert E. Fossier, *New Orleans, the Glamour Period, 1800–1840,* 26–30, 35–40.

36. George M. Brooke Jr., "The Role of the United States Navy in the Suppression of the African Slave Trade," 28–41.

37. Porter to Secretary of the Navy, January 1, 1810, and May 4, 1810, Navy Letters Received; Porter to Secretary of the Navy, April 30, 1808, June 26, 1808, August 5 and 11, 1808, September 1, 1808, November 24, 1808, December 17 and 26, 1808, February 15 and 19, 1809, March 25, 1809, April 5, 1809, Navy Letters Received; Secretary of the Navy to Porter, December 26, 1808, and David Porter to John Henley, August 10, 1810, John Henley Papers, Nimitz Library, United States Naval Academy; Charles Goldsborough to Thomas Jefferson, August 16, 1808, Thomas Jefferson Papers, Library of Congress; Gene A. Smith, "U.S. Navy Gunboats and the Slave Trade in Louisiana Waters, 1808–1811," 135–47; McMillin, *The Final Victims,* 39; Catterall, ed., *Judicial Cases,* 3:445; Howard, *American Slavers and the Federal Law,* 72; David F. Long, *Nothing Too Daring: A Biography of Commodore David Porter, 1780–1843,* 40, 45, 52.

38. Among the more significant Supreme Court decisions that protected the property of citizens was the 1809 case of *U.S. v. Peters* and the 1810 case of *Fletcher v. Peck.* For example, see Alfred Kelly, *The American Constitution: Its Origins and Development,* 186. See also Catterall, ed., *Judicial Cases,* 3:446.

39. Eugene C. Barker, "The African Slave Trade in Texas," 146; Joe G. Taylor, "Foreign Slave Trade," 38–39; William C. Davis, *Three Roads to the Alamo,* 53; DeGrummond, *Renato Beluche,* 38, 50–51, 97–99.

40. Proclamation of James Madison, February 6, 1815, in Richardson, ed., *Messages and Papers,* 2:544–45.

41. "Petition in French by Eugene Marchand to Major James Mather, 1811 Documents from Louisiana Relating to the Economic, Civil and Legal Status of 'Free Persons of Color' and of Slaves, 1803–1825, Box VIII, Folder B, Part 2, 1811, Heartman Manuscript Collection on Slavery (hereafter cited as HMS); Porter to Paul Hamilton, March 21, 1810, in Casper F. Goodrich, "Our Navy and the West Indian Pirates," 42; DeGrummond, *Renato Beluche,*

12, 38–42, 55–56; Gwendolyn Midlo Hall, *Louisiana Slave Database: Afro-Louisiana History and Genealogy, 1718–1820,* www.ibiblio.org.

42. *U.S. v. Pereira,* May 25, 1815, Cases of the United States District Court of New Orleans, RG 21, Regional National Archives, Fort Worth, Texas (hereafter cited as U.S. District Court of New Orleans).

43. *Missouri Gazette,* June 11, 1814; *Louisiana Gazette,* July 12, September 6, 1814; William C. Davis, "The Laffites: The Early Louisiana Years," 2–12; Louis-Jean Calvet, "Barataria: The Strange History of Jean Laffite, Pirate," 3–13; LaChance, "Politics of Fear," 173, 185; Joe G. Taylor, "Foreign Slave Trade," 47; John Smith Kendall, "The Huntsmen of Black Ivory," 19; Mitchell V. Charnley, *Jean Lafitte Gentleman Smuggler,* 23–28; Theresa M. Hunter, *The Saga of Jean Lafitte: From Pirate to Patriot and Back Again,* 13–17; William C. Davis, *Three Roads to the Alamo,* 52–62; DeGrummond, *Renato Beluche,* 17.

44. Gwendolyn Midlo Hall, *Louisiana Slave Database.*

45. Jean L. Epperson, "Burrill Franks: A Lafitte Man," 3–4; Kendall, "The Huntsmen of Black Ivory," 19.

46. For a sense of the recorded slave transactions of the Lafittes, see Hall, *Louisiana Slave Trade Database,* www.ibiblio.org. Sam Steer to John Minor, August 3, 1818, William J. Minor and Family Papers, Department of Archives, Louisiana State University; Gene A. Smith, "U.S. Navy Gunboats," 144; Joe G. Taylor, "Foreign Slave Trade," 38; William C. Davis, *Three Roads to the Alamo,* 54.

47. "The Road to War," William Shaler to James Monroe, October 5, 1812, Document 5246.01, 5246.02. 5246.03, Gilder Lehrman Institute of American History, Middle Tennessee State University, Murfreesboro, Tennessee; Frank Lawrence Owsley, *Struggle for the Gulf Borderlands: The Creek War and the Battle of New Orleans 1812–1815,* 18, 40.

48. Owsley, *Struggle for the Gulf Borderlands,* 107–8; W. Jeffrey Bolster, *Black Jacks: African American Seamen in the Age of Sail,* 107, 113.

49. *Missouri Gazette,* February 4, 1815, June 29, 1816; *Charleston Courier,* February 20, 1815; Owsley, *Struggle for the Borderlands,* 131; DeGrummond, *Renato Beluche,* 92–99.

50. Gudmestad, *A Troublesome Commerce,* 148–52, 165.

51. Edward Cutbush, *Observations on the Means of Preserving the Health of Soldiers and Sailors,* 126–27; Harold D. Langley, "The Negro in the Navy and Merchant Service, 1789–1860," 273–86.

52. Joseph G. Tregle Jr., "Andrew Jackson and the Continuing Battle of New Orleans," 375; Bolster, *Black Jacks,* 115–17.

53. Bolster, *Black Jacks,* 190–91.

54. Affidavits of Pedro Thomasin and Pedro Esnandez, 1812, 1813, Box VIII, Folder C, Part l, HMS; William Grimes, *Life of Grimes,* 104–6.

55. Catterall, ed., *Judicial Cases,* 6:399.

56. Catterall, ed., *Judicial Cases,* 4:267–68, 505.

57. Deposition of George Clark and Thomas Dailey, 1811 and 1813, Box VIII, Folder B, Part 2, HMS; Deposition of Captain Thomas Coates, 1817, Box VIII, Folder D, Part 3, HMS; Deposition of James Robertson, 1818, Box VIII, Folder D, Part 4, HMS; Bolster, *Black Jacks,* 75–76, 112–13; John Hope Franklin and Loren Schweninger, *Runaway Slaves: Rebels on the Plantation,* 26–27, 33.

58. John Houston McIntosh to Secretary of the Treasury William Crawford, July 30, 1817, *American State Papers, Documents, Legislative and Executive, of the Congress of the United States,* 128, cited in T. Frederick Davis, "MacGregor's Invasion," 39. The same letter appeared in the *Savannah Republican,* November 8, 1817, cited in David Bushnell, "Florida Republic," 25, and in the *Niles Weekly Register,* January 3, 1818; and the *Savannah Republican,* January 3, 1818. See Robert C. Vogel, "Rebel without a Cause: The Adventures of Louis Aury," 2–12; Jean L. Epperson, "Jean Laffite and Corsairs on Galveston Bay," 3–5; Jean L. Epperson, "Testimony of Three Escaped Prisoners from Galveston in 1818," 4–5; Catterall, ed., *Judicial Cases,* 4:524; Robbins, "Slave Trade into Texas," 81–82; Jane Landers, *Black Society in Spanish Florida,* 246; Hugh Thomas, *Slave Trade,* 615.

59. Bolster, *Black Jacks,* 31–32.

60. Deposition of Michael Brown, 1811, Box VIII, Folder B, Part 2, HMS; Deposition of John R. Myrick, 1817, Box VIII, Folder D, Part 3, HMS; Deposition of Lewis Barnes, 1817, Box VIII, Folder D, Part 3, HMS; Deposition of William Dey, 1817, Box VIII, Folder D, Part 3, HMS.

61. Affidavit of Captain William Story, 1813, Box VIII, Folder C, Part 2, HMS; Deposition of Captain Charles Rugan, 1817, Box VIII, Folder D, Part 3, HMS; Deposition by Captain Samuel Ordiome, 1817, Box VIII, Folder D, Part 3, HMS.

62. See Julius Scott, "The Common Wind: Currents of Afro-American Communications in the Era of the Haitian Revolution"; Michael J. Jarvis, "Maritime Masters and Seafaring Slaves in Bermuda, 1680–1783," 585–622; Bolster, *Black Jacks,* 159, 214, 219, 222–23. See also James Baker Farr, *Black Odyssey: The Seafaring Traditions of Afro-Americans*; and Martha S. Putney, *Black Sailors: Afro-American Merchant Seamen and the Whalemen Prior to the Civil War.*

63. Minutes of the New Orleans City Council Meeting, 1812, Box VIII, Folder C, Part 1, HMS; Affidavits of Thomas Harman and James Bradley, 1813, Box VIII, Folder C, Part 2, HMS.

64. Statement of Jean Simon Stuart, 1813, Box VIII, Folder C, Part 2, HMS; Deposition of Marie Joseph Piron, 1816, Box VIII, Folder D, Part 2, HMS; Deposition of S. M. Reynaud, 1816, Box VIII, Folder D, Part 2, HMS; Deposition of Petronille Moizard, 1816, Box VIII, Folder D, Part 2, HMS; Deposition of Alexander F. de Bodin, 1816, Box VIII, Folder D, Part 2, HMS; Deposition of Domique York, 1816, Box VIII, Folder D, Part 2, HMS; Deposition of Alexander Harang, 1817, Box VIII, Folder D, Part 3, HMS; Deposition of Honore Fortier, 1817, Box VIII, Folder D, Part 3, HMS.

65. *Courier of Louisiana,* February 6, 1816; Jefferson to Senate and House, December 3, 1805, in Richardson, ed., *Message and Papers,* 1:371–72; "A History of the Enforcement in the United States Customs Service, 1789–1875," in *Special Customs Bicentennial Reissue,* 9–24; John Wilds, *Collectors of Customs at the Port of New Orleans,* 13.

66. Wilds, *Collectors of Customs at the Port of New Orleans,* 12–13.

67. John G. Clark, *New Orleans, 1718–1812,* 317; William C. Davis, *Three Roads to the Alamo,* 53.

68. Chew to Roffignac, Box IX, Folder A, Part 2, 1822, HMS; *Courier of Louisiana,* February 6, 1816; Robbins, "Slave Trade into Texas," 51–55; Catterall, ed., *Judicial Cases,* 324; John G. Clark, *New Orleans, 1718–1812,* 317; Joe G. Taylor, "Foreign Slave Trade," 38–39.

69. Consolidating the collective works of Elizabeth Donnan's *Documents Illustrative of the History of the Slave Trade to America,* Jay Coughtry's *The Notorious Triangle: Rhode Island and the African Slave Trade, 1700–1807,* and David Eltis, David Richardson, Stephen D. Behrendt, and Herbert S. Klein's *The Transatlantic Slave Trade,* James A. McMillin was able to arrive at an estimate of slaves that Chew & Relf sold or traded between 1804 and 1807. See McMillin, *The Final Victims,* 123–24. Also see John G. Clark, *New Orleans, 1718–1812,* 330–33.

CHAPTER 2

1. Joe G. Taylor, "Foreign Slave Trade," 39; William C. Davis, *Three Roads to the Alamo,* 58; Hugh Thomas, *Slave Trade,* 614; "Personalities of Louisiana: Beverley Chew 1773–1851," www.enlou.com/no_people/chewb-bio.htm.

2. Andrew Fede, "Legal Protection for Slave Buyers in the U.S. South: A Caveat concerning Caveat Emptor," 324.

3. Catterall, ed., *Judicial Cases,* 3:396–97; Judith K. Schafer, *Slavery, the Civil Law, and the Supreme Court of Louisiana,* 1–6; Paul Finkelman, ed., *Slavery and the Law,* 14; Gilbert C. Din, *Spaniards, Planters, and Slaves,* 8.

4. Schafer, *Slavery, the Civil Law, and the Supreme Court of Louisiana,* 153–62.

5. John Dick to Edwin Lorrain, January 25, 1819, Letters Received by the United States Attorney General, RG 60, National Archives, Washington, D.C. (hereafter cited as Attorney General Letters Received). John Dick to William C. C. Claiborne, February 10, 1819, Attorney General Letters Received.

6. DeGrummond, *Renato Beluche,* 160–70; Catterall, ed., *Judicial Cases,* 3:462.

7. DeGrummond, *Renato Beluche,* 160–70; Catterall, ed., *Judicial Cases,* 3:462.

8. Bernard H. Nelson, "The Slave Trade as a Factor in the British Foreign Policy, 1815–1862," 192–209.

9. *Kingston Royal Gazette,* April 11–18, 1818; *Louisiana Gazette,* May 25, 1818; DeGrummond, *Renato Beluche,* 160, 171–84.

10. Act of March 22, 1794, Sections 1–2, 1 *United States Statutes at Large,* 347–49; Act of May 10, 1800, Sections 2-3, 2 *United States Statutes at Large,* 70–71; Act of April 20, 1818, Sections 2-3, 3 *United States Statutes at Large,* 451; Joe G. Taylor, "Foreign Slave Trade," 39; William C. Davis, *Three Roads to the Alamo,* 58; Hugh Thomas, *Slave Trade,* 614.

11. *United States v. William Lee,* May 7, 1818, U.S. District Court of New Orleans; John Dick to Edwin Lorrain, January 25, 1819, Attorney General Letters Received.

12. *Sam Glover v. Three Negroes,* June 8, 1819, U.S. District Court of New Orleans; Inward Manifest, March 4, 1819.

13. For more on Abaco, see Stephen D. Becker, *Abaco: The History of an Out Island and Its Cays.*

14. Becker, *Abaco.*

15. Inward Manifest, January–December 1819; Roger Anstey, "The Volume of the North American Slave-Carrying Trade," 56–62; McMillin, *The Final Victims,* 31, 40, 56, 57, 120.

16. Inward Manifest, December 9 and 12, 1818; K. Jack Bauer, *The New American State Papers,* 2:274; 2:276–77.

17. Wesley, "Manifests of Slave Shipments," 160; Howard, *American Slavers,* 25–27.

18. Robbins, "Slave Trade into Texas," 73–74.

19. Epperson, "Jean Laffite and Corsairs on Galveston Bay," 2–4; Andrew W. Hall, "Champ D' Asile French Filibusters on the Texas Frontier," 14–18; William Bollaert, "Life of Jean Lafitte," '440; Jack Autry Dabbs, "Additional Notes on the Champ d' Asile," 350–55; Jesse Reeves, "The Napoleonic Exiles in America," 22, 80–88; William C. Davis, *Three Roads to the Alamo,* 54–55.

20. Dispatches from the U.S. Consul in Galveston, August 30, 1817, Records of the United States Department of State, RG 59, National Archives, Washington, D.C. (hereafter cited as U.S. Dispatches). U.S. House of Representatives, House Document no. 100, 15th Cong., 2d sess., serial no. 22, "Letter of Collector of Customs Beverly Chew Regarding Galveston Pirates"; James Madison to Senate and House, March 3, 1812, in Richardson, ed., *Messages and Papers,* 2:483; First Annual Message of James Monroe, December 2, 1817, in Richardson, ed., *Messages and Papers,* 2:583; Morris to Secretary of the Navy, June 10, 1817, in Bauer, *New American State Papers,* 2:274; Lancaster E. Dabney, "Louis Aury: First Governor of Texas," 108–16; Owsley, *Struggle for the Gulf Borderlands,* 120–68; Frank Lawrence Owsley and Gene A. Smith, *Filibusters and Expansionists,* 40–41.

21. Jean Lafitte to Commandant of the *U.S. Lynx,* November 7, 1819, Box 3, File 15, Jean & Pierre Lafitte Collection, Sam Houston Regional Library & Research Center, Liberty, Texas (hereafter cited as Jean & Pierre Lafitte Collection); J. R. Madison to Jean Lafitte, November 8, 1819, Box 3, File 15, Jean & Pierre Lafitte Collection; Extract from "Report of Attempt to Halt Smuggling of Slaves," June 28, 1817, in Bauer, *New American State Papers,* 2:275.

22. J. McIntosh to General James Long, November 10, 1819, Box 3, File 16, Jean & Pierre Lafitte Collection; John G. Clark, *New Orleans, 1718–1812*, 50–51.

23. Dabney, "Louis Aury," 108–16; Landers, *Black Society in Spanish Florida*, 245–46.

24. *Niles Weekly Register*, November 29, 1817; "Belton A. Copp, Collector of Port of St. Mary's, Ga.," cited in T. Frederick Davis, "MacGregor's Invasion of Florida, 1817,": 3–71; Jane Landers, *Black Society in Spanish Florida*, 180–81, 245.

25. Translation of a letter from Pierre Lafitte on Galveston Island to his brother Jean Lafitte in New Orleans, July 23, 1817. The printed document (Letter No. 111, Legajo 492, No. 18,688) was taken from a text of publications from the National Archive of Cuba, LIII, entitled *Documentos Para la Historia de México*, compiled and arranged by José L. Franco, Havana, Cuba, 1961, pp. 134–35; "Letters From the National Archive of Cuba, translated from the Spanish by Dorothy Karilanovic," 6–11 all found in the Jean and Pierre Lafitte Collection.

26. Translation of a letter signed "No. 13," New Orleans, Louisiana, dated September 1, 1817. Printed document (Letter No. 115, Legajo 492, No. 18,688) from a text of publications from the National Archive of Cuba LIII, titled *Documentos Para la Historia de México*, compiled and arranged by José L. Franco, Havana, Cuba, 1961, pp. 138–41; "Letters From the National Archive of Cuba, translated from the Spanish by Dorothy Karilanovic," 6–11 all found in the Jean and Pierre Lafitte Collection.

27. Owsley and Smith, *Filibusters and Expansionists;* Harris G. Warren, *The Sword Was Their Passport: A History of American Filibustering in the Mexican Revolution*, 216–20; Philip Coolidge Brooks, *Diplomacy and the Borderlands: The Adams-Onís Treaty of 1819*, 123.

28. Gudmestad, *A Troublesome Commerce*, 50–51; see Michael A. Morrison, *Slavery and the American West: The Eclipse of Manifest Destiny and the Coming of the Civil War*, 45–46; Gregg Cantrell, *Stephen F. Austin: Empresario of Texas*, 57–58.

29. José Antonio de Rengel to Domingo Cabello, May 19, 1785, Bexar Archives, Center for American History, University of Texas at Austin; Jefferson to Senate and House, December 3, 1805, in Richardson, ed., *Messages and Papers*, 1:370–73; Stanley Faye, "Privateersmen of the Gulf and Their Prizes," 1012–13; Patrick J. Carroll, *Blacks in Colonial Veracruz: Race, Ethnicity, and Regional Development*, 64–65.

30. David J. Weber, *The Mexican Frontier, 1821–1846: The American Southwest under Mexico*, 122–25.

31. Weber, *The Mexican Frontier*, 148–49.

32. Inward Manifest, December 18, 20, and 21, 1819, January 13, 1820, February 1 and 4, 1820, May 19 and 20, 1820, June 7, 15, and 26, 1820, September 7, 1820.

33. Inward Manifest, August 27, 1820.

34. Wilds, *Collectors of Customs,* 11.

35. U.S. Congress, *American State Papers, Foreign Relations,* House Doc., 15th Cong., 2d sess., no. 100, serial 22, 12; Robbins, "Slave Trade into Texas," 77–80.

36. According to the 1870 census, Louisiana recorded 374 African-born persons. Georgia claimed 286, while Texas tallied 231. Although these census numbers, in all likelihood, do not account for all African-born persons, it does establish a pattern that reflects the probabilities of where most Africans were deposited through legal or illegal means. See Ninth Census of the United States 1870; Jerome S. Handler and JoAnn Jacoby, "Slave Names and Naming in Barbados, 1650–1830," 685–88; Hall, *Slavery and African Ethnicities in the Americas,* 52–54.

37. Ninth Census of the United States 1870; Handler and Jacoby, "Slave Names and Naming in Barbados, 1650–1830"; Hall, *Slavery and African Ethnicities in the Americas.*

38. Fogel and Engerman, *Time on the Cross,* 44, 62, 173, 198–99; Randolph B. Campbell, *An Empire for Slavery,* 33–34.

39. Gwendolyn Midlo Hall, *Database for the Study of Afro-Louisiana History and Genealogy*; Cantrell, *Stephen F. Austin,* 317–18; William C. Davis, *Three Roads to the Alamo,* 52–53; J. Frank Dobie, "James Bowie," 4–13.

40. "Introduction of African Slaves into the Spanish Province," Box 2, FF1, Ben C. Stuart Papers; Robbins Galveston and Texas History Center, Rosenberg Library, Galveston, Texas (hereafter cited Stuart Papers), "Slave Trade into Texas," 156; William C. Davis, *Three Roads to the Alamo,* 57–62; Joe G. Taylor, "Foreign Slave Trade," 39; Eugene C. Barker, "The African Slave Trade in Texas," 148.

41. Juliet L. Galonska, "African-American Deputy Marshals in Arkansas," 6–7; and Bauer, *New American State Papers,* 2:152.

42. Rentz, "The Public Life of David B. Mitchell," 87–113; Shingleton, "David Brydie Mitchell," 327.

43. David Mitchell to Secretary of State James Monroe, July 17, 1812, cited in Alexander, "Ambush of Captain John Williams"; "Statement Relative to Creek Agent David B. Mitchell and the Smuggling of African Negroes at the Creek Agency," undated, Box 18, folder 37, document 01, Southeastern Native American Documents, 1730–1842, Keith Read Collection, Hargrett Rare Book and Manuscript Library, University of Georgia at Athens (hereafter cited as Read Collection); article concerning General David B. Mitchell's alleged involvement in smuggling African slaves into Georgia, Box 9, folder 37, document 01, Read Collection; article concerning the dismissal of General David B. Mitchell by the President of the United States, Box 19, folder 37, document 01, Read Collection; David Kendall to John Clark, March 19, 1820, Box 48, folder 04, document 01, Telamon Cuyler Collection, Hargrett Rare Book and Manuscript Library, University of

Georgia at Athens; Thomas, *Slave Trade,* 614–15. See also Thomas Henry Rentz, "The Public Life of David B. Mitchell," 95–113; Royce Gordon Shingleton, "David Brydie Mitchell and the African Importation Case of 1820," 327–40; Landers, *Black Society in Spanish Florida,* 222.

44. Beverly Chew to William Wirt, January 26, July 31, 1821, November 18, 1824, Attorney General Letters Received. See also Joseph Anderson to Chew, March 14, 1820, Attorney General Letters Received; *New Orleans Times Picayune,* August 22, 1937, quotes the U.S. District Court in New Orleans, which indicated that on January 16, 1810, Pierre Lafitte was a deputy marshal. Catterall, ed., *Judicial Cases,* 3:478; William C. Davis, *Three Roads to the Alamo,* 59; Joe G. Taylor, "Foreign Slave Trade," 38–39; Frederick S. Calhoun, *The Lawmen: The United States Marshals and Their Deputies, 1789–1989,* 2–3; Stanley W. Campbell, *The Slave Catchers.*

45. *New Hampshire Gazette,* March 20, 1821; "Pirates in Corpus Christi," *Corpus Christi Caller,* June 4, 1940; Reginald Wilson, "Charles Nathan Tilton Privateer with Jean Laffite," 6–7.

46. *Courrier de la Louisiane,* May 22, November 29, 1821; *Niles Weekly Register,* June 1, 1822; Jean L. Epperson, "The Final Years of Jean Laffite," 2–6; Jean L. Epperson, "Some Background concerning Laffite's Departure from Galveston," 7–9; Pam Keyes, "One Man's Death Sparks U.S. War against Piracy in 1822," 21–23.

47. "Fugitive Slaves from the United States, captured in Texas by the Expedition against Long: Trial at Monterrey, April 17, 1820," Charles Ramsdell Collection (hereafter cited as Ramsdell Collection); *Salem* (Massachusetts) *Gazette,* June 2, 1820. Upon his surrender, Long was taken to Mexico City where a soldier allegedly shot and killed him accidentally. See Owsley and Smith, *Filibusters and Expansionists,* 17–80.

48. "Declaration of Negro Slave Juan Pedro," April 24, 1820, transcripts; "Declaration of Negro Slave Martin," April 24, 1820, transcripts; and "Declaration of the Negro Slave Ricardo Moran," April 25, 1820, all found in Ramsdell Collection; Jean L. Epperson, "Testimony of Three Escaped Prisoners from Galveston in 1818," 4–5.

49. Cantrell, *Stephen F. Austin,* 7–9; Gudmestad, *A Troublesome Commerce,* 18.

50. Margaret Swett Henson, *Samuel May Williams: Early Texas Entrepreneur,* 1–18; Cantrell, *Stephen F. Austin,* 146–52; Randolph B. Campbell, *Sam Houston and the American Southwest,* 92.

51. "A Joint Resolution Authorizing the President to Negotiate with Foreign Powers on the Means of Abolishing the African Slave Trade," U.S. Congress, House of Representatives Proceedings and Debates, 16th Cong., May 20, 1820, p. 2216; "A Joint Resolution Authorizing the President to Negotiate with Foreign Powers on the Means of Abolishing the African Slave Trade," U.S. Congress, Senate Proceedings and Debates, 16th Cong., May 19, 1820, 697–98; Hugh Thomas, *Slave Trade,* 616.

52. Hugh Thomas, *Slave Trade,* 598.

53. Records of slave sales in Mexico date as far back as 1659. The city of Saltillo, in particular, recorded numerous transactions between slave sellers and buyers. For example, see Carlos Manuel Valdes and Ildefonso Davila, *Esclavos Negros en Saltillo Siglos XVII a XIX,* 106–41; Zoie Odom Newsome, "Antislavery Sentiment in Texas, 1821–1861," 9–11; Cantrell, *Stephen F. Austin,* 104–31.

54. George Nixon to Stephen F. Austin, November 14, 1823, in *Austin Papers,* 3 vols., ed. Eugene C. Barker, 1:707; Eugene C. Barker, "The Influence of Slavery in the Colonization of Texas," 5–6; Lester G. Bugbee, "Slavery in Early Texas," 394–97; Zoie Odom Newsome, "Antislavery Sentiment in Texas, 1821–1861," 12–14; Weber, *Mexican Frontier,* 97; Randolph B. Campbell, *An Empire for Slavery,* 14–16.

55. Randolph B. Campbell, *An Empire for Slavery,* 16–17.

56. William Calderhead, "The Role of the Professional Slave Trader in a Slave Economy: Austin Woolfolk, A Case Study," 194.

57. See *Life and Adventures of the Accomplished Forger and Swindler Colonel Monroe Edwards;* Edna Rowe, "The Disturbances at Anahuac in 1832," 265–99.

58. "Slave Purchases and Indentures, 1820–1830," Box 2, FF2–28, Stuart Papers; Outward Slave Manifest for the Port of New Orleans, January 20, 1822, RG 36, U.S. Customs Service Records for the Port of New Orleans, National Archives, Washington, D.C. (hereafter cited as Outward Manifest); Bugbee, "Slavery in Early Texas," 393–95; Zoie Odom Newsome, "Antislavery Sentiment in Texas, 1821–1861," 11–13; Eugene C. Barker, "The Influence of Slavery in the Colonization of Texas," 4–5; Randolph B. Campbell, *An Empire for Slavery,* 15–16.

59. James A. E. Phelps to Stephen F. Austin, January 16, 1825; and Charles Douglas to Stephen F. Austin, February 15, 1825, both in Austin Papers, ed. Eugene C. Barker, 1:1020–21, 1047, 1067; Randolph B. Campbell, *An Empire for Slavery,* 17–18.

60. Weber, *Mexican Frontier,* 24, 26.

61. Don Manuel Gomez Pedraza to the Inhabitants of Texas concerning Laws, October 17, 1825, Inventory 23-0022, Galveston and Texas History Center, Rosenberg Library, Galveston, Texas; Randolph B. Campbell, *An Empire for Slavery,* 17–19.

62. Richardson, ed., *Messages and Papers,* 2:758–65.

63. Hugh Thomas, *Slave Trade,* 618–19; John T. Noonan Jr., *The Antelope: The Ordeal of the Recaptured Africans in the Administrations of James Monroe and John Quincy Adams,* 50.

64. Hugh Thomas, *Slave Trade,* 618–19.

65. Dispatches from the U.S. consul in Galveston, August 30, 1817, U.S. Dispatches; James Madison to Senate and House, March 3, 1812, in Richardson, ed., *Messages and Papers,* 2:483; First Annual Message of James

Monroe, December 2, 1817, in Richardson, ed., *Messages and Papers,* 2:583; Dabney, "Louis Aury," 108–16; Owsley, *Struggle for the Gulf Borderlands,* 120–68; Owsley and Smith, *Filibusters and Expansionists,* 40–41.

66. Catterall, ed., *Judicial Cases,* 3:132.

67. Noonan, *The Antelope,* 112–13.

68. Richardson, ed., *Messages and Papers,* 2:875–76.

69. Richardson, ed., *Messages and Papers,* 3:1030.

70. *New Orleans Bee,* February 11, April 3, July 9, September 23, October 21, 1828; Richardson, ed., *Messages and Papers,* 3:958, 960.

71. Ramon Eduardo Ruiz, *Triumphs and Tragedy: A History of the Mexican People,* 206–7; Wendell G. Addington, "Slave Insurrections in Texas," 408–34.

72. Randolph B. Campbell, *An Empire for Slavery,* 25.

CHAPTER 3

1. "James Bowie," *New Handbook of Texas,* www.tsha.utexas.edu/handbook/.

2. Stephen F. Austin to Samuel May Williams, February 19, 1831, entry 23-0582, and April 16, 1831, entry 23-0649, Samuel May Williams Papers, Galveston and Texas History Center, Rosenberg Library, Galveston, Texas (hereafter cited as Williams Papers); Bugbee, "Slavery in Early Texas," 389–412, 648–68; Randolph B. Campbell, *An Empire for Slavery,* 26–28; Weber, *Mexican Frontier,* 150.

3. Weber, *Mexican Frontier,* 150.

4. "Slave Purchases and Indentureds, 1820–1830," Box 2, FF2-28, entries 31-0011, 31-0014, 31-0096, 31-0097, 31-0098, 31-0099, 31-0100, 31-0101, 31-0109, James Morgan Papers, Galveston and Texas History Center, Rosenberg Library, Galveston, Texas (hereafter cited as Morgan Papers); Feris A. Bass Jr., and B. R. Brunson, eds., *Fragile Empires: The Texas Correspondence of Samuel Swartwout and James Morgan, 1836–1856.*

5. See Bessie Lucille Letts, "A. George Fisher"; *New Handbook of Texas,* 2:1010.

6. Bauer, *New American State Papers,* 2:153.

7. Richard Royall to Samuel May Williams, June 24, 1830, Transcript 23-0033, Williams Papers. See also John H. Jenkins, ed., *The Papers of the Texas Revolution, 1835–1836.*

8. Randolph B. Campbell, *An Empire for Slavery,* 27–28, including quotes.

9. Outward Manifest, April 19, 1830; William Truit to Samuel May Williams, May 9, 1831, entry 23-0704, Williams Papers; John Austin to Samuel May Williams, March 1, 1831, entry 25-1531, Williams Papers.

10. For a focused look at the role of the Brazos in the global economy during the nineteenth century, see Sean Michael Kelley, "Plantation Frontiers: Race, Ethnicity, and Family along the Brazos River of Texas, 1821–1886." See also John Hebron Moore, *The Emergence of the Cotton*

Kingdom in the Old Southwest: Mississippi, 1770–1860, 118; Sidney W. Mintz, *Sweetness and Power: The Place of Sugar in Modern History;* Immanuel Wallerstein, *The Modern World-System: Capitalist Agriculture and the Origins of the World-Economy in the Sixteenth Century,* 87–90; Peter Kolchin, *Unfree Labor: American Slavery and Russian Serfdom,* 1–35; Bowman, *Masters and Lords,* 46–52.

11. Outward Manifest, February 19, April 24, May 4, June 30, November 30, December 24, 1830; October 30 and 31, 1831.

12. Outward Manifest, January 7, February 19, March 31, April 13, May 17 and 18, July 19, September 17, 1831; April 3, March 1, December 29, 1832; March 27, 1833.

13. "Slave Purchases and Indentureds, 1820–1830," Box 2, FF2-28, entries 31-0011, 31-0014, 31-0096, 31-0097, 31-0098, 31-0099, 31-0100, 31-0101, 31-0109, Morgan Papers; Outward Manifest, March 31, April 1 and 13, May 17 and 18, June 2, July 19, September 17, 1831; Thomas Lee Smith to James Morgan, November 21, 1835, Morgan Papers. See also Robbins, "Slave Trade into Texas," 105; Bass and Brunson, *Fragile Empires.*

14. Bauer, *The New American State Papers.*

15. *New Orleans Bee,* February 8, 1830.

16. Randolph B. Campbell, *An Empire for Slavery,* 34, 36–40.

17. Paul D. Lack, "Slavery and the Texas Revolution," 181–84; Ronnie C. Tyler, "Fugitive Slaves in Mexico," 2; Weber, *Mexican Frontier,* 147–48.

18. Randolph B. Campbell, *An Empire for Slavery,* 36–39.

19. See E. D. Adams, *British Diplomatic Correspondence concerning the Republic of Texas, 1838–1846,* 256–57. Adams's study was the first comprehensive work on British diplomatic policy. Adams argued that British policy regarding Texas was rooted in its desire to maintain peaceful and friendly relations with the United States and to restrict U.S. expansion. Although later historians developed different ideas about the subject, they have not deviated from Adams's basic premise. Lelia M. Roeckell is one exception. Roeckell argues that British response to issues in Texas was driven mainly by its economic interests in Mexico. See Roeckell, "Bonds over Bondage," 257–78.

20. Edward Henrick to Samuel May Williams, August 28, 1832, Williams Papers; Robbins, "Slave Trade into Texas," 99–109; Henson, *Samuel May Williams;* and Jenkins, *Papers of the Texas Revolution.*

21. *Houston Telegraph,* July 5, 1843; *Texas Register,* July 5, 1843; "History of Johnson's Bayou, Louisiana," *Cameron Parish Centennial Commission,* 1970 ; W. F. Gray, *From Virginia to Texas;* Adams, *British Correspondence,* 257; Nancy Barker, *The French Legation in Texas,* 122.

22. Outward Manifest, March 22, April 9, November 4, 1835; United States Consulate at Brazoria to the United States Department of State, September 15, 1834, U.S. Dispatches; Robbins, "Slave Trade into Texas," 102–5. See *Life and Adventures of the Accomplished Forger and Swindler Colonel*

Monroe Edwards, 20–50; William C. Binkley, *Official Correspondence of the Texas Revolution, 1835–1836,* 1:477; Randolph B. Campbell, *An Empire for Slavery,* 36.

23. Harbert Davenport, "The Men of Goliad," 1–41; Ruby C. Smith, "James W. Fannin, Jr., in the Texas Revolution," 79–80; Stephen L. Hardin, *Texian Iliad: A Military History of the Texas Revolution, 1835–1836;* Henson, *Samuel May Williams;* Jenkins, *Papers of the Texas Revolution.*

24. Davenport, "The Men of Goliad," 1–41; Ruby C. Smith, "James W. Fannin, Jr., in the Texas Revolution," 79–80; Stephen L. Hardin, *Texian Iliad;* Henson, *Samuel May Williams;* Jenkins, *Papers of the Texas Revolution.*

25. Alex Dienst, "The Navy of the Republic of Texas," 165–66.

26. Lack, "Slavery and the Texas Revolution," 195–97; Tyler, "Fugitive Slaves in Mexico," 2–3; Weber, *Mexican Frontier,* 147–48.

27. See *Life and Adventures of the Accomplished Forger and Swindler Colonel Monroe Edwards;* Rowe, "Disturbances at Anahuac," 265–99; Bass and Brunson, *Fragile Empires.*

28. John Forsyth to Mexican government, July 24, 1837, RG 59, entry T-151 and T-153, U.S. Dispatches.

29. Diplomatic Correspondence, March 20, 1838, entry 2-9/9; May 20, 1838, entry 2-9/9; April 26 and 28, 1840, entries 2566, 2567, Republic of Texas Diplomatic Correspondence, Texas State Archives, Austin, Texas (hereafter cited as DC); Republic of Texas Navy Records, 2D61, p. 102, Texas State Archives, Austin, Texas (hereafter cited as ROT Navy).

30. Ward to Canning, September 6, 1825, British Foreign Office Records 50/14, Public Records Office, London, England (hereafter cited as F.O.); Ward to Canning, March 18, 1826, F.O. 50/20; Roeckell, "Bonds over Bondage," 257–78.

31. DC, May 20, 1838, entry 2-9/9; DC, April 26 and 28, 1840, entries 2566, 2567; ROT Navy, p. 102.

32. DC, December 26, 1839, entries 2537, 2538; DC, February 27, April 21, 1940, entries 2564, 2565; DC, April 2, 1841, entry 2597; David Turnbull, *Travels in the West. Cuba; With Notices of Porto Rico, and the Slave Trade,* 64, 149, 171, 391; J. S. Buckingham, *The Slave States of America,* 2:485; Randolph B. Campbell, *An Empire for Slavery,* 53.

33. DC, entries 2537, 2538, December 26, 1839; DC, entries 2564, 2565, February 27, April 21, 1840; DC, entries 2597, April 2, 1841; DC, entries 2583, 2584, November 6, 1840; Randolph B. Campbell, *An Empire for Slavery,* 53.

34. *Houston Morning Star,* August 6, 1840. See also James Walvin, *England, Slaves and Freedom, 1776–1838;* J. F. Johnson, *Proceedings of the General Anti-Slavery Convention;* Miers, *Ending of the Slave Trade;* W. E. F. Ward, *The Royal Navy and the Slavers;* Tenzer, *Forgotten Causes,* esp. chapter 4. On the origins and development of the slave trade in Mozambique, see Joseph C.

Miller, *Way of Death: Merchant Capitalism and the Angolan Slave Trade, 1730–1830.*

35. First quote is found in Hugh Thomas, *Slave Trade,* 619. Second quote is found in Tenzer, *Forgotten Cause,* 166.

36. "An Act for Carrying into effect the Treaty between Her Majesty and the Republic of Texas for the Suppression of the African Slave Trade," November 16, 1840, DC, entry 2527; E. D. Adams, *British Interests,* 58–60. Mary Lee Spence, "British Interests and Attitudes Regarding the Republic of Texas and Its Annexation by the United States," 1–10, 58–60.

37. See Seymour Drescher, *Capitalism and Antislavery.*

38. Republic of Texas Navy Muster Rolls, May–August 1938, 401-1313, ROT Navy; Samuel May Williams to Secretary of the Republic of Texas Navy, October 9, 1838, 2D61, ROT Navy, 67–69; James Hamilton to Secretary of the Republic of Texas Navy, October 9, 1838, 2D61, ROT Navy, 69; 2D61, ROT Navy, 49–61; Thomas F. McKinney to Samuel May Williams, October 22, 1838, entry 23-1610, Williams Papers; N. T. Bumley to Samuel May Williams, October 22, 1838, entry 23-1609, Williams Papers.

39. George F. Fuller, "Sketches of the Texas Navy," 223–34.

40. G. W. Hill to Sam Houston, January 1, 1844, DC; Ashbel Smith to Anson Jones, June 30, 1842, DC, entry 2612; Ashbel Smith to Spanish Foreign Minister, September 7, 1842, DC, entry 2693; Ashbel Smith to Anson Jones, September 8, 1842, DC, entry 2691–92; G. W. Hill to F. T. Wells, January 17, 1844, entry 16026, DC; Officers of the Republic of Texas Navy to the Senate and House of Representatives, January 9, 1844, DC; *National Register Extra,* April 12, 1839; *Houston Morning Star,* August 22, 1840; Adams, *British Interests and Activities in Texas,* 81–83.

41. Thomas F. McKinney to Samuel May Williams, October 22, 1838, entry 23-1610, Williams Papers; Outward Manifest, February 19 and 20, March 8, 12, and 24, April 2, 12, 16, 24, June 8, 10, 15, 19, July 21, August 1, September 18, October 29, November 4 and 26, December 1 and 31, 1838; March 23, May 10 and 25, 1839; *Houston Morning Star,* April 9, 1839; *Pendleton Messenger,* February 1839; Randolph B. Campbell, *An Empire for Slavery,* 53.

42. John G. Tod Papers, MC037, Inventory 33.2-1, 33.2-2, 33.2-3, 33.2-4, 33.2-6, San Jacinto Museum of History, Houston, Texas. See also James Henry Leach, "The Life of Reuben Marmaduke Potter"; Dienst, "Navy of the Republic of Texas"; and Tom Henderson Wells, Commodore Moore, and the Texas Navy.

43. On the activities of black abolitionists in Great Britain, see R. J. M. Blackett, *Building an Antislavery Wall: Black Americans in the Atlantic Abolitionist Movement, 1830–1860.*

44. For Williams's New Year's Day sermon, see Peter Williams Jr., "Oration on the Abolition of the Slave Trade delivered in the African Church in the City of New York, January 1, 1808," in Herbert Aptheker, *A Documentary*

History of the Negro People in the United States, 51. Also see Peter Williams Jr.,
"Abolition of the Slave Trade: A Sermon by Peter Williams, Jr.," in Philip S.
Foner, *The Voice of Black America: Major Speeches by Negroes in the United States,
1791–1971,* 20–25, 28–32; Patrick Curtis Kennicott, "Negro Antislavery
Speakers in America," 26, 31–35; *Freedom's Journal,* April 6, 1827; George E.
Walker, *The Afro-American in New York City, 1827–1860,* 19, 89, 93, 100, 150;
William W. Story, ed., *Life and Letters of Joseph Story,* 1:335; David Eltis,
Economic Growth and the Ending of the Transatlantic Slave Trade, 54–56.

45. Foner, *The Voice of Black America,* 43–47; Carter G. Woodson, *Negro
Orators and Their Orations,* 77–81.

46. *New Orleans Bee,* April 24, 1842; Bolster, *Black Jacks,* 200–203;
Theodore Dwight Weld, *American Slavery as It Is: Testimony of a Thousand,* 140,
142; Carol Wilson, *Freedom at Risk: The Kidnapping of Free Blacks in America,
1780–1865,* 1, 18, 35, 114, 116. For instances of gangs kidnapping free blacks
and free mulattoes, see Winfield H. Collins, *The Domestic Slave Trade of the
Southern States,* 95.

47. *New Orleans Picayune,* April 9, August 21, September 9, 1842; *Pendleton
Messenger,* April 9, August 21, September 9, 1842; *Houston Telegraph,* July 23,
October 4, 1851.

48. See Howard Jones, *Mutiny on the* Amistad: *The Saga of a Slave Revolt and
Its Impact on American Abolition, Law, and Diplomacy.*

49. David L. Lightner, "The Interstate Slave Trade in Antislavery Politics,"
119–20; Landers, *Black Society in Spanish Florida,* 229–48. See also Ronald G.
Walters, *The Antislavery Appeal: American Abolitionism after 1830.*

50. *Houston Morning Star,* July 7, 1840. See also *Life and Adventures of the
Accomplished Forger and Swindler Colonel Monroe Edwards.*

51. *New Orleans Picayune,* August 11, November 1, 1841; *Houston Morning
Star,* April 10, 1839; *Telegraph and Texas Register,* November 16, 1836, October
4, 1837, February 17, 1838, March 24, 1838. Outward Manifest, February 14
and 24, March 21, April 1, 10, 27, 28, 29, May 9 and 16, June 13 and 15, July
8, August 15, November 2 and 24, December 19 and 24, 1840; Marjorie
Browne Hawkins, "Runaway Slaves in Texas from 1830 to 1860," 34; Peter P.
Hinks, ed., *David Walker's Appeal to the Coloured Citizens of the World,* 107.

52. *New Orleans Picayune,* August 11, November 1, 1841; *Houston Morning
Star,* April 10, 1839; *Telegraph and Texas Register,* November 16, 1836.

53. Catterall, ed., *Judicial Cases,* 5:272. See also Addington, "Slave
Insurrections in Texas"; Paul D. Lack, "Slavery and Vigilantism in Austin,
Texas, 1840–1860," 1–20; Lack, "Slavery and the Texas Revolution," 196–97;
Bill Ledbetter, "Slave Unrest and White Panic: The Impact of Black
Republicanism in Antebellum Texas," 335–50; Harold Schoen, "The Free
Negro in the Republic of Texas," 292–308, 26–34.

54. See Landers, *Black Society in Spanish Florida,* 3, 229–37; K. W. Porter,
The Black Seminoles: A History of a Freedom-Seeking; K. W. Porter, *The Negro on*

the American Frontier; Kevin Mulroy, *Freedom on the Border: The Seminole Maroons in Florida, the Indian Territory, Coahuila and Texas;* Richard Price, *Maroon Societies: Rebel Slave Communities in the Americas.*

55. Outward Manifest, January 15, 21, 25, February 6, 10, 26, March 3, 6, 20, 27, 29 April 7, 10, 17, May 1, October 1, 1841; Carlo Barinetti, *A Voyage to Mexico and Havana; Including some General Observations on the United States,* 82–84.

56. Dispatches from United States Consuls in Havana, April 1839 to March 1842, U.S. Dispatches; Jones, *Mutiny on the* Amistad, 21, 55.

CHAPTER 4

1. Judith K. Schafer, "New Orleans Slavery in 1850 as Seen in Advertisements," 33.

2. *New Orleans Daily Picayune,* July 6, 1840, December 6, 1844.

3. *New Orleans Daily Picayune,* July 6, 1840, December 6, 1844; Outward Manifest, January 3, 1844; January 6, June 3, 1845.

4. Outward Manifest, January 18, 1843, April 8, 1843; Howard, *American Slavers and the Federal Law,* 42, 239, 282.

5. *New Orleans Daily Picayune,* September 20, 26, 1844; January 6, 1845.

6. *New Orleans Daily Picayune,* January 1, 1840.

7. *Niles National Register,* May 1, 1847; *Houston Morning Star,* August 6, 1840; Pascoe Grenfell Hill, *Fifty Days on Board a Slave Vessel in the Mozambique Channel,* 46–54. For more on Galinhas, see Adam Jones, *From Slaves to Palm Kernels: A History of the Galinhas Country (West Africa) 1730–1890.*

8. *Niles National Register,* November 6, 1847; *State Gazette,* March 20, 1852. In 1809 nine Africans reported to be slaves on a Portuguese ship were rescued from a Liverpool prison where they had been incarcerated "for debt" pending the departure of their ship. In a show of support, the white prisoners prevented the Portuguese ship's captain from taking the Africans until a group of abolitionists could arrive. See Drescher, *Capitalism and Antislavery,* 45; Dow, *Slave Ships and Slaving,* 181–87. Also, Roger Anstey and P. E. H. Hair, eds., *Liverpool, the African Slave Trade, and Abolition.*

9. Outward Manifest, January 3, March 5, 1842; January 27, February 17, June 2, 1843; February 22, 1845.

10. Outward Manifest, July 22, August (no date), September 9, October 2, 1845; *New Orleans Picayune,* April 29, October 27, 1844; *Pendleton Messenger,* April 29, October 27, 1844.

11. *New Orleans Picayune,* August 21, 1843.

12. Outward Manifest, December 31, 1845.

13. Outward Manifest, January 5, February 21, April 21, June 2, 1842; January 2, 16, 26, February 25, July 13, 1843; January 2, 23, 25, 26, 27, February 3, 7, March 8, 18, 26, April 6, 8, December 27, 1844; January 26, 1845.

14. Outward Manifest, January (no date), February 1, 14, 26, 1846; Randolph B. Campbell, *An Empire for Slavery,* 51–66; Binkley, *The Expansionist Movement in Texas, 1836–1850.*

15. Outward Manifest, June 7, 1843; May 18, June 8, 1844; January 8, March 18, May 3, June 7, October 10, 1845.

16. *Niles National Register,* June 19, December 25, 1847; Kevin S. Reilly, "Slavers in Disguise: American Whaling and the African Slave Trade, 1845–1862," 181.

17. Outward Manifest, January 14, February 9, 17, 21, April 7, 11, 20, 23, 25, May 4, June 10, 15, 23, 26, July 7, 11, October 13, 21, 24, November 13, 21, 25, December 1, 2, 3, 10, 11, 15, 16, 21, 29, 1846; *Democratic Telegraph* and *Texas Register,* August 18, 1846; Howard, *American Slavers and the Federal Law,* 215.

18. See Lack, "Slavery and Vigilantism," 1–20; John H. Schroeder, "Annexation or Independence: The Texas Issue in American Politics, 1836–1845," 137–64; David M. Pletcher, *The Diplomacy of Annexation: Texas, Oregon, and the Mexican War;* Ruiz, *Triumphs and Tragedy,* 211–14. Several speeches on slavery and the U.S.-Mexican conflict emerged during the late 1840s which expressed a wide range of opinions. A few included David S. Kaufman, "'The Slavery Question': A Speech Delivered in the House of Representatives," February 10, 1847; Daniel R. Tilden, "'The Mexican War and Slavery': A Speech Delivered in the House of Representatives," February 4, 1847; A. Birdsall, "'The Wilmot Proviso-Martin Van Buren': A Speech Delivered in the House of Representatives," July 21, 1848; Reverend John Dudley, "'The Mexican War and American Slavery': A Sermon Preached on Fast Day," April 10, 1847.

19. Outward Manifest, January 9, 10, 24, 31, February 2, 6, 7, March 14, 19, 20, April 7, 18, June 16, August 17, November 2, 30, 1850; January 22, June 26, August 19, October 24, November 1, December 13, 17, 18, 20, 1851; June 12, November 24, December 4, 1852, January 7, 8, 22, 31, February 16, March 4, 1853; *Niles National Register,* September 4, 1847; Murphy Givens, "Slavery Was Not Widespread Here."

20. "Father Refused Freedom: Interviews with Former Slave Sketch Early History of City," African American History Special Collection, Corpus Christi Public Library, Corpus Christi, Texas; Interview of Walter Rimm, in *Slave Narratives: A Folk History of Slavery in the United States from Interviews with Former Slaves,* transcribed by Eleanor Wyatt in Ronnie C. Tyler and Lawrence R. Murphy, eds., *The Slave Narratives of Texas; State Gazette,* March 13, 1852; Franklin and Schweninger, *Runaway Slaves,* 25–28, 91, 115; Quintard Taylor, *In Search of the Racial Frontier: African Americans in the American West, 1528–1990,* 60.

21. *New Orleans Daily Picayune,* December 4, 1840, February 7, 1844; *State Gazette,* September 9, 1854.

22. *New Orleans Daily Picayune,* December 4, 1840, February 7, 1844; *State Gazette,* September 9, 1854; *State Gazette,* February 16, 1850, September 9, 1854.

23. *New Orleans Daily Picayune,* May 14, 1840 December 4, 1840, February 7, 1844; *State Gazette,* September 9, 1854; *Texas National Register,* January 11, 1844; *Houston Telegraph,* July 18, 1851; *State Gazette,* September 9, 1854; Hawkins, "Runaway Slaves in Texas," 64–74; Tyler, "Fugitive Slaves in Mexico," 2–3; Franklin and Schweninger, *Runaway Slaves,* 228–29.

24. Franklin and Schweninger, *Runaway Slaves,* 94.

25. *New Orleans Daily Picayune,* December 5, 1848; *Niles National Register,* May 8, 1847.

26. Tyler, "Fugitive Slaves in Mexico," 3; Quintard Taylor, *Racial Frontier,* 60.

27. Tyler, "Fugitive Slaves in Mexico," 5.

28. See Leo Morgan Hauptman, *Martin Stowell,* 58, 61. Also, see John Crittenden Duval, *The Adventures of Big Foot Wallace, the Texas Ranger and Hunter;* Andrew Jackson Sowell, *Life of "Bigfoot" Wallace, the Great Texas Ranger Captain;* Stanley Vestal, *Bigfoot Wallace: A Biography.*

29. *State Gazette,* February 16, 1850, September 9, 1854.

30. *Houston Morning Star,* April 10, 1839; *State Gazette,* April 3, 1852, September 16, 1854; Quintard Taylor, *Racial Frontier,* 59; Tyler, "Fugitive Slaves in Mexico," 5.

31. *New Orleans Daily Picayune,* May 21, 1844; *State Gazette,* February 17, 1852.

32. Catterall, ed., *Judicial Cases,* 3:381–82.

33. *New Orleans Picayune,* August 4, 1841. For more on Canada and the Underground Railroad, see Michael Wayne, "The Black Population of Canada West on the Eve of the American Civil War: A Reassessment based on the Manuscript Census of 1861," 465–86; Peggy Bristow, ed., "We're rooted here and they can't pull us up," in *Essays in African Canadian Women's History;* Gary Collison, "Loyal and Dutiful Subjects of Her Gracious Majesty, Queen Victoria: Fugitive Slaves in Montreal, 1850–66," 59–70; Owen Thomas, *Niagara's Freedom Trail: A Guide to African-Canadian History on the Niagara Peninsula;* C. Peter Ripley, ed., *The Black Abolitionist Papers,* 2:181. Daniel Hill, *The Freedom Seekers: Blacks in Early Canada;* and Robin W. Winks, *The Blacks in Canada: A History.*

34. Aaron Mahr Yanez, "The UGRR on the Rio Grande," 41–44; Hilary Russell, "Underground Railroad Parks: A Shared History," 15–21.

35. *State Gazette,* August 25, 1849. See also Harbert Davenport, "The Life and Background of William Alfred Neale," 63–66.

36. Outward Manifest, January 4, 9, 13, 16, 22, 27, February 10, 26, March 22, April 26, May 21, July 1, 2, August 14, October 22, 27, November 9, 10, 23, December 6, 14, 1847; January 21, May 22, June 2, 10, 15, 30, July 19, August 8, 19, September 11, 15, 18, 28, October 28, November 9, 13, 18, December 15, 29, 1848.

37. Earl W. Fornell, "Texans and Filibusters in the 1850's," 411–12.

38. For more on New Mexico and slavery, see Hubert Howe Bancroft, *History of Arizona and New Mexico, 1539–1888*; Robert W. Larson, *New Mexico's Quest for Statehood, 1846–1912*; Warren Beck, *New Mexico: A History of Four Centuries*; and Martin Hardwick Hall, *Sibley's New Mexico Campaign*.

39. Ruiz, *Triumphs and Tragedy*, 211.

40. Charles R. Schultz, "The Gold Rush Voyage of the Ship *Pacific*: A Study in Ship Management," 190–200.

41. Schultz, "The Gold Rush Voyage of the Ship *Pacific*," 190–200.

42. U.S. Bureau of the Census, 1850. Gwendolyn Midlo Hall, *Slavery and African Ethnicities in the Americas,* 113, 116. Quote is found in Albert S. Broussard, "Civil Rights, Racial Protest, and Anti-Slavery Activism in San Francisco, 1850–1865," 2.

43. Outward Manifest, July 12, October 25, 1849; Catterall, ed., *Judicial Cases,* 3:600; Hugh Thomas, *Slave Trade,* 577, 598.

44. Outward Manifest, January 11, 14, February 25, 26, 27, March 5, 14, 25, April 13, 17, May 14, 28, 1850; July 12, December 4, 24, 30, 1851; December 6, 1852; January 6, 17, 21, February 5, 21, 1853; Hugh Thomas, *Slave Trade,* 237; Walter Johnson, *Soul by Soul,* 47–48; Randolph B. Campbell, *An Empire for Slavery,* 52–53.

45. Quintard Taylor, *Racial Frontier,* 77–78; Morrison, *Slavery and the American West,* 96–98.

46. Outward Manifest, November 22, 1850; Quintard Taylor, *Racial Frontier,* 83–89.

47. Outward Manifest, January 11, 14, February 25, 26, 27, March 5, 14, 25, April 13, 17, May 14, 28, 1850; July 12, December 4, 24, 30, 1851; December 6, 1852; January 6, 17, 21, February 5, 21, 1853; Hugh Thomas, *Slave Trade,* 237.

48. John Haskell Kemble, *The Panama Route, 1848–1869,* 182–87.

49. Reilly, "Slavers in Disguise," 177–78.

50. Dispatches from United States Consuls in Havana, April 1839 to March 1842, U.S. Dispatches.

51. *Niles Register Recorder,* January 14, 1847; January 15, 1848; Reilly, "Slavers in Disguise," 177–78; Hugh Thomas, *Slave Trade,* 237, 631; Quintard Taylor, *Racial Frontier,* 83–89.

52. Henry G. Kuper, July 16, September 17, November 28, 1856, F.O. 84/999; Bartlett, February 3, 1857, F.O. 84/ 1027; Edward W. Mark, May 29, 1858, F.O. 84/1059; Reilly, "Slavers in Disguise," 178; Laura A. White, "The South in the 1850s as Seen by British Consuls," 31–34, 36; Jones, *Mutiny on the Amistad,* 21, 55.

53. Pakenham, August 5, 1836, F.O. 84/206.

54. Pakenham, March 7, 13, 1836, F.O. 84/206; Ashburnam, June 24, 1838, F.O. 50/114; Roeckell, "Bonds over Bondage," 259–60.

55. Pakenham, August 5, September 6, 27, 1836, F.O. 84/206.

56. José Maria Ortiz, March 12, 1836, F.O. 84/206.

57. Lord Palmerston to Thomas Spring Rice (private), October 9, 1837, Broadland Papers, GC/MO/129; Roeckell, "Bonds over Bondage," 257, 270.

58. Pakenham, March 4, April 4, May 1, 1837, F.O. 84/225; John Parkinson, September 18, 30, October 3, 1837, F.O. 84/225.

59. Pakenham, May 11, 1841, F.O. 84/374; Wlson, April 2, 1844, F.O. 84/534.

60. Lord Aberdeen, May 11, November 24, 1841, F.O. 84/374; Pakenham, August 9, 1841, F.O. 84/374; Sebastian Camacho, August 16, 1841, F.O. 84/374; Doyle, July 31, 1843, F.O. 84/481.

61. Doyle, July 31, 1843, F.O. 84/481.

62. Lord Aberdeen, October 10, 1843, F.O. 84/481; May 28, 1844, F.O. 84/532; Elliot, March 15, 1844, F.O. 84/532.

63. Lord Aberdeen to British Consul at New Orleans, May 30, 1843, F.O. 84/485; Bunch, June 1, December 13, 1858, F.O. 84/1059; January 12, April 21, 1859, F.O. 84/1086.

64. Bunch, May 1, 1858, F.O. 5/534; MacTavish, September 30, 1851, F.O. 5/534; Mark, May 29, 1858, F.O. 84/1059; Tulin, July 12, August 9, 1860, F.O. 84/1112.

65. Bunch, May 1, 1858, F.O. 5/534; James, March 24, October 3, 1853, F.O. 5/570; February 10, 1854, F.O. 5/602; Laura A. White, "The South in the 1850s as Seen by British Consuls," 30–31.

66. James, October 19, 1850, F.O. 84/814; February 24, 1851, F.O. 5/534; June 9, 18, 1855, F.O. 5/626; May 26, 1856, F.O. 84/999; Henry G. Kuper, July 16, September 17, November 28, 1856, F.O. 84/999; White, 30–31.

67. Bunch, June 8, 1854, F.O. 5/601; January 11, 1854, F.O. 84/948; November 29, December 22, 29, 1853, F.O. 5/570; November 28, December 21, 1855, F.O. 5/626; November 29, 1856, F.O. 5/649; February 7, 1860, F.O. 5/745; Ogilby, January 20, 1842, F.O. 5/383; Mathew, June 16, December 28, 1850, F.O. 5/518; February 10, 23, 25, November 20, 30, 1851; Petigru, March 26, 1851, F.O. 5/535; March 18, 1853, F.O. 5/570; White, 33–36.

68. Bunch, May 31, June 1, 1858, F.O. 84/1059; January 12, 1859, F.O. 84/1059, January 12, 1859 F.O. 84/1086; July 27, 28, 1859, F.O. 84/1086; Archibald, July 27, 1859, F.O. 84/1086.

69. Bunch, December 22, 1860, F.O. 84/1112.

70. Mure, January 21, April 17, 1860, F.O. 84/1112.

71. Dispatches from the U.S. Consul in Galveston, August 30, 1817, U.S. Dispatches; U.S. House of Representatives, House Document no. 100, 15th Cong., 2d sess., serial no. 22, "Letter of Collector of Customs Beverly Chew Regarding Galveston Pirates."

72. British Consulate at Tampico, September 18, 1837, F.O. 84/225.

73. Mure, February 28, 1850, F.O. 5/519; December 31, 1855, F.O. 5/627; March 5, April 14, 1858, F.O. 84/1059; March 31, August 17, 1859, F.O.

5/721; May 16, 1859, F.O. 84/1086; May 18, 1860, F.O. 84/1112; February 16, March 24, 1860, F.O. 5/744; White, 34.

74. Mure, March 5, 18, 1858, F.O. 84/1059; Lynn, July 15, 1856, F.O. 5/651; June 18, August 31, 1860, F.O. 84/1112; White, 31.

75. Mure, May 18, June 20, 1860, F.O. 84/1112; Warren Howard, *American Slavers and the Federal Law,* 76.

76. Lynn, August 31, 1860, F.O. 84/1112; Warren Howard, *American Slavers and the Federal Law,* 252–61.

77. Bunch, October 20, November 13, 17, 23, 24, 29, Dec, 8, 14, 15, 1860, F.O. 5/745; White, 42–43.

78. Mathew, June 16, November 27, 1850, F.O. 5/518; March 4, October 30, 1851, F.O. 5/535.

79. Mure, December 13, 1860, F.O. 5/744; White, 46–47.

CHAPTER 5

1. For an in-depth analysis on the history of filibustering in the United States, see Robert B. May, *Manifest Destiny's Underworld: Filibustering in Antebellum America,* 179. Also see Tom Chaffin, "'Sons of Washington': Narciso Lopez, Filibustering, and U.S. Nationalism, 1848–1851," 79–108; Eugene D. Genovese, *The Political Economy of Slavery: Studies in the Economy and Society of the Slave South,* 248; John McCardell, *The Idea of a Southern Nation: Southern Nationalists and Southern Nationalism, 1830–1860,* 235–36; Charles H. Brown, *Agents of Manifest Destiny: The Lives and Times of the Filibusters,* 41.

2. Hugh Thomas, *Slave Trade,* 752–53.

3. *New Orleans Picayune,* June 12, 1854; Fanny Juda, "California Filibusters: A History of Their Expeditions into Hispanic America"; Robert B. May, *John A. Quitman,* 314–15; May, *Manifest Destiny's Underworld,* 63.

4. Thomas McCoy to Caleb Cushing, December 18, 1855, Attorney General Letters Received; Ronnie C. Tyler, "Slave Owners and Runaway Slaves in Texas," 22; Randolph B. Campbell, *An Empire for Slavery,* 180; Frederick Law Olmsted, *A Journey through Texas; or, a Saddle-Trip on the Southwestern Frontier,* 324; May, *Manifest Destiny's Underworld,* 139.

5. Clack to Black, December 26, 1857, Attorney General Letters Received; May, *Manifest Destiny's Underworld,* 50, 179–80.

6. Tyler, "Slave Owners and Runaway Slaves in Texas," 2–6; Ronnie C. Tyler, "The Callahan Expedition of 1855: Indians or Negroes," 574–76; Patsy McDonald Spaw, ed., *The Texas Senate, vol. 1: Republic to the Civil War, 1836–1861,* 236; May, *Manifest Destiny's Underworld,* 260.

7. John Salmon Ford, *Rip Ford's Texas,* ed. Stephen B. Oates, 196, 205; Tyler, "Fugitive Slaves," 6; Bob Cunningham and Harry P. Hewitt, "A 'lovely land full of roses and thorns': Emil Langberg and Mexico, 1835–1866,"

402–3; Mulroy, *Freedom on the Border*, 70; May, *Manifest Destiny's Underworld*, 260.

8. James H. Callahan to Elisha M. Pease, October 13, 1855, Elisha M. Pease Papers, Austin History Center, Austin Public Library; John S. Ford to John A. Quitman, July 2, 1855, John A. Quitmam Papers, University of Virginia, Charlottesville; Tyler, "Callahan Expedition," 576, 579–80; Ford, *Rip Ford's Texas*, 214–15; Walter V. Scholes, *Mexican Politics during the Juarez Regime, 1855–1872*, 3, 8; Mulroy, *Freedom on the Border*, 78–80.

9. Arthur T. Lynn, British Consul in Galveston, to Sir H. L. Bulwer, British Foreign Office, May 13, 1850, May 31, 1856, and July 12, 1850, F.O. 5/651. Lynn, a British citizen, maintained a small trading firm in Galveston. He was retained for many years by the British government to serve as England's consul for Texas. He played a significant role in monitoring his government's interests in Texas during the 1850s and early 1860s and was one of the few foreigners allowed to remain in the Confederacy during the Civil War. See also Fornell, "Texans and Filibusters in the 1850s," 411–13; *Houston Telegraph*, October 10, 1856; *Galveston News*, February 26, 1857; *Harper's Weekly* 1, January 10, 1857, p. 23.

10. Arthur T. Lynn to J. F. Crompton, February 18, 1855, F.O. 5/651; *Houston Telegraph*, March 19, 26, 31, 1856, and October 10, 1856; *Galveston Civilian*, May 26 and 28, 1856; *New York Herald*, December 25, 1856; *New York Daily Tribune*, April 3, 1857; *Harper's Weekly* 1, January 10, 1857, p. 23; Fornell, "Texans and Filibusters in the 1850s," 414–15.

11. *Houston Telegraph*, March 31, 1856; Arthur T. Lynn to J. Saville Lamley, June 25, 1856, F.O. 5/651. In this dispatch Lynn identified the names of volunteers and a list of fifty-six persons who contributed money. Among them were leading Texans, such as B. B. Nichols, F. R. Lubbock, W. Henley, W. Richardson, J. H. Sydnor, M. M. Potter, O. C. Hartley, ex-governor G. Wood, J. C. Shaw, M. Menard, and H. Stuart. Fornell, "Texans and Filibusters in the 1850s," 416–17.

12. Arthur T. Lynn to Henry Bulwer, May 13, 1850; July 12, 1850; July 7, 1852, F.O. 5/651; Arthur T. Lynn to J. F. Crompton, British Minister to Washington, February 18, 1854, May 31, 1856, F.O. 651; *Philadelphia Ledger*, August 1 and 6, 1851; Fornell, "Texans and Filibusters in the 1850s," 415–16.

13. Logan Hunton to Reverdy Johnson, June 28, 1850, Attorney General Letters Received; J. F. H. Claiborne, *Life and Correspondence of John A. Quitman*, 2:74–101; May, *John A. Quitman*, 236–52; Stanley W. Campbell, *The Slave Catchers*, 3–25; Mark J. Stegmaier, *Texas, New Mexico, and the Compromise of 1850*, 5–20; Morrison, *Slavery and the American West*, 96–125.

14. May, *Manifest Destiny's Underworld*, 22–23.

15. May, *Manifest Destiny's Underworld*, 256.

16. *New Orleans Picayune*, May 11, 1855.

17. Robert E. May, "John A. Quitman and His Slaves: Reconciling Slave Resistance with the Proslavery Defense," 551–70; May, *John A. Quitman,* 19–28, 165–70, 325–26.

18. Chester Stanley Urban, "New Orleans and the Cuban Question during the Lopez Expeditions of 1849–1851: A Local Study in 'Manifest Destiny,'" 1122–23; James T. Wall, *Manifest Destiny Denied: America's First Intervention in Nicaragua,* 52; Basil Rauch, *American Interest in Cuba, 1848–1855,* 121; May, *Manifest Destiny's Underworld,* 179–80, 256–57.

19. Chief Clerk of the United States Attorney Generals Bureau to Logan Hunton, May 6, 1851, Attorney General Letters Received; J. F. H. Claiborne, *Life and Correspondence,* 2:75; Richard D. Yonger, "Southern Grand Juries and Slavery," 166–78.

20. "Proceedings of a Public Meeting in Galveston, Texas, July 7, 1856," *Texas Slave Laws,* 8–9, Center for American History, University of Texas at Austin; John A. Moretta, *William Pitt Ballinger: Texas Lawyer, Southern Statesman, 1825–1888,* 39–41.

21. Moretta, *William Pitt Ballinger,* 39–40.

22. For a fuller discussion on Robert J. Walker, see James Patrick Shenton, *Robert John Walker: A Politician from Jackson to Lincoln,* 113, 135; Calhoun, *The Lawmen,* 55–58.

23. Moretta, *William Pitt Ballinger,* 40–41.

24. May, *Manifest Destiny's Underworld,* 140–41, 175. See also James P. Baughman, *Charles Morgan and the Development of Southern Transportation;* S. G. Reed, *A History of Texas Railroads.*

25. McCay to Cushing, April 9 and 10, 1856, Attorney General Letters Received; May, *Manifest Destiny's Underworld,* 133.

26. *True Delta,* October 6, 1857; Ronnie C. Tyler and Lawrence R. Murphy, eds., *The Slave Narratives of Texas,* 3, 134; May, *Manifest Destiny's Underworld,* 133; Bauer, *New American State Papers,* 2:289–91.

27. Howard, *American Slaves and the Federal Law,* 120–21, 176, 253.

28. Howard, *American Slaves and the Federal Law,* 253; Joseph C. Miller, *Way of Death,* 1730–1830, 229, 432, 517–18.

29. *Niles National Register,* June 19, December 25, 1847; Reilly, "Slavers in Disguise," 181; Johnson, *Soul by Soul,* 47–48; Howard, *American Slavers and the Federal Law,* 49–50.

30. *New Orleans Picayune,* June 10, 1844; *Pendleton Messenger,* June 10, 1844; Reilly, "Slavers in Disguise," 178–80.

31. James Farr, "A Slow Boat to Nowhere: The Multi-Racial Crews of the American Whaling Industry," 159; Bolster, *Black Jacks,* 28, 161–65, 176–79.

32. Eric Walther, *The Shattering of the Union: America in the 1850s,* 155–56; Calhoun, *The Lawmen,* 80–81; Ronald T. Takaki, *A Pro-Slavery Crusade: The Agitation to Reopen the African Slave Trade,* 201–26.

33. Walther, *Shattering of the Union,* 156.

34. Ben C. Stuart, "Last of the African Slave Ships," MSS 29, Box 2, FF2, Stuart Papers.

35. Ben C. Stuart, "Last of the African Slave Ships," MSS 29, Box 2, FF2, Stuart Papers; Barton J. Bernstein, "Southern Politics and Attempts to Reopen the African Slave Trade," 16.

36. *Southern Intelligencer,* April 28, September 8, 1858, February 16, March 16, 1859; May, *Manifest Destiny's Underworld,* 325–26; Takaki, *Pro-Slavery Crusade,* 1–85; *Congressional Globe,* 34th Cong., 3d sess., 123–26.

37. *Southern Intelligencer,* February 16, 1858; J. H. Easterby, "The Charleston Commercial Convention of 1854," 184; W. J. Carnathan, "The Proposal to Reopen the African Slave Trade in the South, 1854–1860," 413; Harvey Wish, "The Revival of the African Slave Trade in the United States, 1856–1860," 571; John G. Va Deusen, *The Ante-Bellum Southern Commercial Conventions,* 21–27, 62; Robert R. Russell, *Economic Aspects of Southern Sectionalism, 1840–1861,* 127, 131, 142–43; *DeBow's Review* 1, January 1846, 10–13; Herbert Wender, *The Southern Commercial Conventions,* 11, 15, 21; Takaki, *Pro-Slavery Crusade,* 15, 23, 178.

38. Wish, "The Revival of the African Slave Trade," 570–83; Takaki, *Pro-Slavery Crusade,* 148–49.

39. Takaki, *Pro-Slavery Crusade,* 150–51.

40. *New Orleans Daily Delta,* January 31, February, 5, 1858, in Stella Herron, "The African Apprentice Bill," 138–39; "Official Journal of the House of Representatives of the State of Louisiana, Session of 1858," 64–65; *Baton Rouge Daily Advocate,* in *Richmond Enquirer,* April 9, 1858; *Jackson Semi-Weekly Mississippian,* March 23, 1858; Takaki, *Pro-Slavery Crusade,* 170–71.

41. *Galveston News,* August 29, 1857; *Houston Telegraph,* April 4, 1859; *Texas Christian Advocate,* October 18, 1860; Robbins, "Slave Trade into Texas," 112–14; Lewis M. Purifoy, "The Southern Methodist Church and the Proslavery Argument," 325; Walter Brownlow Posey, "Influence of Slavery upon the Methodist Church in the Early South and Southwest."

42. *Galveston News,* December 1, 1857, January 9, 1858, May 7, 1859; Peter Gray, *An Address of Judge Peter W. Gray to the Citizens of Houston, on the African Slave Trade, May 30, 1859,* Judge Peter W. Gray Papers, Woodson Research Center, Rice University, Houston, Texas; Takaki, *Pro-Slavery Crusade,* 181–83.

43. Bauer, *New American State Papers,* 2:292–96; Eli S. Shorter to A. W. Starke, August 29, 1859, in the *Charleston Mercury,* September 24, 1859.

CHAPTER 6

1. Henry G. Kuper, July 16, September 17, November 28, 1856, F.O. 84/999; Bartlett, February 3, 1857, F.O. 84/1027; Edward W. Mark, May 29, 1858, F.O. 84/1059; Reilly, "Slavers in Disguise," 178, 180–82; Laura A. White, "The South in the 1850s as Seen by British Consuls," 31–34, 36.

"The Slave Trade in New York," *DeBow's Review* 18 (February 1855): 224–25; Robert Ralph Davis Jr., "James Buchanan and the Suppression of the Slave Trade, 1858–1861," 447–48; Howard, *American Slavers and the Federal Law,* 49–50.

2. British Foreign Office Memo, April 6, 1858, 84/1059; *Richmond Reporter,* June 14, 1859; Laura A. White, "The South in the 1850's as Seen by British Consuls," 38.

3. *Mobile Mercury,* August 5, 1860; *Mobile Press Register,* March 1890; Wish, "The Revival of the African Slave Trade in the United States, 1856–1860," 582, 585.

4. S. H. M. Byers, "The Last Slave Ship," 113, 744; James D. Lockett, "The Last Ship That Brought Slaves from Africa to America: The Landing of the *Clotilde* at Mobile in the Autumn of 1859," 159–63; Rufus Clark, *The African Slave Trade,* 90; Emma M. Roche, *Historical Sketches of the South,* 72–73.

5. For more on the 1859 Delegate Convention in Matagorda, Texas, see E. W. Winkler, ed., *Journal of the Secession Convention of Texas;* Wish, "The Revival of the African Slave Trade in the United States, 1856–1860," 585–86.

6. Elbert B. Smith, *The Presidency of James Buchanan,* 14–15, 37, 70.

7. Robert Ralph Davis Jr., "James Buchanan," 449–52.

8. Robert Ralph Davis Jr., "James Buchanan," 453–55.

9. Kenneth M. Stampp, *America in 1857: A Nation on the Brink,* 5–6.

10. Caleb Cushing, "Speech Delivered in City Hall, Newburyport, Massachusetts," *Boston Post,* October 1857; Stampp, *America in 1857: A Nation on the Brink,* 105–9.

11. Howard, *American Slavers and the Federal Law,* 37–39; Catterall, ed., *Judicial Cases,* 4:445.

12. Catterall, ed., *Judicial Cases,* 4:393–96; Howard, *American Slavers and the Federal Law,* 38–39.

13. Catterall, ed., *Judicial Cases,* 4:410–11.

14. Catterall, ed., *Judicial Cases,* 4:411–12.

15. Catterall, ed., *Judicial Cases,* 4:412.

16. Howard, *American Slavers and the Federal Law,* 38–39.

17. Du Bois, *Suppression of the African Slave-Trade,* 181–82; Catterall, ed., *Judicial Cases,* 2:390, 4:351; Takaki, *Pro-Slavery Crusade,* 200–201.

18. *New York Herald,* August 5, 1860; *New York Times,* February 22, 1862; *New York Journal of Commerce,* cited by Du Bois, *Suppression of the African Slave-Trade,* 172, 179; Robert Ralph Davis Jr., "James Buchanan," 447–48; Wish, "The Revival of the African Slave Trade in the United States, 1856–1860," 582; William Law Mathiesen, *Great Britain and the Slave Trade, 1839–1865,* 165; Rufus Clark, *The African Slave Trade,* 90.

19. *New York Evening Post,* August 15, 1833, March 9, 11, 1850, August 30, September 18, 1852; Howard R. Floan, "The *New York Evening Post* and the Ante-bellum South," 243–53.

20. Howard, *American Slavers and the Federal Law,* 50–51.

21. Harold Holzer, ed., *State of the Union: New York and the Civil War,* 19–20.

22. Obituary of Moses F. Odell, January 1867, *The Ladies' Repository: A Monthly Periodical. Devoted to Literature, Arts, and Religion,* 27, no. 1, 1867; Robert Ralph Davis Jr., "James Buchanan," 449.

23. For a discussion of Powell and more detail on Africans in New York, see George E. Walker, *The Afro-American in New York City, 1827–1860,* 24–25, 56, 71–72, 125, 173–74. Also, Adrian Cook, *The Annies of the Streets: The New York City Draft Riots of 1863,* 80; and Holzer, *State of the Union,* 20.

24. Walker, *The Afro-American in New York City,* 178; Holzer, *State of the Union,* 20; Howard, *American Slavers and the Federal Law,* 248–51.

25. Walker, *The Afro-American in New York City,* 178; Holzer, *State of the Union,* 20; Howard, *American Slavers and the Federal Law,* 248–51.

26. Howard, *American Slavers and the Federal Law,* 248–51.

27. Howard, *American Slavers and the Federal Law,* 248–51.

28. Howard, *American Slavers and the Federal Law,* 249–50; Catterall, ed., *Judicial Cases,* 4:407–8.

29. Catterall, ed., *Judicial Cases,* 4:249–52.

30. Catterall, ed., *Judicial Cases,* 4:249–52.

31. *New York Daily Tribune,* February 1, 15, 19, 1851, November 27, 1856, June 1, 1860; Howard, *American Slavers and the Federal Law,* 227.

32. Catterall, ed., *Judicial Cases,* 6:409.

33. *New York Daily Tribune,* February 1, 15, 19, 1851; Howard, *American Slavers and the Federal Law,* 227.

34. *New York Daily Tribune,* June 17, 18, 19, 1856; Howard, *American Slavers and the Federal Law,* 155–69.

35. Gregory to Hillyer, December 26, 1857, August 14, 1858, RG 206, Letters Received by the Solicitor of the Treasury, National Archives, Washington, D.C.; *New York Daily Tribune,* June 25, 26, July 15, 16, 17, 18, September 11, 12, 13, 17, 24, 26, December 4, 5, 8, 10, 1856; *New Orleans Daily Picayune,* May 22, June 10, 1857, May 29, 1859; *New Orleans Weekly Picayune,* April 27, 1859; Howard, *American Slavers and the Federal Law,* 227–35.

36. "Eulogy on Henry Clay at Springfield, July 6, 1852" in *Abraham Lincoln: Speeches and Writings, 1832–1858* (hereafter cited as *Lincoln: Speeches and Writings*), 270. Also, "Speech on Kansas-Nebraska Act," October 16, 1854, *Lincoln: Speeches and Writings,* 325–26, 330, 335–38, 343; "House Divided" Speech at Springfield, June 16, 1858, 433; "Speech at Chicago," *Lincoln: Speeches and Writings,* July 10, 1858, 447–52; "First Lincoln-Douglas Debate," Ottawa, Illinois, August 21, 1858, *Lincoln: Speeches and Writings,* 511; "Seventh Lincoln-Douglas Debate," Alton, Illinois, October 15, 1858, *Lincoln: Speeches and Writings,* 800–801.

37. On Lincoln's election, see David M. Potter, *The Impending Crisis, 1848–1861,* 405–47; Allan Nevins, *The Emergence of Lincoln,* vol. 2, *Prologue to Civil War, 1859–1861,* 287–317.

38. *Baton Rouge Daily Gazette and Comet,* November 9, 1860; *Port Allen Sugar Planter,* November 17, 1860; *Alexandria Constitutional,* November 17 and December 8, 15, 1860; *Opelousas Courier,* November 24, 1860; Willie Malvin Caskey, *Secession and Restoration of Louisiana,* 12.

39. *Daily Delta,* July 31, 1860; Caskey, *Secession and Restoration of Louisiana,* 3–4, 24–25, 121–22.

40. *Marshall Texas Republican,* November 24, 1860. A list of the leaders of the Texas secession movement and a description of their actions can be found in John Salmon Ford, "The Memoirs of John Salmon Ford," John Salmon Ford Papers, Center for American, History, Austin, Texas; Roberts, "Political, Legislative, and Judicial History of Texas," 85–115. Also see Frank H. Smyrl, "Unionism in Texas, 1856–1861," 172–95; Maher, "Sam Houston and Secession," 451–58; Walter L. Buenger, *Secession and the Union in Texas,* 119–40.

41. "First Inaugural Address," March 4, 1861, *Lincoln: Speeches and Writings,* 221.

42. "Annual Message to Congress," December 3, 1861, *Lincoln: Speeches and Writings,* 290.

43. U.S. Circuit Court for the Southern District of New York, *The United States v. Nathaniel Gordon,* Indictment G. 14, filed August 1, 1838, National Archives, New York Branch (hereafter cited U.S. District Court of New York); United States Congress, Senate Executive Documents, 35th Cong., 2d sess., 1861, 3, pt. I: 8–9; House Executive Document, 35th Cong., 2nd sess., 9 (1861), 5–6, 10, 19. No lengthy scholarly history of Captain Nathaniel Gordon or his trial exists, but two good accounts are William S. Fitzgerald, "Make Him an Example," 40–45; James A. Rawley, "Captain Nathaniel Gordon, The Only American Executed for Violating the Slave Trade Laws," 216–24; Howard, *American Slavers and the Federal Law,* 85–90, 137; Philip D. Curtin, *The Atlantic Slave Trade: A Census.*

44. House Executive Documents, 34th Cong., 1st sess., 1861, 56–57.

45. House Executive Documents, 36th Cong., 2nd sess., 1861, 596–97; *New York Daily Tribune,* November 10, 1861; Rawley, "Captain Nathaniel Gordon," 220.

46. Senate Executive Document, 37th Cong., 2nd sess., 1861, 2; *New York Daily Tribune,* June 21, November 8, 1861.

47. For Smith's arrest, trial, and sentence, see *New York Daily Tribune,* September 21, October 2, November 6, 7, 9, 10, 21, 1854; January 26, May 17, 18, 1855; July 17, 1856; June 9, 1857; Rawley, "Captain Nathaniel Gordon," 220–21; Howard, *American Slavers and the Federal Law,* 194–95.

48. U.S. District Court of New York, *The United States v. Nathaniel Gordon,* filed October 29, 1860; Rawley, "Captain Nathaniel Gordon," 221–22; Catterall, ed., *Judicial Cases;* Howard, *American Slavers and the Federal Law,* 199–204.

49. Howard, *American Slavers and the Federal Law,* 200.

50. Rawley, "Captain Nathaniel Gordon," 221–22.

51. *United States v. Nathaniel Gordon,* Federal Case 15,231, vol. 25, 1364–68, U.S. District Court of New York; E. Delafield Smith to George C. Whiting, October 17, 1861, Attorneys' Letters; *New York Daily Tribune,* November 7, 8, 9; December 2, 1861; February 24, 1862.

52. Federal Cases, 1367–68, U.S. District Court of New York; Edward Bates to Abraham Lincoln, February 4, 1862, Robert Todd Lincoln Papers, Library of Congress, Washington, D.C.; *New York Daily Tribune,* December 2, 1861; *New York Times,* February 21, 1861; *New York Times,* February 19, 1862; *The Diary of Edward Bates, 1859–1866,* ed. Howard K. Beale, 229–30; Roy P. Basler, ed., *The Collected Works of Abraham Lincoln,* 5:128–29; John R. Spears, *The American Slave Trade,* 220; Carl B. Swisher, "The Taney Period, 1836–64," in *History of the Supreme Court of the United States,* 5:706; J. S. Black, *Reports of Cases Argued and Determined in the Supreme Court of the United States at December Term, 1861,* 1:503–6.

53. *New York Daily Tribune,* February 22, 24, 1862; Howard, *American Slavers and the Federal Law,* 202.

54. Howard, *American Slavers and the Federal Law,* 202.

55. William M. Malloy, ed., *Treatiesm, Conventions, International Acts, Protocols and Agreements between the United States and Other Powers,* 2 vols., 1:650–56; A. Taylor Milne, "The Lyons-Seward Treaty of 1862," 511–25; Rawley, "Captain Nathaniel Gordon," 223–24.

56. Lizzie Neblett to Will H. Neblett, January 3, 1864, in Lizzie Neblett Papers, Center for American History, University of Texas, Austin; Estates of Abram Sheppard, Matagorda County Probate Records (Transcribed Will Record), Matagorda County, Texas; Randolph B. Campbell, *An Empire for Slavery,* 240.

57. Estate of Sidney Phillips, Brazoria County Probate Records (Wills, etc., Book D), Brazoria County, Texas; Randolph B. Campbell, *An Empire for Slavery,* 241.

Bibliography

ARCHIVES, LIBRARIES, MANUSCRIPT COLLECTIONS

African-American History and Culture
  A Remembering. Special Collection. Kansas State University
Austin History Center, Austin Public Library, Austin, Texas
  Elisa M. Pease Papers
  Eugene C. Barker, ed. Austin Papers. 3 vols.
Brazoria County Probate Records, Brazoria County, Texas. Estate of Sidney
  Phillips
British Public Record Office, London, England
  British Foreign Office Records, Group 84
Center for American History, University of Texas at Austin
  Bexar Archives
  Lizzie Neblett Papers
  Charles Ramsdell Collection, Archivo General de Mexico: Historia
  Tomo 96
  John Salmon Ford Papers
  Proceedings of a Public Meeting in Texas, Texas State Laws
  Republic of Texas Navy Newspaper Clippings, Dients Arrangement,
  2D61
  Richard Royster Royall, Family History
Charles F. Heartman Collection, 1724–1897 (HMS), Xavier University
  Archives and Special Collections, New Orleans
Corpus Christi Public Library, Corpus Christi, Texas
  African American History Special Collection
Galveston and Texas History Center, Rosenberg Library, Galveston, Texas
  Ben C. Stuart Papers
  James Morgan Papers
Georgia Historical Society
  Clay, Telfair and Co. Letter Book
  Savannah City Council Minutes
Gilder Lehrman Institute of American History, Middle Tennessee State,
  University, Murfreesboro, Tennessee
Hagrett Rare Book and Manuscript Library, University of Georgia at Athens
  Telamon Cuyler Collection
  Keith Read Collection
Hartley Library, Southhampton University, Southhampton, England
  Broadland Papers

Historic New Orleans Collection, New Orleans, Louisiana
    Brugman Privateer Papers
John A. Quitman Papers, University of Virginia, Charlottesville
Leo Morgan Hauptman, Archival Collection, Peru State College Library,
    Peru, Nebraska
Louisiana State University, Department of Archives, Baton Rouge, Louisiana
    William J. Minor Family Papers
Matagorda County Probate Records, Matagorda County, Texas. Estate of
    Abram Sheppard
National Archives, Fort Worth, Texas
    U.S. District Court Records of New Orleans, RG 21
National Archives, New York, U.S. District Court Records for the Southern
    District of New York, Indictment G.14.
National Archives, Washington, D.C.
    Letters Received by the Secretary of the Navy from Commanders, RG
        45, 1804–1886
    U.S. Customs Service Records for the Port of New Orleans, RG 36,
        Inward Slave Manifest for the Port of New Orleans
    U.S. Customs Service Records for the Port of New Orleans, RG 36,
        Outward Slave Manifest for the Port of New Orleans
    Records of the U.S. Department of Justice, 1809–1870, RG 60. Attorney
        General Letters Received, entry 9
    Records of the Solicitor of the Treasury, RG 206, National Archives,
        Washington, D.C. Letters Received by the Solicitor of the Treasury
    Records of the U.S. Department of State, RG 59, National Archives,
        Washington, D.C.
Naval Historical Foundation, Library of Congress, Washington, D.C.
    John Shaw Papers
New York Historical Society, New York, New York
    Slavery Papers, Box 1
Nimitz Library, United States Naval Academy, Annapolis, Maryland
    John Henley Papers
Sam Houston Regional Library and Research Center, Liberty, Texas
    Jean and Pierre Lafitte Collection
San Jacinto Museum of History, Houston, Texas
    John G. Tod Papers
Texas State Archives, Austin, Texas
    Republic of Texas Navy Records
    Republic of Texas, Diplomatic Correspondence
Thomas Jefferson Papers. Library of Congress. Washington, D.C.
U.S. Bureau of the Census, 1850. Government Printing Office, Washington,
    D.C., 1850
Whittlesey-Resley Family Collection, University of Texas at El Paso

Woodson Research Center, Rice University, Houston, Texas
    Judge Peter W. Gray Papers

NEWSPAPERS

Alexandria Constitutional
Baton Rouge Daily Advocate
Baton Rouge Daily Gazette and Comet
Boston Post
Charleston Courier
Congressional Globe
Corpus Christi Caller
Courier of Louisiana
Democratic Telegraph and Texas Register
Domestic Telegraph and Texas Register
Galveston Civilian
Galveston News
Georgia Gazette
Harper's Monthly Magazine
Harper's Weekly
Houston Morning Star
Houston Telegraph
Houston Telegraph and Texas Register
Jackson Semi-Weekly Mississippian
Kingston Royal Gazette
London Times
Louisiana Gazette
Missouri Gazette
Mobile Mercury
Mobile Press Register
National Register Extra
New Hampshire Gazette
New Orleans Bee
New Orleans Daily Delta
New Orleans Daily Picayune
New Orleans Picayune
New Orleans Times Picayune
New Orleans Weekly Picayune
New York Daily Tribune
New York Herald
New York Times
Niles National Register
Opelousas Courier

Pendleton Messenger
Philadelphia Ledger
Port Allen Sugar Planter
Providence Gazette
Richmond Enquirer
Richmond Reporter
Salem (Massachusetts) Gazette
Southern Intelligencer
State Gazette
Telegraph and Texas Register
Texas Christian Advocate
Texas National Register
Texas Republican
True Delta

BOOKS, ARTICLES, AND DATABASES

Adams, E. D. *British Diplomatic Correspondence concerning the Republic of Texas, 1838–1846.* LaCrosse, Wisc.: Northern Micrographics, 2001.

Adams, E. D. *British Interests and Activities in Texas, 1836–1846.* Gloucester, Mass.: Peter Smith, 1963.

Addington, Wendell G. "Slave Insurrections in Texas." *Journal of Negro History* (October 1950): 408–34.

Aimes, Hubert H. S. *A History of Slavery in Cuba, 1511–1868.* New York: Octagon, 1967.

Allen, Joseph. *The Navigation Laws of Great Britain: Historically and Practically Considered.* London, 1849.

Anstey, Roger. "The Volume of the North American Slave-Carrying Trade from Africa, 1761–1810." *Revue Francaise D'histoire D'outre-mer* 62, 2 (1975).

Anstey, Roger, and P. E. H. Hair, eds. *Liverpool, the African Slave Trade, and Abolition.* Liverpool: Historic Society of Lancashire and Cheshire, 1976

Aptheker, Herbert. *A Documentary History of the Negro People in the United States.* 3 vols. New York: Citadel Press, 1966–1973.

Bailyn, Bernard. *The Ideological Origins of the American Revolution.* Cambridge: Harvard University Press, 1967.

Bancroft, Frederic. *Slave-Trading in the Old South.* Baltimore: J. H. Furst Company, 1931.

Bancroft, Hubert Howe. *History of Arizona and New Mexico, 1530–1888.* San Francisco: The History Co., 1889.

Baptist, Edward B. *Creating an Old South: Middle Florida's' Plantation Frontier before the Civil War.* Chapel Hill: University of North Carolina Press, 2002.

Barinetti, Carlo. *A Voyage to Mexico and Havanna; Including some General Observations on the United States.* New York: C.Vintoh, 1841.

Barker, Eugene C. "The African Slave Trade in Texas." *Southern Historical Quarterly* 6 (October 1902): 145–58.

Barker, Eugene C. "The Influence of Slavery in the Colonization of Texas." *Missouri Valley Historical Review* 11, 1 (June 1924): 4–5.

Barker, Nancy. *The French Legation in Texas.* Austin: Texas State Historical Association, 1973.

Basler, Roy P., ed. *The Collected Works of Abraham Lincoln.* New Brunswick, N.J.: Rutgers University Press, 1953.

Bass, Feris A., and B. R. Brunson, eds. *Fragile Empires: The Texas Correspondence of Samuel Swartwout and James Morgan, 1836–1856.* Austin: Shoal Creek, 1978.

Bates, Edward. *The Diary of Edward Bates, 1859–1866.* Ed. Howard K. Beale. Washington, D.C.: U.S. Government Printing Office, 1933.

Bauer, K. Jack, ed. *The New American State Papers,* vol. 2, *Naval Affairs.* Wilmington, Del.: Scholarly Resources, Inc., 1981.

Baughman, James P. *Charles Morgan and the Development of Southern Transportation.* Nashville: Vanderbilt University Press, 1968.

Beck, Warren. *New Mexico: A History of Four Centuries.* Norman: University of Oklahoma Press, 1962.

Becker, Stephen D. *Abaco: The History of an Out Island and Its Cays.* North Miami, Fla.: Tropic Isle Publications, 1983.

Beeman, Richard R., Stephen Botein, and Edward Carlos Carter, eds. *Beyond Confederation: Origins of the Constitution and American National Identity.* Chapel Hill: University of North Carolina Press, 1987.

Berlin, Ira, and Ronald Hoffman, eds. *Slavery and Freedom in the Age of the American Revolution.* Charlottesville: University of Virginia Press, 1983.

Bernstein, Barton J. "Southern Politics and Attempts to Reopen the African Slave Trade." *Journal of Negro History* 51, 1 (January 1966): 16–35.

Binkley, William C. *The Expansionist Movement in Texas, 1836–1850.* Berkeley and Los Angeles: University of California Press, 1925.

Binkley, William C., ed. *Official Correspondence of the Texas Revolution, 1835–1836.* 2 vols. New York: D. Appleton-Century, 1936.

Birdsall, A. "'The Wilmot Proviso-Martin Van Buren': A Speech Delivered in the House of Representatives, July 21, 1848.* Washington, D.C.: Congressional Globe Office, 1848.

Black, J. S. *Reports of Cases Argued and Determined in the Supreme Court of the United States at December Term, 1861* (Washington, D.C.: W. H. & O. H. Morrison, 1862), 1:503–6.

Blackett, R. J. M. *Building an Antislavery Wall: Black Americans in the Atlantic Abolitionist Movement, 1830–1860.* Baton Rouge: Louisiana State University Press, 1983.

Bollaert, William. "Life of Jean Lafitte." *Littell's Living Age* 32 (March 1852): 433–46.

Bolster, Jeffery W. *Black Jacks: African American Seamen in the Age of Sail.* Cambridge: Harvard University Press, 1997.

Bontemps, Arna, ed. *Five Black Lives: The Autobiographies of Venture Smith, James Mars, William Grimes, the Rev. G. W. Offley, James L. Smith.* Middletown: Wesleyan University Press, 1971.

Bowman, Shearer Davis. *Masters and Lords: Mid-19th-Century U.S. Planters and Prussian Junkers.* New York: Oxford University Press, 1993.

Brasseaux, Carl A., and Glenn R. Conrad, eds. *The Road to Louisiana: The Saint-Dominque Refugees, 1792–1809.* Lafayette: Center for Louisiana Studies, University of Southwestern Louisiana, 1992.

Brewer, John. *The Sinews of Power: War, Money, and the English State, 1688–1783.* Cambridge: Harvard University Press, 1990.

Bristow, Peggy, ed. "We're rooted here and they can't pull us up." *Essays in African Canadian Women's History.* Toronto: University of Toronto Press, 1994.

Brooke, George M., Jr. "The Role of the United States Navy in the Suppression of the African Slave Trade." *American Neptune: Quarterly Journal of Maritime History* 21, 1 (1961): 28–41.

Brooks, Philip Coolidge. *Diplomacy and the Borderlands: The Adams-Onis Treaty of 1819.* Berkeley and Los Angeles: University of California Press, 1939.

Broussard, Albert S. "Civil Rights, Racial Protest, and Anti-Slavery Activism in San Francisco, 1850–1865." San Francisco: National Maritime Museum, 1999. Pp. 1–50.

Brown, Charles H. *Agents of Manifest Destiny: The Lives and Times of the Filibusters.* Chapel Hill: University of North Carolina Press, 1980.

Buckingham, J. S. *The Slave States of America.* 2 vols. New York: Negro Universities Press, 1968.

Buenger, Walter. *Secession and the Union in Texas.* Austin: University of Texas Press, 1984.

Bugbee, Lester G. "Slavery in Early Texas." *Political Science Quarterly* 13 (1898): 389–412, 648–68. Bureau of the Census. Ninth Census of the United States. Washington, D.C.: Government Printing Office, 1870.

Byers, S. H. M. "The Last Slave Ship." *Harper's Monthly Magazine* 113 (October 1906): 742–46.

Calderhead, William. "The Role of the Professional Slave Trader in a Slave Economy: A Case Study." *Civil War History* 23 (September 1977): 195–211.

Calhoun, Frederick S. *The Lawmen: The United States Marshals and Their Deputies, 1789–1989.* Washington, D.C.: Smithsonian Institution Press, 1989.

Calvet, Louis-Jean. "Barataria: The Strange History of Jean Laffite, Pirate." *Laffite Chronicles* 9, 2 (October 2003): 3–13.

Campbell, Randolph B. *An Empire for Slavery: The Peculiar Institution in Texas, 1821–1865.* Baton Rouge: Louisiana State University Press, 1989.

Campbell, Randolph B. *Sam Houston and the American Southwest.* New York: Harper Collins Publishers, 1993.

Campbell, Stanley W. *The Slave Catchers.* Chapel Hill: University of North Carolina Press, 1970.

Cantrell, Gregg. *Stephen F. Austin: Empresario of Texas.* New Haven, Conn.: Yale University Press, 1999.

Carnathan, W. J. "The Proposal to Reopen the African Slave Trade in the South, 1854–1860." *South Atlantic Quarterly* 25, 4 (1926): 414–32.

Carroll, Patrick J. *Blacks in Colonial Veracruz: Race, Ethnicity, and Regional Development.* Austin: University of Texas Press, 1991.

Caskey, Willie Malvin. *Secession and Restoration of Louisiana.* New York: Da Capo Press, 1970.

Catterall, Helen Tunncliff, ed. *Judicial Cases concerning American Slavery and the Negro.* 5 vols. Washington, D.C.: Carnegie Institution of Washington, 1926–37.

Caughey, John. "Bernardo de Galvez and the English Smugglers on the Mississippi, 1777." *Hispanic American Historical Review* 12 (February 1932): 46–58.

Chaffin, Tom. "'Sons of Washington': Narciso Lopez, Filibustering, and U.S. Nationalism, 1848–1851." *Journal of the Early Republic* 15, 1 (Spring 1995): 79–108.

Chambers, Douglas B. *Jamaican Runaways: A Compilation of Fugitive Slaves, 1718–1817,* CD-ROM, in possession of author.

Chamley, Mitchell V. *Jean Lafitte, Gentleman Smuggler.* New York: Viking Press, 1934.

Chidsey, Donald Barr. *Louisiana Purchase.* New York: Crown Publishers, 1972.

Claiborne, J. F. H. *Life and Correspondence of John A. Quitman: Major-General, U.S.A. and Governor of the State of Mississippi.* New York: Harper & Brothers, 1860.

Claiborne, W. C. C. *Official Letter books of W. C. C. Claiborne, 1801–1816.* Edited by Rowland Dunbar. Jackson, Miss.: State Department of Archives and History, 1917.

Clark, John G. *New Orleans, 1718–1812: An Economic History.* Baton Rouge: Louisiana State University Press, 1970.

Clark, Rufus. *The African Slave Trade.* Boston: American Tract Society, 1860.

Collins, Winfield H. *The Domestic Slave Trade of the Southern States.* 1904. Reprint, Port Washington, N.Y.: Kennikat Press, 1969.

Collison, Gary. "Loyal and Dutiful Subjects of Her Gracious Majesty, Queen Victoria: Fugitive Slaves in Montreal, 1850–1866." *Québec Studies* 19 (1993): 59–70.

Colloque International sur la Traite des Noirs. *De la Traite L'esciavage; Actes du*

Colloque International sur la Traite des Noirs, Nantes, 1985. Nantes, France: Centre de Recherche sur L'histoire du Monde Atlantique, 1988.

Conrad, Robert Edgar. *World of Sorrow: The African Slave Trade to Brazil.* Baton Rouge: Louisiana State University Press, 1986.

Cook, Adrian. *The Armies of the Streets: The New York City Draft Riots of 1863.* Lexington: University Press of Kentucky, 1974.

Corbitt, D.C. "Shipments of Slaves from the United States to Cuba, 1789–1807." *Journal of Southern History* 7 (1941): 540–49.

Creel, Margaret Washington. *"A Peculiar People": Slave Religion and Community Culture among the Gullahs.* New York: New York University Press, 1998.

Cunningham, Bob, and Harvey P. Hewett. "A 'lovely land full of roses and thorns': Emil Landberg and Mexico, 1835–1866." *Southwestern Historical Quarterly* 98 (January 1995): 387–425.

Curtin, Philip D. *The Atlantic Slave Trade: A Census.* Madison: University of Wisconsin Press, 1969.

Cutbush, Edward, *Observations on the Means of Preserving the Health of Soldiers and Sailors* (Philadelphia, 1808).

Dabbs, Jack Autry. "Additional Notes on the Champ d'Asile." *Western Historical Quarterly* 54 (1950–51): 347–58.

Dabney, Lancaster E. "Louis Aury: First Governor of Texas." *Southwestern Historical Quarterly* (October 1938): 108–16.

Dalleo, Peter T. "Africans in the Caribbean: A Preliminary Assessment of Recaptives in the Bahamas, 1811–1860." *Journal of the Bahamas Historical Society* 6 (1984): 15–24.

Davenport, Harbert. "The Men of Goliad." *Southwestern Historical Quarterly* 43, 1 (July 1939): 1–41.

Davenport, Harbert. "The Life and Background of William Alfred Neale." *Southwestern Historical Quarterly* 47, 1 (July 1943): 63–66.

Davis, Darien J., ed. *Slavery and Beyond: The African Impact on Latin America and the Caribbean.* Wilmington, Del.: SR Books, 1995.

Davis, David Brion. *The Problem of Slavery in the Age of Revolution, 1770–1823.* Ithaca, N.Y.: Cornell University Press, 1975.

Davis, Robert Ralph, Jr. "James Buchanan and the Suppression of the Slave Trade, 1858–1861." *Pennsylvania History* 33, 4 (October 1966): 446–59.

Davis, T. Frederick. "MacGregor's Invasion of Florida, 1817." *Florida Historical Quarterly* 7 (July 1928): 3–71.

Davis, William C. *Three Roads to the Alamo: The Lives and Fortunes of David Crockett, James Bowie, and William Barret Travis.* New York: Harper-Collins, 1998.

Davis, William C. "The Laffites: The Early Louisiana Years." *Laffite Society Chronicles* 10, 1 (February 2004): 2–12.

DeBow, J. D. B. "Texas: A Province, Republic, and State." *DeBow's Review* 23 (1857): 243.

DeBow, J. D. B. *Statistical View of the United States, Embracing Its Territory, Population—White, Free Colored, and Slave—Moral and Social Condition, Industry, Property, and Revenue; The Detailed Statistics of Cities, Towns and Counties: Being a Compendium of the Seventh Census, to which Are Added the Results of Every Previous Census, Beginning with 1790, in Comparative Tables, with explanatory and illustrative notes, Based upon the Schedules and other Official Sources of Information.* Washington, D.C.: A. O. P. Nicholson, Public Printer, 1854.

DeConde, Alexander. *This Affair of Louisiana.* New York: Scribner, 1976.

Deerr, Noel. *The History of Sugar.* 2 vols. London: Chapman and Hall, 1950.

DeGrummond, Jane Lucas. *Baratarians and the Battle of New Orleans.* Baton Rouge: Louisiana State University Press, 1961.

DeGrummond, Jane Lucas. *Renato Beluche: Smuggler, Privateer and Patriot, 1780–1860.* Baton Rouge: Louisiana State University Press, 1983.

Dienst, Alex. "The Navy of the Republic of Texas." *Southwestern Historical Quarterly* 12, 3 (June 1909): 165–66.

Din, Gilbert C. *Spaniards, Planters, and Slaves: The Spanish Regulation of Slavery in Louisiana, 1763–1803.* College Station: Texas A&M University Press, 1999.

Dobie, J. Frank. "James Bowie." *American West* 2, 2 (Spring 1965): 4–13.

Donnan, Elizabeth, ed. *Documents illustrative of the History of the Slave Trade to America.* 4 vols. Washington, D.C.: Carnegie Institution of Washington, 1930–35.

Douglas, C. L. *James Bowie: The Life of a Bravo.* Dallas, Tex.: Upshaw, 1944.

Dow, George F. *Slave Ships and Slaving.* Port Washington, N.Y.: Kennikat Press, 1969.

Drescher, Seymour. *Capitalism and Antislavery: British Mobilization in Comparative Perspective.* New York: Oxford University Press, 1987.

Du Bois, W. E. B. "The Enforcement of the Slave Trade Laws." In *Annual Report of the American Historical Association for the Year 1891.* Washington, D.C.: Smithsonian Institution Press, 1892.

Du Bois, W. E. B. *The Suppression of the African Slave Trade in the United States of America, 1638–1870.* Millwood, N.Y.: Kraus-Thomson, 1973.

Dudley, John. *"'The Mexican War and American Slavery': A Sermon Preached on Fast Day, April 10, 1847.* Hanover: Dartmouth Press, 1847.

Duval, John Crittenden. *The Adventures of Big Foot Wallace, the Texas Ranger and Hunter.* Macon, Ga.: Burke, 1870.

Easterby, J. H. "The Charleston Commercial Convention of 1854." *South Atlantic Quarterly* 25, 2 (April 1926): 181–97.

Ekman, Ernest. "Sweden, the Slave Trade and Slavery, 1784–1847." *Revue Francaise D 'histoire D'outre-mer* 62 (1975): 221–31.

Eltis, David. "The British Trans-Atlantic Slave Trade after 1807." *Maritime History* 4, 1 (Spring 1974): 1–11.

Eltis, David. *Economic Growth and the Ending of the Transatlantic Slave Trade.* New York: Oxford University Press, 1987.

Eltis, David. "The Traffic in Slaves between the British West Indies Colonies, 1807–1833." *Economic History Review* 25, 1 (February 1972): 55–64.

Eltis, David, and James Walvin. *The Abolition of the Atlantic Slave Trade: Origins and Effects in Europe, Africa, and the Americas.* Madison: University of Wisconsin Press, 1981.

Eltis, David, David Richardson, Stephen d. Behrandt, and Herbert S. Klein, eds., *The Trans-Atlantic Slave Trade: A Database on CD-ROM.* Cambridge: Cambridge University Press, 1999.

Epperson, Jean L. "Burrill Franks: A Lafitte Man." *Laffite Society Chronicles* 1, 1 (January 1995): 3–4.

Epperson, Jean L. "Jean Laffite and Corsairs on Galveston Bay." *Laffite Society Chronicles* 3, 2 (July 1997): 3–5.

Epperson, Jean L. "Some Background concerning Laffite's Departure from Galveston." *Laffite Society Chronicles* 5, 2 (August 1999): 7–9.

Epperson, Jean L. "Testimony of Three Escaped Prisoners from Galveston in 1818." *Laffite Society Chronicles* 4, 1 (February 1998): 4–5.

Farr, James Baker. *Black Odyssey: The Seafaring Traditions of Afro-Americans.* New York: P. Lang, 1989.

Farr, James Baker. "A Slow Boat to Nowhere: The Multi-Racial Crews of the American Whaling Industry." *Journal of Negro History* 68, 2 (Spring 1983): 159–70.

Faulk, Odie B. *The Last Years of Spanish Texas, 1778–1821.* London: Mouton & Co., 1964.

Faye, Stanley. "Privateersmen of the Gulf and Their Prizes." *Louisiana Historical Quarterly* 22 (1939): 1012–94.

Fede, Andrew. "Legal Protection for Slave Buyers in the U.S. South: A Caveat concerning Caveat Emptor." *American Journal of Legal History* 31, 4 (October 1987): 322–58.

Federal Writers Project. *Slave Narratives: A Folk History of Slavery in the United States from Interviews with Former Slaves.* 17 vols. St. Clair Shores, Mich: Scholarly Press, 1936–1976.

Fehrenbacher, Don E. *The Slaveholding Republic: An Account of the United States Government's Relations to Slavery.* Oxford: Oxford University Press, 2001.

Fitzgerald, William S. "Make Him an Example." *American History Illustrated* 17, 9 (1983): 40–45.

Floan, Howard R. "The *New York Evening Post* and the Ante-bellum South." *American Quarterly* 8, 3 (Autumn 1956): 243–53.

Fogel, Robert William, and Stanley Engerman. *Time on the Cross: The Economics of American Negro Slavery.* Boston: Little, Brown, 1974.

Fogel, Robert William, Ralph A. Galantine, Richard L. Manning, and Nicholas Scott Cardell. *Without Consent or Contract: The Rise and Fall of American Slavery—Evidence and Methods.* New York: W. W. Norton, 1989.

Foner, Philip S. *The Voice of Black America: Major Speeches by Negroes in the United States, 1791–1971.* New York: Simon and Schuster, 1972.

Ford, John Salmon. *Rip Ford's Texas.* Edited by Stephen B. Oats. Austin: University of Texas Press, 1963.

Fornell, Earl W. "Texans and Filibusters in the 1 850's." *Southwestern Historical Quarterly* 59, 4 (April 1956): 411–12.

Fossier, Albert E. *New Orleans, the Glamour Period, 1800–1840.* New Orleans: Pelican Publishing Co., 1957.

Fowler, William M., Jr. *Jack Tars and Commodores: The American Navy, 1783–1815.* Boston: Houghton Mifflin Company, 1984.

Franklin, John Hope, and Loren Schweninger. *Runaway Slaves: Rebels on the Plantation.* New York: Oxford University Press, 1999.

Freudenberger, Herman, and Jonathan B. Pritchett. "The Domestic United States Slave Trade: New Evidence." *Journal of Interdisciplinary History* 21, 3 (Winter 1991): 449–50.

Fuller, George F. "Sketches of the Texas Navy." *Quarterly of the Texas State Historical Association* 7, 3 (January 1904): 223–34.

Galonska, Juliet L. "African-American Deputy Marshals in Arkansas." *Cultural Resource Management* 6, 2 (1997): 6–7.

Garrett, Julia Kathryn. *Green Flag over Texas.* New York: Pemberton Press, 1969.

Geggus, David P. *The Impact of the Haitian Revolution in the Atlantic World.* Columbia: University of South Carolina Press, 2001.

Genovese, Eugene D. *The Political Economy of Slavery: Studies in the Economy and Society of the Slave South.* New York: Vintage Books, 1967.

Givens, Murphy. "Slavery Was Not Widespread Here." *Corpus Christi Caller* (October 21, 1998): 1.

Goodrich, Casper F. "Our Navy and the West Indian Pirates." *United States Naval Institute Proceedings* 42 (1916): 1171–79, 1461–83, 1923–39.

Gray, W. F. *From Virginia to Texas.* Houston: Fletcher Young, 1965.

Grimes, William. *Life of Grimes: The Runaway Slave.* Chapel Hill: University of North Carolina Press, 2000.

Gudmestad, Robert H. *A Troublesome Commerce: The Transformation of the Interstate Slave Trade.* Baton Rouge: Louisiana State University Press, 2003, 18–20.

Haggard, J. Villasana. "The Counter-Revolution of Bexar, 1811." *Southwestern Historical Quarterly* 43 (October 1939): 222–35.

Hall, Gwendolyn Midlo. *Africans in Colonial Louisiana: The Development of Afro-Creole Culture in the Eighteenth Century.* Baton Rouge: Louisiana State University Press, 1992.

Hall, Gwendolyn Midlo. *Africans in the Americas: Continuities of Ethnicities and Regions.* Chapel Hill: University of North Carolina Press, 2001.

Hall, Gwendolyn Midlo. *Slavery and African Ethnicities in the Americas: Restoring the Links.* Chapel Hill: University of North Carolina Press, 2005.

Hall, Gwendolyn Midlo. *Louisiana Slave Database: Afro-Louisiana History and*

Genealogy, 1719–1820, www.ibiblio.org. *Database for the Study of Afro-Louisiana History and Genealogy, 1719–1860: Computerized Information from Original Manuscript Sources: A Compact Disk Publication* (Baton Rouge: Louisiana State University Press, 2000).

Hall, Martin Hardwick. *Sibley's New Mexico Campaign.* Austin: University of Texas Press, 1960.

Handler, Jerome S., and JoAnn Jacoby. "Slave Names and Naming in Barbados, 1650–1830." *William and Mary Quarterly,* 3rd Series, 52, 4 (October 1996): 685–728.

Hardin, Stephen L. *Texian Iliad: A Military History of the Texas Revolution, 1835–1836.* Austin: University of Texas Press, 1994.

Hauptman, Leo Morgan. *Martin Stowell.* Peru, NE: Peru State College, 1928.

Henson, Margaret Swett. *Samuel May Williams: Early Texas Entrepreneur.* College Station: Texas A&M University Press, 1976.

Herron, Stella. "The African Apprentice Bill." *Proceedings of the Mississippi Valley Historical Association* 8 (1914–1915): 138–39.

Higham, Barry W. *Slave Populations of the British Caribbean, 1807–1834.* Baltimore: Johns Hopkins University Press, 1984.

Hill, Daniel. *The Freedom Seekers: Blacks in Canada. A History.* Montreal: McGill-Queens University Press, 1971.

Hill, Pascoe Grenfell. *Fifty Days on Board a Slave Vessel in the Mozambique Channel.* London: John Murray, 1844.

Hinks, Peter P., ed. *David Walker's Appeal to the Coloured Citizens of the World.* University Park: Pennsylvania State University Press, 2000.

"History of Johnson's Bayou, Louisiana." Cameron Parish Centennial Commission, 1970.

Holt, Francis Ludlow. *A System of Shipping and Navigation Laws of Great Britain.* London, 1820.

Holzer, Harold, ed., *State of the Union: New York and the Civil War.* New York: Fordham University Press, 2002.

Howard, Warren S. *American Slavers and the Federal Law, 1837–1862.* Berkeley and Los Angeles: University of California Press, 1963.

Howe, John. *Journal kept by John Howe while he was employed as a British Spy, during the Revolutionary War, also while he was engaged in the Smuggling Business during the late War.* Concord, N.H.: Luther Roby, 1827.

Hunter, Theresa M. *The Saga of Jean Lafitte: From Pirate to Patriot and Back Again.* San Antonio: Naylor Company, 1940.

Ingersoll, Thomas N. "The Slave Trade of St. Dominique and the Ethnic Diversity of Louisiana's Slave Community." *Louisiana History* 37 (Spring 1996): 133–36.

Inikori, J. E. *Forced Migration: The Impact of the Export Slave Trade on African Societies.* New York: Africana, 1982.

Jarvis, Michael J. "Maritime Masters and Seafaring Slaves in Bermuda, 1680–1783." *William and Mary Quarterly 59*, 3 (July 2002): 585–622.

Jenkins, John H. *The Papers of the Texas Revolution, 1835–1836.* 10 vols. Austin: Presidial Press, 1973.

Johnson, David R. *Policing the Urban Underworld: The Impact of Crime on the Development of the American Police, 1800–1887.* Philadelphia: Temple University Press, 1979.

Johnson, J. F. *Proceedings of the General Anti-Slavery Convention.* Miami: Mnemosyne Publishing Co., 1969.

Johnson, Walter. *Soul by Soul: Life inside the Antebellum Slave Market.* Cambridge: Harvard University Press, 1999.

Jones, Howard. *Mutiny on the* Amistad: *The Saga of a Slave Revolt and Its Impact on American Abolition, Law, and Diplomacy.* Oxford: Oxford University Press, 1987.

Juda, Fanny. "California Filibusters: A History of Their Expeditions into Hispanic America." *Grizzly Bear* 21, 4 (February 1919).

Kaplan, Lawrence S. *Thomas Jefferson: Westward the Course of Empire.* Wilmington, Del.: Scholarly Resources, 1999.

Karilanovic, Dorothy. *Lafitte Society Chronicles* 5, 1 (February 1999): 6–11.

Karras, Alan L. "Caribbean Contraband, Slave Property, and the State, 1767–1792." *Pennsylvania History: A Journal of Mid-Atlantic Studies* 64 (Summer 1997): 250–69.

Karras, Alan L. "'Custom Has the Force of Law': Local Officials and Contraband in the Bahamas and the Floridas, 1748–1779." *Florida Historical Quarterly* 80, 3 (Winter 2002): 281–311.

Kaufman, David S. "'The Slavery Question': A Speech Delivered in the House of Representatives, February 10, 1847.* Washington, D.C.: Government Printing Office, 1847.

Keats, John. *Eminent Domain: The Louisiana Purchase and the Making of America.* New York: Charterhouse, 1973.

Kelly, Alfred H. *The American Constitution: Its Origins and Development.* New York: W. W. Norton & Company, 1983.

Kemble, John Haskell. *The Panama Route, 1848–1869.* New York: DaCapo Press, 1972.

Kendall, John Smith. "The Huntsmen of Black Ivory." *Louisiana Historical Quarterly* 24, 1 (January 1941): 9–34.

Keyes, Pam. "One Man's Death Sparks U.S. War against Piracy in 1822." *Laffite Society Chronicles* 9, 1 (February 2003): 21–23.

King, James Ferguson. "Latin-American Republics and the Suppression of the Slave Trade." *Hispanic American Historical Review* 24, 3 (August 1944): 387–411.

Kiple, Kenneth F. *Blacks in Colonial Cuba, 1774–1899.* Gainesville: University Presses of Florida, 1976.

Klein, Herbert S. *African Slavery in Latin America and the Caribbean.* New York: Oxford University Press, 1986.

Kolchin, Peter. *Unfree Labor: American Slavery and Russian Serfdom.* Cambridge, Mass.: Harvard University Press, 1987.

Kotlikoff, Laurence J., and Sebastian Pinera. "The Old South's Stake in the Inter-Regional Movement of Slaves, 1850–1860." *Journal of Economic History* 37, 2 (June 1977): 434–50.

Kulikoff, Allan. "Uprooted Peoples. Black Migrants in the Age of Revolution, 1790–1820." In *Slavery and Freedom in the Age of American Revolution,* ed. Ira Berlin and Ronald Hoffman. Urbana: University of Illinois Press, 1983.

Labbé, Dolores Egger. *The Louisiana Purchase and Its Aftermath, 1800–1830.* Lafayette: Center for Louisiana Studies, University of Louisiana, 1998.

LaChance, Paul F. "The 1809 Immigration of Saint-Domingue Refugees to New Orleans: Reception, Integration, and Impact." *Louisiana History* 29, 2 (Spring 1988): 109–42.

LaChance, Paul F. "The Politics of Fear: French Louisianans and the Slave Trade, 1786–1809." *Plantation Societies* 1, 2 (June 1979): 162–97.

LaChance, Paul F. "Repercussions of the Haitian Revolution in Louisiana." In *The Impact of the Haitian Revolution in the Atlantic World.* Ed. David P. Geggus. Columbia: University of South Carolina Press, 2001.

Lack, Paul D. "Slavery and the Texas Revolution." *Southwestern Historical Quarterly* 89, 2 (October 1985): 181–202.

Lack, Paul D. "Slavery and Vigilantism in Austin, Texas, 1840–1860." *Southwestern Historical Quarterly* 85, 1 (July 1981): 1–20.

Landers, Jane. *Black Society in Spanish Florida.* Urbana: University of Illinois Press, 1999.

Langley, Harold D. "The Negro in the Navy and Merchant Service, 1789–1860." *Journal of Negro History* 52, 4 (October 1967): 273–86.

Larson, Robert W. *New Mexico's Quest for Statehood, 1846–1912.* Albuquerque: University of New Mexico Press, 1968.

Ledbetter, Bill. "Slave Unrest and White Panic: The Impact of Black Republicanism in Antebellum Texas." *Texana* 10, 4 (1972): 335–50.

Life and Adventures of the Accomplished Forger and Swindler, Colonel Monroe Edwards. New York: H. Long and Bros., 1848.

Lightner, David L. "The Founders of the Interstate Slave Trade." *Journal of the Early Republic* 22, 1 (Spring 2002): 25–51.

Lightner, David L. "The Interstate Slave Trade in Antislavery Politics." *Civil War History* 36, 2 (1990): 119–20.

Lincoln, Abraham. *Abraham Lincoln: Speeches and Writings, 1832–1858.* New York: Viking Press, 1989.

Lloyd, Christopher. *The Navy and the Slave Trade: The Suppression of the African Slave Trade in the Nineteenth Century.* London: Longman, Green, 1968.

Lockett, James D. "The Last Ship That Brought Slaves from Africa to

America:The Landing of the *Clotilde* at Mobile in the Autumn of 1859."
   Western Journal of Black Studies 22, 3 (Fall 1998): 159–63.

Löffler, Michael. *Preussens und Sachsens Beziehungen zu den US.A. während des Sezessionskrieges, 1860–1865.* Münster: Lit.Verlag, 1999.

Long, David F. *Nothing Too Daring: A Biography of Commodore David Porter, 1780–1843.* Annapolis, Mich.: United States Naval Institute Press, 1970.

Lyon, Elijah Wilson. *Louisiana in French Diplomacy, 1759–1804.* 1934.
   Reprint, Norman: University of Oklahoma Press, 1974.

Maher, Edward R. "Sam Houston and Secession." *Southwestern Historical Quarterly* 55 (1952): 451–58.

Malloy, William M., ed. *Treaties, Conventions, International Acts, Protocols and Agreements between the United States and Other Powers.* 2 vols. (Washington, D.C.: Government Printing Office, 1910), 1:650–56.

Martinez-Fernandez, Luis. *Fighting Slavery in the Caribbean: The Life and Times of a British Family in Nineteenth-Century Havana.* Armonk, N.Y.: M. E. Sharpe, 1998.

Mathieson, William L. *Great Britain and the Slave Trade, 1839–1865.* New York: Octagon Books, 1967.

May, Robert E. *John A. Quitman: Old Southern Crusader.* Baton Rouge: Louisiana State University Press, 1985.

May, Robert E. "John A. Quitman and His Slaves: Reconciling Slave Resistance with the Proslavery Defense." *Journal of Southern History,* 46, 4 (November 1980): 551–70.

May, Robert E. *Manifest Destiny's Underworld: Filibustering in Antebellum America.* Chapel Hill: University of North Carolina Press, 2002.

McCardell, John. *The Idea of a Southern Nation: Southern Nationalists and Southern Nationalism, 1830–1860.* New York: W. W. Norton and Co., 1979.

McMillin, James A. *The Final Victims: Foreign Slave Trade to North America, 1783–1810.* Columbia: University of South Carolina Press, 2004.

Miers, Suzanne. *Britain and the Ending of the Slave Trade.* New York: Africana Publishing Company, 1975.

Miller, Joseph C. *Way of Death: Merchant Capitalism and the Angolan Slave Trade, 1730–1830.* Madison: University of Wisconsin Press, 1988.

Miller, William L. "A Note on the Importance of the Interstate Slave Trade of the Ante Bellum South." *Journal of Political Economy* 73, 2 (April 1965): 181–87.

Milne, A. Taylor. "The Lyons–Seward Treaty of 1862." *American Historical Review* 38 (April 1933): 511–25.

Mintz, Sidney W. *Sweetness and Power: The Place of Sugar in Modern History.* New York: Penguin Books, 1985.

Moore, John Hebron. *The Emergence of the Cotton Kingdom in the Old Southwest: Mississippi, 1770–1860.* Baton Rouge: Louisiana State University Press, 1988.

Moretta, John A. *William Pitt Ballinger: Texas Lawyer, Southern Statesman, 1825–1888*. Austin: Texas State Historical Association, 2000.

Morrison, Michael A. *Slavery and the American West: The Eclipse of Manifest Destiny and the Coming of the Civil War*. Chapel Hill: University of North Carolina Press, 1997.

Nelson, Bernard H. "The Slave Trade as a Factor in the British Foreign Policy, 1815–1862." *Journal of Negro History* 27, 2 (April 1942): 192–209.

Nevins, Allan. *The Emergence of Lincoln*. Vol. 2. *Prologue to the Civil War, 1859–1861*. New York: Scribner, 1950.

New Handbook of Texas. Austin: Texas State Historical Association, 1996.

Nolte, Vincent. *Fifty Years in Both Hemispheres*. New York: Redfield, 1854.

Noonan, John T., Jr. *The Antelope: The Ordeal of the Recaptured Africans in the Administrations of James Monroe and John Quincy Adams*. Berkeley and Los Angeles: University of California Press, 1977.

Norregard, Georg. *Danish Settlements in West Africa, 1658–1850*. Boston: Boston University Press, 1966.

Olmsted, Frederick Law. *A Journey through Texas; or a Saddle-Trip on the Southwestern Frontier*. New York: Dix, Edwards, 1857.

Owsley, Frank Lawrence. *Struggle for the Gulf Borderlands: The Creek War and the Battle of New Orleans, 1812–1815*. Gainesville: University Presses of Florida, 1981.

Owsley, Frank Lawrence, and Gene A. Smith. *Filibusters and Expansionists: Jeffersonian Manifest Destiny, 1800–1821*. Tuscaloosa: University of Alabama Press, 1997.

Phelan, John Leedy. "Authority and Flexibility in the Spanish Imperial Bureaucracy." *Administrative Science Quarterly* 5 (June 1960): 47–65.

Pletcher, David M. *The Diplomacy of Annexation. Texas, Oregon, and the Mexican War*. Columbia: University of Missouri Press, 1973.

Porter, K. W. *The Black Seminoles: A History of a Freedom-Seeking People*. Gainesville: University Presses of Florida, 1996.

Porter, K. W. *The Negro on the American Frontier*. New York: Arno Press, 1971.

Posey, Walter Brownlow. "Influence of Slavery upon the Methodist Church in the Early South and Southwest." *Mississippi Valley Historical Review* 17, 4 (March 1931): 530–42.

Potter, David M. *The Impending Crisis, 1848–1861*. New York: Harper & Row, 1972.

Price, Richard. *Maroon Societies: Rebel Slave Communities in the Americas*. Baltimore: Johns Hopkins University Press, 1979.

Purifoy, Lewis M. "The Southern Methodist Church and the Proslavery Argument." *Journal of Southern History* 32, 3 (August 1966): 325–41.

Putney, Martha S. *Black Sailors: Afro-American Merchant Seamen and the Whalemen Prior to the Civil War*. New York: Greenwood Press, 1987.

Ratchford, Fannie E., ed. *The Story of Champ d'Asile as Told by Two of the*

Colonists. Translated by Donald Joseph. Austin: Steck-Vaughn Company, 1969.

Rauch, Basil. *American Interest in Cuba, 1848–1855.* New York: Columbia University Press, 1948.

Rawley, James A. "Captain Nathaniel Gordon: The Only American Executed for Violating the Slave Trade Laws." *Civil War History* 39, 3 (September 1993): 216–24.

Reed, S. G. *A History of Texas Railroads.* New York: Arno Press, 1981.

Reeves, Jesse. "The Napoleonic Exiles in America: A Study in American Diplomatic History, 1815–1819." *Johns Hopkins University Studies* 22, 9–10 (1905): 80–88.

Reilly, Kevin S. "Slavers in Disguise: American Whaling and the African Slave Trade, 1845–1862." *American Neptune* 53, 3 (Summer 1993): 177–89.

Riordan, Patrick. "Finding Freedom in Florida: Native Peoples, African Americans, and Colonists, 1670–1816." *Florida Historical Quarterly* 75 (Summer 1996): 34–40.

Ripley, Peter, ed. *The Black Abolitionist Papers.* 5 vols. Chapel Hill: University of North Carolina Press, 1986.

Roberts, Oran Milo. "Political, Legislative, and Judicial History of Texas." *Southwestern Historical Quarterly* 2, 1 (1899): 85–115.

Robertson, James Alexander. *Louisiana under the Rule of Spain, France, and the United States, 1785–1807.* Freeport, N.Y.: Books for Libraries Press, 1969.

Roche, Emma M. *Historical Sketches of the South.* New York: Knickerbocker Press, 1914.

Rowe, Edna. "The Disturbances at Anahuac in 1832." *Quarterly of the Texas State Historical Association* 6, 4 (April 1903): 265–99.

Rowland, Dunbar, ed. *Official Letter Books of W. C. C. Claiborne, 1801–1816.* 6 vols. Jackson, Miss.: State Department of Archives and History, 1917.

Ruiz, Ramon Eduardo. *Triumphs and Tragedy; A History of the Mexican People.* New York: W. W. Norton & Company, 1992.

Russell, Hilary. "Underground Railroad Parks: A Shared History." *Cultural Resource Management,* 20. Washington, D.C.: National Park Service, 1997, 15–21.

Russell, Robert R. *Economic Aspects of Southern Sectionalism, 1840–1861.* New York: Russell & Russell, 1960.

Sanders, G. Earl. "Counter-Contraband in Spanish America." *The Americas* 34 (July 1977): 60–78.

Schafer, Judith K. *Slavery, the Civil Law, and the Supreme Court of Louisiana.* Baton Rouge: Louisiana State University Press, 1994.

Schafer, Judith K. "New Orleans Slavery in 1850 as Seen in Advertisements." *Journal of Southern History* 47, 1 (February 1981): 33–56.

Schoen, Harold. "The Free Negro in the Republic of Texas." *Southwestern*

Historical Quarterly 39, 4 (April 1936): 292–308; and 40, 1 (July 1936): 26–34.

Scholes, Walter V. *Mexican Politics during the Juarez Regime, 1855–1872.* Columbus: University of Missouri Press, 1957.

Schroeder, John H. "Annexation or Independence: The Texas Issue in American Politics, 1836–1845." *Southwestern Historical Quarterly* 89, 2 (October 1985): 137–64.

Schultz, Charles R. "The Gold Rush Voyage of the Ship *Pacific:* A Study in Ship Management." *American Neptune* 53, 3 (Summer 1993): 190–200.

Shenton, James Patrick. *Robert John Walker: A Politician from Jackson to Lincoln.* New York: Columbia University Press, 1961.

Shingleton, Royce Gordon. "David Byrdie Mitchell and the African Importation Case of 1820." *Journal of Negro History* 58, 3 (July 1973): 327–40.

Shugerman, Jed Handelsman. "The Louisiana Purchase and South Carolina's Reopening of the Slave Trade in 1803." *Journal of the Early Republic* 22, 2 (Summer 2002): 263–90.

Smith, Elbert B. *The Presidency of James Buchanan.* Lawrence: University of Kansas Press, 1975.

Smith, Gene A. "U.S. Navy Gunboats and the Slave Trade in Louisiana Waters." *Military History of the West* 23, 2 (Fall 1993): 135–47.

Smith, Julia Ford. *Slavery and Rice Culture in Low Country Georgia, 1750–1860.* Knoxville: University of Tennessee Press, 1985.

Smith, Robert. "Napoleon and Louisiana: Failure of the Proposed Expedition to Occupy and Defend Louisiana, 1801–1803." *Louisiana History* 12, 1 (Winter 1971): 21–40.

Smith, Ruby C. "James W. Fannin, Jr., in the Texas Revolution." *Southwestern Historical Quarterly* 23, 2 (October 1919): 79–80.

Smyrl, Frank H. "Unionism in Texas, 1856–1861." *Southwestern Historical Quarterly* 68 (October 1964): 172–95.

Sowell, Andrew Jackson. *Life of "Bigfoot" Wallace, the Great Ranger Captain.* 1899. Reprint, Austin: State House Press, 1989.

Spaw, Patsy McDonald, ed. *The Texas Senate. Vol. 1: Republic to the Civil War, 1836–1861.* College Station, Tex., 1990.

Spears, John R. *The American Slave Trade: An Account of Its Origin, Growth and Suppression.* New York: C. Scribner's Sons, 1900.

Special Customs Bicentennial Reissue. San Francisco: United States Treasury Department, 1988.

Stampp, Kenneth M. *America in 1857: A Nation on the Brink.* New York: Oxford University Press, 1990.

Stegmaier, Mark J. *Texas, New Mexico, and the Compromise of 1850.* Kent, Ohio: Kent State University Press, 1996.

Story, Joseph. *The Life and Letters of Joseph Story.* 2 vols. Ed. William W. Story. Boston: Little, Brown, 1851.

Swisher, Carl B. "The Taney Period, 1836–64." *History of the Supreme Court of the United States.* Vol. 5. New York: Macmillan Press, 1974.

Tadman, Michael. *Speculators and Slaves: Masters, Traders, and Slaves in the Old South.* Madison: University of Wisconsin Press, 1989.

Takaki, Ronald T. *A Pro-Slavery Crusade: The Agitation to Reopen the African Slave Trade.* New York: Free Press, 1971.

Taylor, Alrutheus. "The Movement of Negroes from the East to the Gulf States from 1830 to 1850." *Journal of Negro History* 8, 4 (October 1923): 367–93.

Taylor, Joe G. "The Foreign Slave Trade in Louisiana after 1808." *Louisiana History* 1 (Winter 1960): 36–45.

Taylor, Quintard. *In Search of the Racial Frontier: African Americans in the American West.* New York: W. W. Norton, 1998.

Tenzer, Lawrence R. *The Forgotten Cause of the Civil War: A New Look at the Slavery Issue.* Manahawkin, N.J.: Scholars' Publishing House, 1997.

Thomas, Hugh. *The Slave Trade: The Story of the Atlantic Slave Trade, 1440–1870.* New York: Simon & Schuster, 1997.

Thomas, Owen. *Niagara's Freedom Trail: A Guide to African-Canadian History on the Niagara Peninsula.* Niagara Falls: The Region Niagara Tourists Council, 1995.

Thrasher, J. S. "Cuba and the United States." *DeBow's Review* 17 (July 1854): 46.

Tilden, Daniel R. "'The Mexican War and Slavery.'" *A Speech Delivered to the House of Representatives, February 4, 1847.* Washington, D.C.: Office of Blair and Rives, 1847.

Toplin, Robert Brent, ed. *Slavery and Race Relations in Latin America.* Westport, Conn.: Greenwood Press, 1974.

Tregle, Joseph G. "Andrew Jackson and the Continuing Battle of New Orleans." *Journal of the Republic* 1, 4 (Winter 1981): 373–93.

Turner, Frederick Jackson. *The Frontier in American History.* New York: H. Holt, 1920.

Tyler, John W. *Smugglers and Patriots: Boston Merchants and the Advent of the American Revolution.* Boston: Northeastern University Press, 1986.

Tyler, Ronnie C. "Fugitive Slaves in Mexico." *Journal of Negro History* 57, 1 (January 1972): 1–12.

Tyler, Ronnie C. "The Callahan Expedition of 1855: Indians or Negroes." *Southwestern Historical Quarterly* 70 (April 1967): 574–85.

Tyler, Ronnie C., and Lawrence R. Murphy, eds. *The Slave Narratives of Texas.* Austin: Encino Press, 1974.

United States Bureau of the Census, Preliminary Report on the Eighth Census, 1860. Washington, D.C.: Government Printing Office, 1862.

United States Congress. House of Representatives Proceedings and Debates. 16th Cong., sess. 1, May 20, 1820.

United States Congress. Senate Proceedings and Debates, 16th Cong., 1st sess., May 20, 1820.

United States Statutes at Large. Dayton, Ohio: Lexis-Nexis, 2001.

Unser, Daniel H., Jr. *Indians, Settlers, and Slaves in a Frontier Exchange Economy.* Chapel Hill: University of North Carolina Press, 1990, 112–16.

Urban, Chester Stanley. "New Orleans and the Cuban Question during the Lopez Expeditions of 1849–1851: A Local Study in 'Manifest Destiny.'" *Louisiana Historical Quarterly* 22 (October 1939): 1095–1167.

Va Deusen, John G. *The Ante-Bellum Southern Commercial Conventions.* Durham: Duke University Press, 1926.

Valdes, Carlos Manuel, and Ildefonso Davila. *Esclavos Negros en Saltillo Siglos XVII a XIX.* Saltillo: Universidad Autonoma de Coahuila, 1990.

Vestal, Stanley. *Bigfoot Wallace: A Biography.* Boston: Houghton Mifflin, 1942.

Vogel, Robert C. "Rebel without a Cause: The Adventures of Louis Aury." *Laffite Society Chronilces* 8, 1 (February 2002): 2–12.

Walker, George E. *The Afro-American in New York City, 1827–1860.* New York: Garland Publishing, 1933.

Wall, James T. *Manifest Destiny Denied: America's First Intervention in Nicaragua.* University Press of America, 1982.

Wallerstein, Immanuel. *The Modern World-System: Capitalist Agriculture and the Origins of the World-Economy in the Sixteenth Century.* New York: Academic Press, 1974.

Walsh, Lorena. "The Chesapeake Slave Trade: Regional Patterns, African Origins, and Some Implications." *William and Mary Quarterly* 58, 1 (2001): 139–70.

Walters, Ronald G. *The Antislavery Appeal: American Abolitionism after 1830.* Baltimore: Johns Hopkins University Press, 1976.

Walther, Eric. *The Shattering of the Union: America in the 1850s.* Wilmington, Del.: Scholarly Resources, 2004.

Ward, W. E. F. *The Royal Navy and the Slavers.* London: Allen and Unwin, 1969.

Warren, Harris Gaylord. "Document Relating to the Establishment of Privateers at Galveston, 1816–1817."

Wax, Donald D. "'New Negroes Are Always in Demand': The Slave Trade in Eighteenth-Century Georgia." *Georgia Historical Quarterly* 68 (Summer 1984): 193–220.

Weber, David J. *The Mexican Frontier, 1821–1846: The American Southwest under Mexico.* Albuquerque: University of New Mexico Press, 1982.

Welborn, C. A. *The Red River Controversy: The Western Boundary of the Louisiana Purchase.* Wichita Falls, Tex.: Nortex Offset Publications, 1973.

Weld, Theodore Dwight. *American Slavery as It Is: Testimony of a Thousand Witnesses.* New York: Arno Press, 1968.

Wells, Tom Henderson. *The Slave Ship* Wanderer. Athens: University of Georgia Press, 1967.

Wender, Herbert. *The Southern Commercial Conventions.* Baltimore: Johns
   Hopkins University Press, 1930.
Wesley, Charles H. "Manifests of Slave Shipments along the Waterways,
   1808–1864." *Journal of Negro History* 27, 2 (April 1942): 155–74.
White, Laura A. "The South in the 1850s as Seen by British Consuls." *Journal
   of Southern History* 1, 1 (February 1935): 29–48.
Wiecek, William M. *The Sources of Antislavery Constitutionalism in America,
   1760–1848.* Ithaca, N.Y.: Cornell University Press, 1977.
Wilds, John. *Collectors of Customs at the Port of New Orleans. U.S. Customs
   Service Historical Study Number 12.* Washington, D.C.: Department of
   Treasury, 1991.
Wilson, Reginald. "Charles Nathan Tilton Privateer with Jean Laffite." *Laffite
   Society Chronicles* 2, 1 (January 1996): 6–7.
Williams, Edwin L., Jr. "Negro Slavery in Florida." *Florida Historical Quarterly*
   28 (October 1949): 93–110.
Williams, Eric. "The British West Indian Slave Trade after Its Abolition in
   1807." *Journal of Negro History* 27, 2 (April 1942): 175–91.
Wilson, Carol. *Freedom at Risk: The Kidnapping of Free Blacks in America,
   1780–1865.* Lexington: University Press of Kentucky, 1994.
Winkley, E. W., ed. *Journal of the Secession Convention of Texas.* Austin: E. W.
   Winkler, 1912.
Winks, Robin W. *The Blacks in Canada: A History.* Montreal: McGill-Queen's
   University Press, 1971.
Wish, Harvey. "The Revival of the African Slave Trade in the U.S.,
   1856–1860." *Mississippi Valley Historical Review* 27 (March 1941): 569–88.
Woodson, Carter G. *Negro Orators and Their Orations.* New York: Russell &
   Russell, 1969.
Yanez, Aaron Mahr. "The UGRR on the Rio Grande." *Cultural Resource
   Management* 4. Washington, D.C.: National Park Service, 1998, 41–44.
Younger, Richard D. "Southern Grand Juries and Slavery." *Journal of Negro
   History* 40, 2 (April 1955): 166–78.

DISSERTATIONS AND THESES

Adderley, Rosanne Marion. "New Negroes from Africa: Culture and
   Community among Liberated Africans in the Bahamas and Trinidad,
   1800(10) to 1900." Ph.D. diss., University of Pennsylvania, 1996.
Behrendt, Stephen D. "The British Slave Trade, 1785–1807: Volume,
   Profitability, and Mortality." Ph.D. diss., University of Wisconsin, 1993.
Bradley, Udolpho Theodore. "The Contentious Commodore: Thomas ap
   Catesby Jones of the Old Navy, 1788–1858." Ph.D. diss., Cornell
   University, 1933.

Hawkins, Marjorie Browne. "Runaway Slaves in Texas from 1830 to 1860." M.A. thesis, Prairie View A&M University, 1952.

Kelley, Sean Michael. "Plantation Frontiers: Race, Ethnicity, and Family along the Brazos River of Texas, 1821–1886." Ph.D. diss., University of Texas at Austin, 2000.

Kennicott, Patrcik Curtis. "Negro Antislavery Speakers in America." Ph.D. diss., Florida State University, 1967.

Leach, James Henry. "The Life of Marmaduke Potter." M.A. thesis, University of Texas, 1939.

Letts, Bessie Lucille. "George Fisher." M.A. thesis, University of Texas, 1928.

Newsome, Zoie Odom. "Antislavery Sentiment in Texas, 1821–1861." M.A. thesis, Texas Tech University, 1968.

Rentz, Thomas Henry, Sr. "The Public Life of David B. Mitchell." M.A. thesis, University of Georgia at Athens, 1955.

Robbins, Fred H. "The Origins and Development of the African Slave Trade into Texas, 1816–1860." M.A. thesis, University of Houston, 1972.

Scott, Julius. "The Common Wind Currents of Afro-American Communications in the Era of the Haitian Revolution." Ph.D. diss., Duke University, 1986.

Spence, Mary Lee. "British Interests and Attitudes Regarding the Republic of Texas and Its Annexation by the United States." Ph.D. diss., University of Minnesota, 1957.

Tyler, Ronnie C. "Slave Owners and Runaway Slaves in Texas." M.A. thesis, Texas Christian University, 1966.

Wayne, Michael. "The Black Population of Canada West on the Eve of the American Civil War: A Reassessment Based on the Manuscript Census of 1861." Unpublished paper in possession of the author.

INTERNET SOURCES

"George Washington Appoints First Marshals, 1789," www.usdoj.gov/marshals/usmshist.htm.

"James Bowie," *New Handbook of Texas,* www.tsha.utexas.edu/handbook/.

"Personalities of Louisiana: Beverley Chew 1773–1851," www.enlou.com/no_people/chewb-bio.htm.

Index

and, 21, 66, 73, 95–97, 99, 134, 138–39;
number imported after 1808, 9–10;
number imported between 1783 and
1810, 9; number imported between
1790 and 1860, 7; population of from
1790-1810, 6; price of, 3, 7, 30, 99, 125;
protection and colonization of in
Mexico, 85; refugees in Mexico, 66, 85,
98, 119–21, 123, 125–27, 148; smuggled
into Georgia in 1780-1783, 17–18; sold
at government auctions, 6, 12, 24, 62,
73, 81, 124–25; total number imported,
9; transported into Florida in post-
Revolutionary period, 18; transshipments of, 12, 20; Underground Railroad
and, 126–27. See *also* Africans, free and
enslaved
slave smugglers. *See* smugglers and traffickers in slaves
slave smuggling. *See* foreign slave trade
slave trade, 27–28, 68. *See also* coastwise
domestic slave trade; domestic slave
trade; foreign slave trade; smugglers and
traffickers in slaves
slave traders, 10, 16. *See also* smugglers and
traffickers in slaves
slave vessels: African seamen on, 40–41;
British interdiction of, 22–23, 24–25,
32, 114, 139, 141, 173; identification of,
24–25; list of names of, 20; number
entering New Orleans after 1808, 10;
recycled used vessels, 11, 144, 145,
156–59, 178–81; seizure of, 156; seizure
off coast of Cuba, 141; seizure of in
post-Revolutionary period, 17, 18; slave
trade with Africa, 24; use of foreign-
registered ships or flags, 24–25; U.S.
seizure of, 11, 24, 32, 50–52, 51, 80,
141, 161–62, 171–72, 178, 179, 184, 186
(*see also* court cases); whale ships refitted
for, 11, 144, 156–60, 180. See *also specific
ship by name*
Slidell, John, 81
Smalley, Adam, 178
Smith (customs agent), 174
Smith, Benjamin Fort, 83
Smith, Charles, 179
Smith, Cotesworth Pickney, 153
Smith, E. Delafield, 187–88, 189
Smith, James McCune, 94, 187
Smith, John, 24
Smith, Levin, 125
Smith, Roger, 17
Smith, Thomas Loughton, 17
Smith, William, *157,* 159

Smugglers' Anchorage, 30
smugglers and traffickers in slaves, 10; activity in Coahuila y Texas, 76–77; African
seamen as, 39, 40–41; alliances with customs officers, 11, 42–45, 59–60;
alliances with filibusters, 11, 62, 144,
155–56; alliances with slaveholders, 11,
144; avoidance of political controversy
over slavery, 57–58; bail skipping and,
180–81; British suppression and, 174,
193; during Civil War, 190; confiscation
of African seamen, 124–25; contribution to Texas's independence movement, 85–86; court cases against, 12, 24,
32–33, 48, 49–51, 72, 139, 153–54,
161–62, 184–85; defense of Gulf coast
in War of 1812, 33–34, 36; disregard for
political fallout from Mexico, 82; extension of slave trade into Mexican
Cession lands, 127–30; fear of free
roaming Africans, 98–99; foreign consuls as, 132–33, 136, 140; on Galveston
Island, 52–56; geographic limits of, 11;
Gordon's execution and, 189–91; government ambivalence encouraging, 6,
21–22, 70–74, 81, 115–16, 154, 170–72;
as informants, 32; Lafitte brothers'
scheme, 4; list of names of, 10–11; in
Louisiana, 16; Lyons-Seward Treaty and,
189–90; Madison's pardon of, 33;
manipulation of judicial process, 11, 13,
47–52; manipulation of marshals, 11;
means of eluding prosecution, 11, 13,
24–25, 28, 41, 44–45, 79, 80, 83,
115–16, 132, 141, 173–74, 180;
Mexican officials as, 136; move into
Mexican Cession, 127–30; movement
beyond American borders, 52–68;
movement of slaves into Mexican Texas,
79–80; Negro-stealing by, 95–97, 99,
134, 138–39; networks of, 5–6; newspapers as source of information for,
110–15; in New York, 167–68; opposition from black Seminoles, 99; patterns
of conduct among, 8; political connections of, 42–44; ports used by, 9–10, 58,
79–80, 82, 116, 117, 119, 131, 167; pos-
ing as abolitionists, 97; in post-
Revolutionary era, 17–18; practices of,
3, 10, 185, 188; relationship with government officials, 3, 11, 42, 80;
Republic of Texas and, 99–100; reuse of
names on slave manifests, 80, 115–16;
routes for transporting slaves, 29–30,
128; searches for escaped slaves, 121,